Supporting Windows Vista

Addendum to A+ Guide to Managing and Maintaining Your PC [Sixth Edition] and A+ Guide to Software [Fourth Edition]

Supporting Windows Vista

Addendum to A+ Guide to Managing and Maintaining Your PC [Sixth Edition] and A+ Guide to Software [Fourth Edition]

Jean Andrews, Ph.D.

THOMSON
COURSE TECHNOLOGY

Australia • Canada • Mexico • Singapore • Spain • United Kingdom • United States

Supporting Windows Vista is published by Thomson Course Technology.

Executive Editor:
Steve Helba

Managing Editor:
Larry Main

Acquisitions Editor:
Nick Lombardi

Senior Product Manager:
Michelle Ruelos Cannistraci

Developmental Editor:
Jill Batistick

Marketing Manager:
Guy Baskaran

Print Buyer:
Justin Palmeiro

Content Project Manager:
Heather Furrow

Technical Editor:
John Bosco, Green Pen QA

Copy Editor:
Andrew Therriault

Proofreader:
Brandy Lilly

Indexer:
Kevin Broccoli

Internal Design:
Betsy Young

Compositor:
Integra

COPYRIGHT © 2008 Thomson Course Technology, a division of Thomson Learning, Inc. Thomson Learning™ is a trademark used herein under license.

Printed in the United States of America
1 2 3 4 5 6 7 8 9 QWD 10 09 08 07

For more information, contact
Thomson Course Technology, 25 Thomson Place,
Boston, Massachusetts, 02210.

Or find us on the World Wide Web at: www.course.com

ALL RIGHTS RESERVED. No part of this work covered by the copyright hereon may be reproduced or used in any form or by any means—graphic, electronic, or mechanical, including photocopying, recording, taping, Web distribution, or information storage and retrieval systems—without the written permission of the publisher.

For permission to use material from this text or product, submit a request online at **www.thomsonrights.com**

Any additional questions about permissions can be submitted by e-mail to **thomsonrights@thomson.com**

Disclaimer
Thomson Course Technology reserves the right to revise this publication and make changes from time to time in its content without notice.

ISBN-13 978-1-4239-0216-4

ISBN-10 1-4239-0216-5

Brief Contents

Table of Contents

Introduction

Supporting Windows Vista contains two new chapters about Microsoft's latest desktop and laptop operating system, Windows Vista. It is meant to accompany *A+ Guide to Managing and Maintaining Your PC*, Sixth Edition, and *A+ Guide to Software*, Fourth Edition. It builds on the material in these core books and provides an in-depth look at installing, maintaining, securing, and troubleshooting Windows Vista. Plenty of screenshots and step-by-step instructions guide students through the process of learning to support this new OS.

CompTIA's 2006 A+ exams currently do not include Windows Vista, but it is expected that Vista will be added to the exams in the upcoming months.

In addition to this book, there are eight new hands-on labs using Windows Vista available on the Course Technology Web site at www.course.com/pcrepair.

For more information about A+ Guide to Managing and Maintaining Your PC or A+ Guide to Software, please contact your sales representative or go to www.course.com/pcrepair.

FEATURES

To make the book function well for the individual reader as well as in the classroom, you'll find these features:

- **Learning Objectives:** Every chapter opens with a list of Learning Objectives that sets the stage for the goals and content of the chapter.
- **Step-by-Step Instructions:** Detailed information on installation, maintenance, optimization of system performance, and troubleshooting are included throughout the book.
- **End-of-Chapter Material:** Each chapter closes with the following features, which reinforce the material covered in the chapter and provide real-world, hands-on testing of the chapter's skill set:
    - **Chapter Summary:** This bulleted list of concise statements summarizes all the major points of the chapter.
    - **Key Terms:** The new, important terms introduced in the chapter are defined at the end of the chapter.
    - **Reviewing the Basics:** A comprehensive set of review questions at the end of each chapter checks your understanding of fundamental concepts.
    - **Thinking Critically:** This section presents you with scenarios that require you to use both real-world common sense and the concepts you've learned in the chapter to solve problems or answer questions.
    - **Hands-On Projects:** Several in-depth, hands-on projects are included at the end of each chapter; they are designed to ensure that you not only understand the material, but also can apply what you've learned.

- **Real Problems, Real Solutions:** These projects give you valuable practice in applying the knowledge you've gained in the chapter to real-world situations, often using your own computer or one belonging to someone you know.

- **Figures:** Where appropriate, photographs of hardware and screenshots of software are provided to increase student mastery of the topic.
- **Notes:** Note icons highlight additional helpful information related to the subject being discussed.

INSTRUCTOR RESOURCES

Answers to all end-of-chapter material, including Review Questions and Critical Thinking questions, are provided to instructors online at the textbook's Web site at www.course.com/pcrepair.

ACKNOWLEDGMENTS

When Microsoft releases a new operating system, we here at Course Technology begin to respond in many ways. Part of that response is making sure that instructors and students have all the materials they need to successfully include the new OS in their curriculum. This book along with the online labs should do just that. The following reviewers all provided invaluable insights and showed a genuine interest in the book's success: Thank you to Joan Wealing, Ivy Tech Community College of Indiana, Lafayette, IN; and to Paul J. Bartoszewicz, Florida Keys Community College, Key West, FL. Thank you to Joy Dark who was here with me making this book happen. I'm very grateful.

This book is dedicated to the covenant of God with man on earth.

— Jean Andrews, Ph.D.

WANT TO WRITE THE AUTHOR?

If you'd like to give any feedback about the book or suggest what might be included in future books, please feel free to e-mail Jean Andrews at jean.andrews@buystory.com.

CHAPTER

1

Installing and Maintaining Windows Vista

In this chapter, you will learn:

- About the new features of Windows Vista and how it differs from its predecessor, Windows XP
- How to install Windows Vista, including upgrades, clean installs, and dual boot systems
- What to do after Vista is installed, including installing hardware and applications, setting up user accounts, and customizing the Vista desktop
- About several of the Windows Vista support tools, including new tools to manage networking

Microsoft considers Windows Vista to be an upgrade to Windows XP because Vista is based on the same basic internal architecture. However, Vista has many new features not found in XP, and even makes some fundamental architectural changes over XP. This chapter assumes you already understand how to use and support Windows XP and have used Windows Vista on a basic level. Its focus is to show you how Vista differs from XP. You will learn about the many changes in Vista and how to take full advantage of its improvements. We will first discuss the new Vista features, and then we will turn our attention to the details of installing and configuring Vista and using the support tools.

Windows Vista is an extremely stable OS. Many technicians remember the horrible days when Windows XP was first released and all the bugs, errors, and faults it had. It was not until after Windows XP Service Pack 2 was available that support technicians were able to relax and enjoy the OS. However, Microsoft did a much better job of testing Windows Vista, and it was released relatively bug-free. What a relief! Instead of dealing with multiple problems, you can now simply enjoy learning to use and support a new OS with tons of new features and support techniques and tools. There are lots of neat improvements in Vista that I believe you are going to like. Enjoy!

A+ Exam Tip

If you have not used Windows Vista, you might want to do Lab 1.3 before you read this chapter. The lab gives you practice exploring and customizing Vista. Labs for this book can be found online at *www.course.com/pcrepair.*

WHAT'S NEW WITH WINDOWS VISTA

New features of Vista include some that are obvious to the user, such as the new look for the user interface (called Aero), and some not so obvious, such as the new tools to troubleshoot a failed boot and the new security features built into the Windows architecture. (Security and troubleshooting are covered in Chapter 2.) In the following sections, you will learn how Windows Vista differs from Windows XP and about the several different versions of Windows Vista.

VISTA IMPROVEMENTS OVER WINDOWS XP

Here is a list of the major Vista improvements that users see, together with a few tips on how to use these improvements:

- Some find the striking and beautiful 3D appearance of the Windows Vista desktop to be distracting. Others find it awesome. This feature, known as the **Aero user interface**, is not available for all Vista versions and requires that you have a video card that supports DirectX 9 graphics and has at least 128 MB of memory.
- The Windows Vista desktop and Start menu are shown in Figure 1-1. Notice that the Windows XP Start button has been replaced by a Vista sphere with the Windows flag.

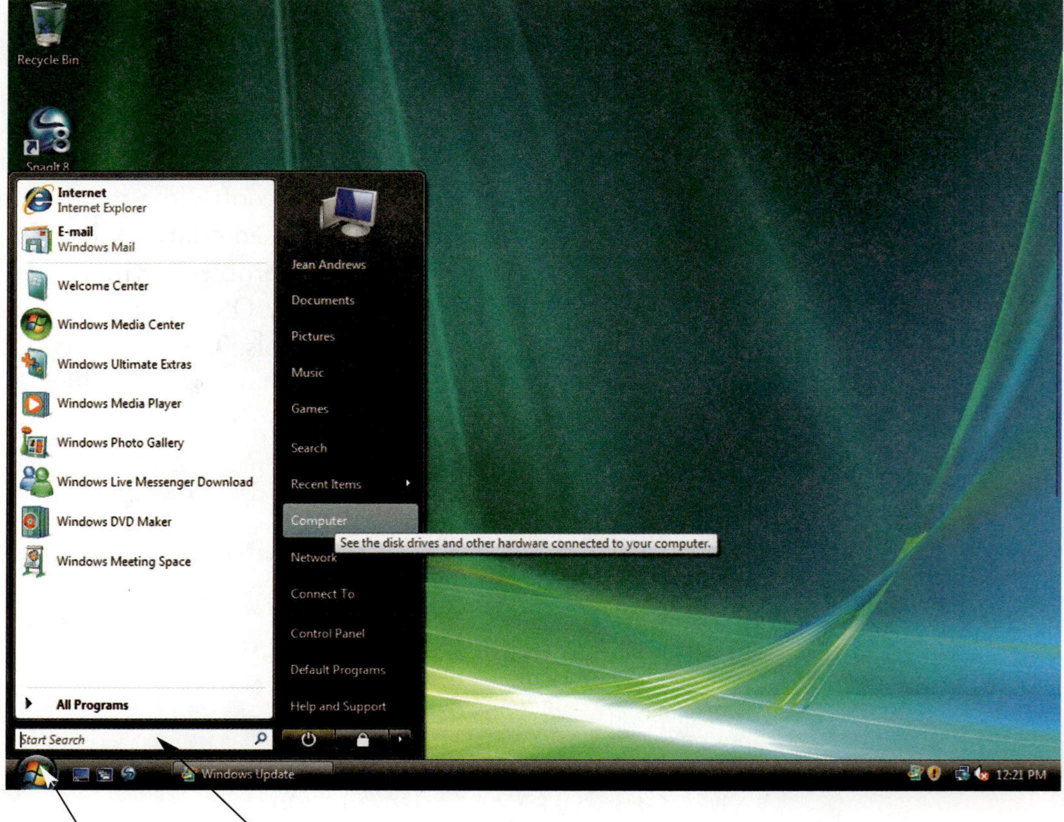

Figure 1-1 Windows Vista desktop and Start menu

- The Vista Start Menu has been reorganized to reduce the time it takes to find an application on the menu or to search for a file or application. For example, when you click Start, All Programs, and Microsoft Office, you will see a sublist of all the Microsoft Office applications, as shown in Figure 1-2.

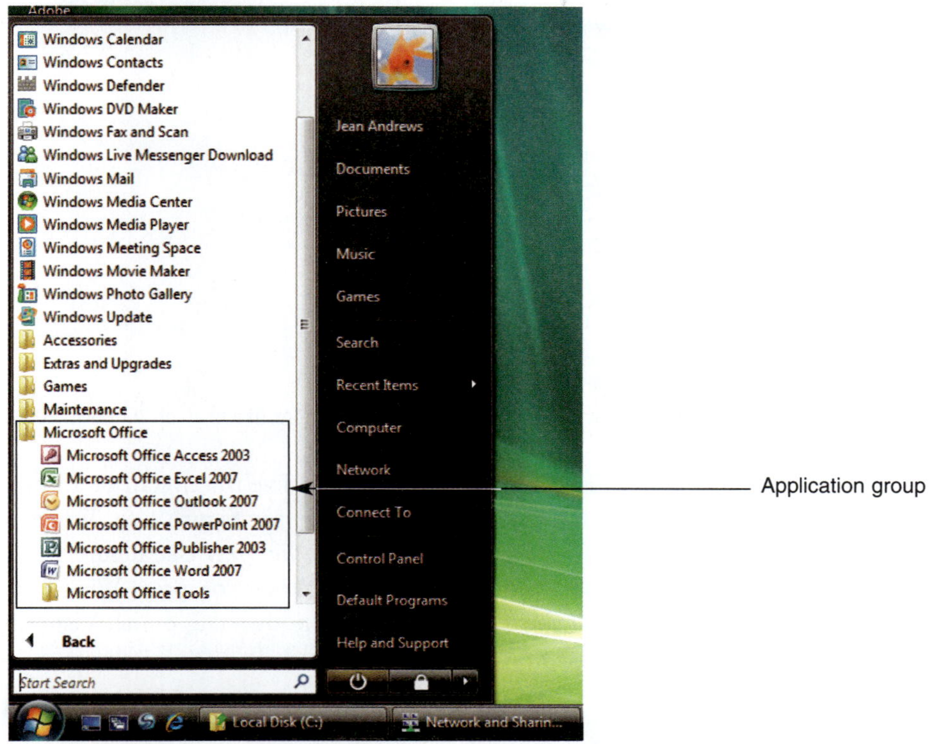

Figure 1-2 The Vista Start menu is organized by groups of applications

- Using Vista Search, you can enter anything from a document name, a program, a URL, or Windows component and Vista will find it and start it up. To perform a search, click Start and enter the item in the search box, shown in Figure 1-3. Use the Search box as you used the Run box in Windows XP to launch a program, such as a command prompt window.
- If you like the Classic Start menu of previous versions of Windows better than the Vista Start menu, you can revert Vista back to the more traditional look. To do that, right-click the Start button and select Properties from the shortcut menu. The Taskbar and Start Menu Properties window opens (see Figure 1-4). Select Classic Start menu and then click Apply.

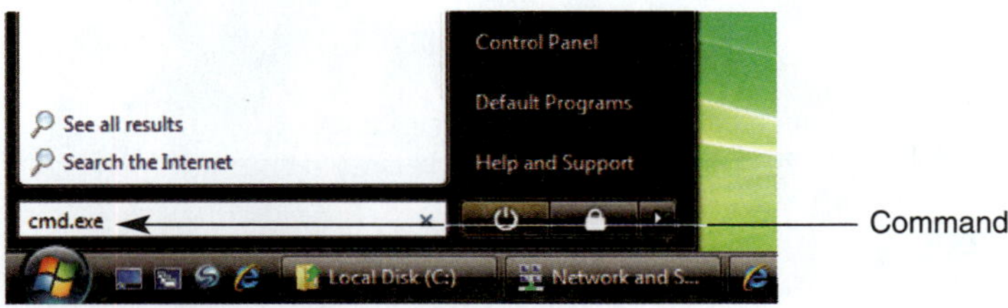

Figure 1-3 Use the Vista Search box to run a command

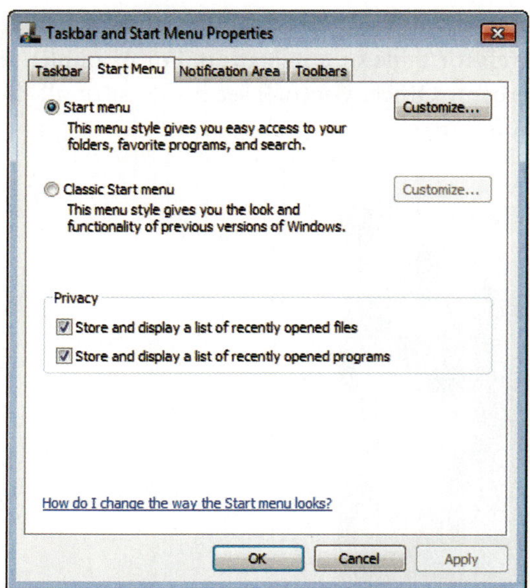

Figure 1-4 Change the Windows Vista Start menu to look more like that of Windows 2000/XP

- The taskbar on the Vista desktop can display a live thumbnail of an open application when you hover over the button in the taskbar (see Figure 1-5). When you press Alt+Tab, Vista displays open applications in a flip view (see Figure 1-6). Press Tab to move from one open application to the next. When you press Win+Tab (on your keyboard, you will see that the Win key has a Windows flag on it), Vista displays the same applications in a flip 3D view (see Figure 1-7).

Figure 1-5 Hover over a button in the taskbar to display a thumbnail of the open application

- Windows Explorer has a new look and feel, including a search box that appears in the upper-right corner of every Explorer window (see Figure 1-8). Explorer displays live icons in the right pane, information about a selected file in the bottom pane, and the

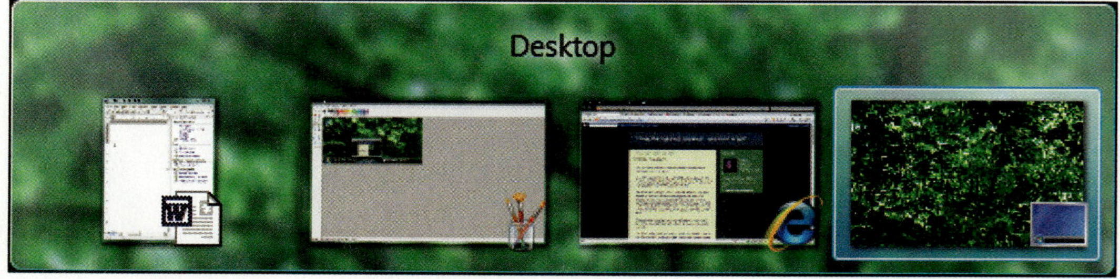

Figure 1-6 Press Alt+Tab to view open applications in a flip view

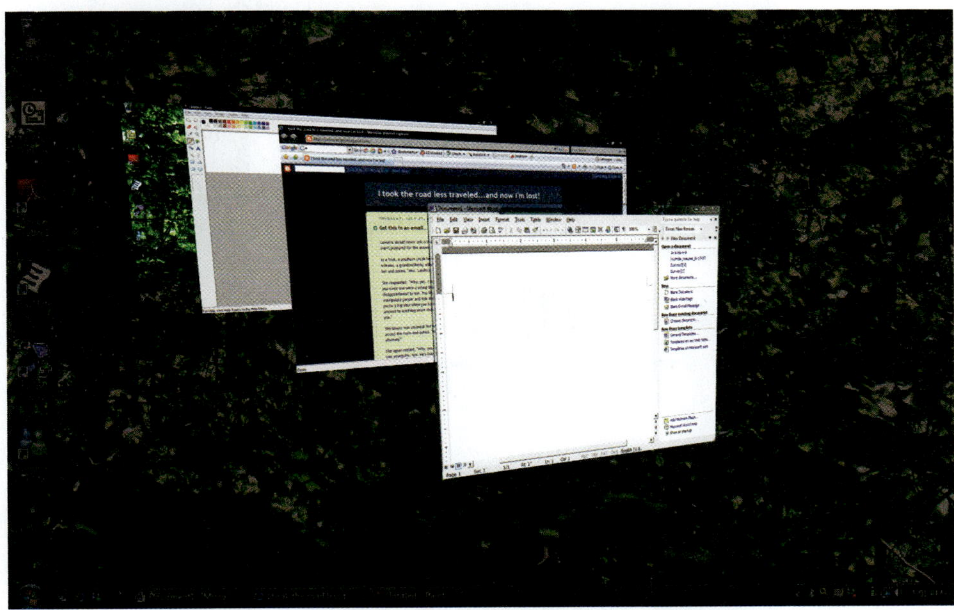

Figure 1-7 Press Win+Tab to view open applications in a flip 3D view

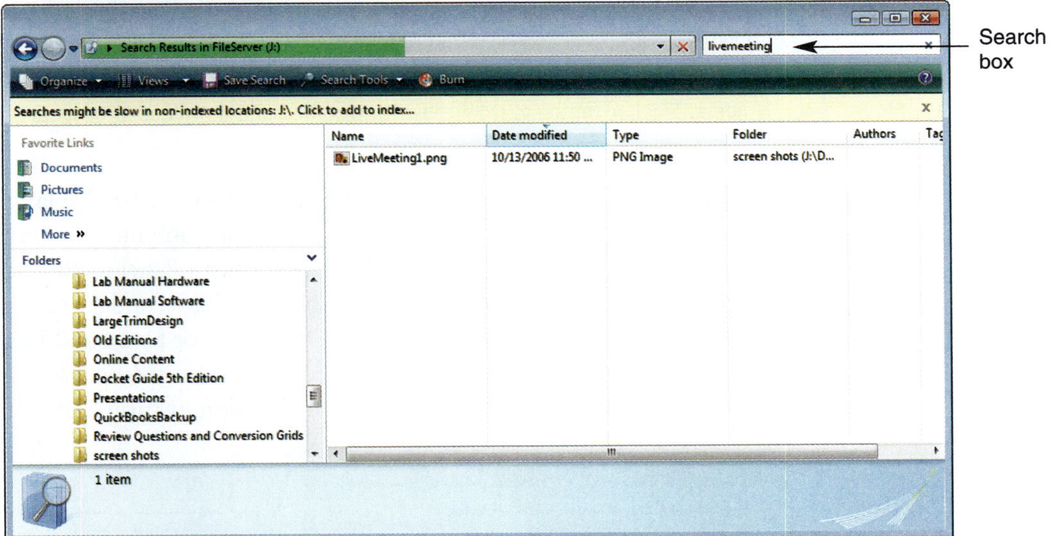

Figure 1-8 Windows Explorer has a search box

address bar at the top of the window. In the left pane, users are strongly encouraged to use the Favorite Links folders for their data, as these folders always appear before other folders.

- You can add the Windows Sidebar and gadgets to your Vista desktop as shown on the right side of Figure 1-9. To add the sidebar, from the Control Panel, select Appearance and Personalization and then select Windows Sidebar Properties. From the properties box, you can choose to start the sidebar each time Windows starts, decide where on the desktop the sidebar appears, and manage the gadgets in the sidebar. To add a new gadget, right-click the sidebar and select Add Gadgets from the shortcut menu. Available gadgets appear as shown in the window in Figure 1-9. To select a new gadget, double-click it.

Figure 1-9 Windows Sidebar can be customized with installed and downloaded gadgets

A+ Exam Tip

If you don't like the way the Vista Control Panel is organized, you can switch it to Classic View by clicking Classic View in the left pane.

- Windows SideShow is a secondary display that is expected to be built into notebook computers by the time this book is in print. You use Control Panel to choose the gadgets you want to display on the secondary screen, which can be provided by the notebook or by a hand-held device, such as a PDA or cell phone. The gadgets work even when the notebook is in hibernation or turned off.

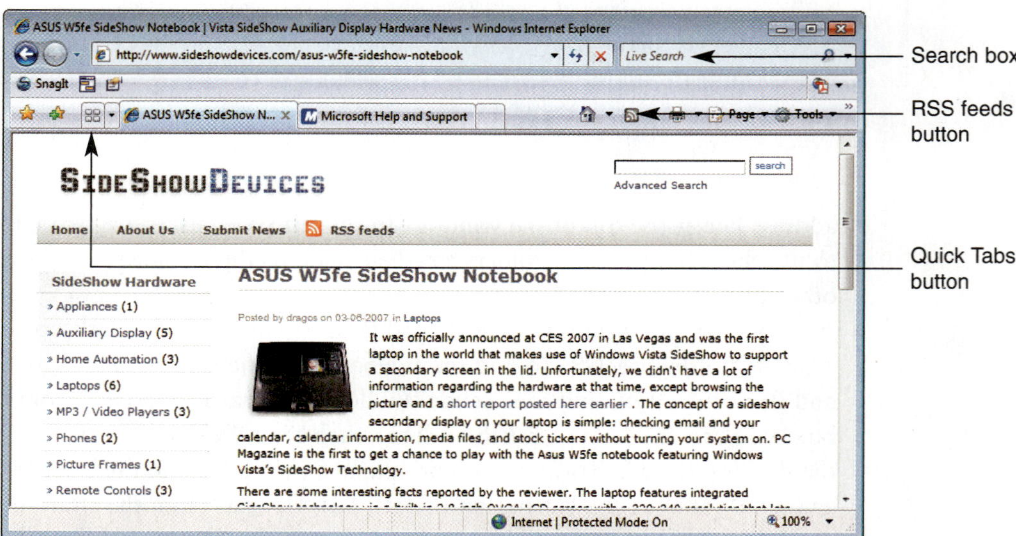

Figure 1-10 Some new features that make Internet Explorer 7 easier to use

- Internet Explorer 7 is an integrated part of Windows Vista. IE 7 can use tabs for browsing instead of separate windows, and includes a search box on the toolbar (see Figure 1-10). Use the Quick Tabs button to display thumbnails of all open windows, and click a thumbnail of a window to expand it. Internet Explorer 7 offers several new security features, which are covered in Chapter 2.
- Using Print Preview in Internet Explorer 7, you can resize the page to print so that wide Web pages can be made to fit the paper. Click the down arrow beside the Print button and then select Print Preview (see Figure 1-11).

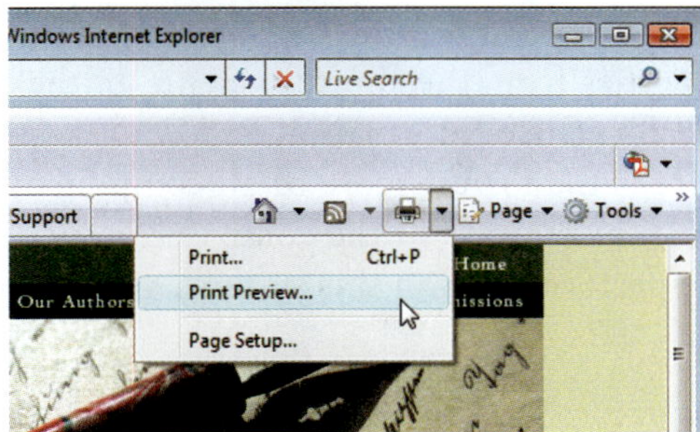

Figure 1-11 Useful icons on the IE Command bar

- Using either a gadget in your sidebar or the Feed button in the IE 7 window (see Figure 1-10), you can subscribe to and view a list of new content for a variety of news and information sites. These lists are called **Really Simple Syndication (RSS) feeds** or simply "feeds".

Behind the scenes, Windows Vista adds several new support tools for the PC support technician and also contains new security enhancements:

- **ReadyBoost** is a feature designed to improve performance that uses a USB flash memory device or secure digital (SD) memory card to speed up a slow hard drive.
- Some high-end hard drives have built-in flash memory that is used to improve performance of the drive in much the same way that ReadyBoost uses flash memory that is external to the drive. Windows Vista **ReadyDrive** makes use of the flash memory installed inside these hybrid drives to speed up startup time and resume time from hibernation.
- Networking with Windows Vista is improved with several components designed to easily configure a network, improve performance, and troubleshoot problems. Network Discovery searches a network and the Network and Sharing Center is used to configure networks and diagnose problems.

> **A+ Exam Tip**
>
> As a leap forward toward the next generation of TCP/IP, Windows Vista includes support for IP version 6 (IPv6), which will ultimately replace the current IPv4. IPv4 uses 32-bit IP addresses, and IPv6 uses 128-bit IP addresses, giving us a much larger number of IP addresses to work with globally. Vista uses either IP address configuration; in most cases, your network will still use IPv4.

- Disk defragmentation happens automatically to improve hard drive performance. By default, defragmentation happens weekly, on Wednesday mornings at 1:00AM. If the computer is off, defragging begins the next time you turn the computer on. You can still manually defrag anytime you like.

- You can use the Disk Management tool to resize partitions without losing data or rebooting the computer.
- BitLocker Drive Encryption encrypts the entire system volume on a hard drive and is intended to be used to lock down the drive if it is stolen from a notebook or desktop computer. BitLocker is designed to be used in conjunction with Encrypted File System (EFS) for high security requirements. EFS encrypts files and folders, and first became available with the Windows 2000 NTFS file system.
- The Windows Experience Index is a summary index designed to measure the overall performance of a system so that you can compare systems and identify performance bottlenecks in a particular system. To display the summary, click Start, right-click Computer, and select Properties from the shortcut menu. In the System window, click Performance. The Performance Information and Tools window appears (see Figure 1-12). The base score is the lowest score of all components and identifies the bottleneck for the system; in the case of the computer in Figure 1-12, this is memory. Therefore, to improve performance on this system, a memory upgrade should be considered.

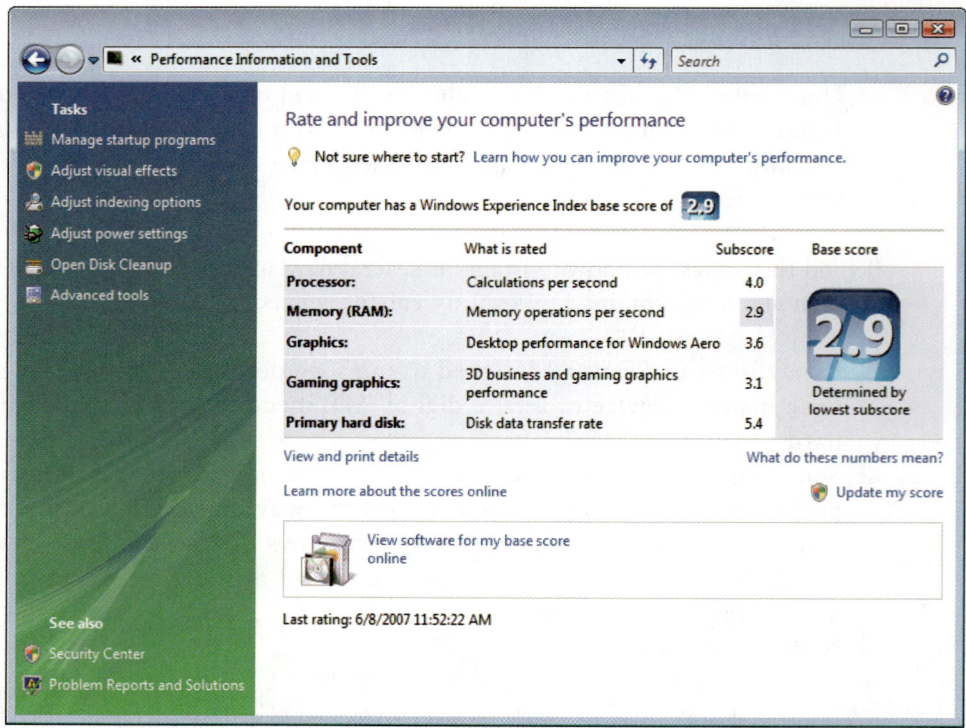

Figure 1-12 Use the Windows Experience Index to get a snapshot of a computer's performance and identify potential bottlenecks

- Windows Vista is designed so that background tasks or services, such as scanning for viruses or defragging the hard drive, can be done using low-priority I/O so that user applications are not slowed down when these services are running. The service must be written specifically for Windows Vista in order to take advantage of this low-priority I/O feature.
- To improve power management, Vista offers sleep mode, which is a hybrid of standby mode and hibernation. When a computer enters sleep mode, most components are

turned off, but the data in memory is maintained. For a notebook computer, if battery power is low or enough time passes by, the notebook will then enter hibernation (the contents of the memory are copied to the hard drive and the system is turned off).

- The Windows Vista backup tool offers new features not available under XP including a **Complete PC backup**, which creates an image of the local drive. Regular backups of files and folders are done using .zip files, which can easily be searched and restored using any operating system. After the initial backup, later backups only back up changed files. Multiple copies of each file are kept so that files that have been lost or corrupted after several incremental backups can still be recovered. One disadvantage Vista backup has is that you have less control over which files and folders you will backup than you did under XP because Vista only allows you to select file types on a volume for backup, rather than letting you select specific folders to back up.
- Hardware device installations are designed so that standard users without administrative privileges are more likely to be able to install previously approved devices without the help of an administrator. Device drivers can be copied to a driver store area, to be used later when the device is first connected to the computer. In 64-bit versions of Vista, digitally signed drivers are required.
- Group Policy has tons of new settings, making it more likely that an administrator can lock down a computer's configuration. You can now use Group Policy to do such things as configure desktop settings, manage updates, secure a wireless network, and configure Internet access.
- **Windows Defender**, Microsoft's anti-spyware software, is an integrated part of Vista.
- A new security feature is the **User Account Control (UAC) dialog box**, shown in Figure 1-13. This box appears each time a user attempts to perform an action that can be done only with administrative privileges. If the user is logged on as an administrator, all s/he has to do is click Continue to close the box and move on. If the user account does not have administrative privileges, the user has the opportunity to enter a password of an administrative account to continue. The purposes of this dialog box are: (1) to prevent malicious background tasks from doing harm when the administrator is logged on, and (2) to make it easier for an administrator to log in using a less powerful user account for normal desktop activities, but still be able to perform administrative tasks while logged in as a regular user. In the next chapter, you will learn how you can disable the UAC dialog box and its underlying security measures.

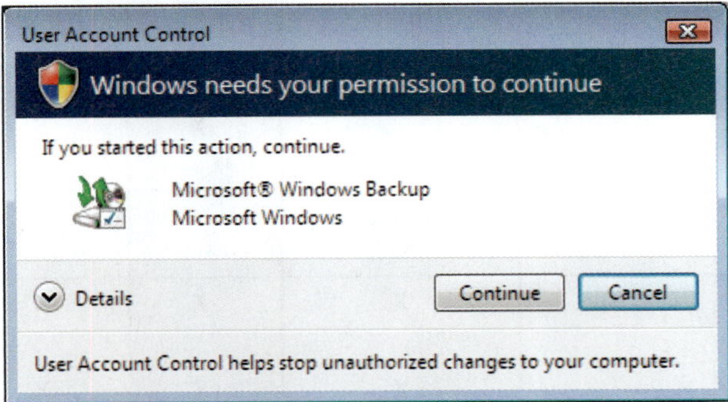

Figure 1-13 The User Account Control box appears each time a user attempts to perform an action requiring administrative privileges

VERSIONS OF VISTA

Microsoft has released several versions of Vista designed to satisfy a variety of consumer needs. All the versions are included on the Vista setup DVD or CDs; the version installed depends on the product key that you enter during the installation. Therefore, upgrading to a better version of Vista can easily be accomplished by using the Windows Anytime Upgrade feature. Here are the Vista versions:

- Windows Vista Starter has the most limited features and is intended to be used in developing nations.
- Windows Vista Home Basic is similar to Windows XP Home Edition and is designed for low-cost home systems that don't require full security and networking features.
- Windows Vista Home Premium is similar to Windows Vista Home Basic but includes additional features.
- Windows Vista Business is intended for business users. Computers can join a domain, support Group Policy, and use the Encrypted File System for better security. You can also purchase volume licenses (also called a multiple site license) for this version. Consumer features not included in Windows Vista Business or Windows Vista Enterprise include Windows Media Center, Movie Maker, DVD Maker, and parental controls.
- Windows Vista Enterprise includes additional features over Windows Vista Business. The major additional security feature is BitLocker, which is useful to secure data stored on a hard drive if the drive is stolen. Volume licensing is available.
- Windows Vista Ultimate includes every Windows Vista feature. You cannot purchase volume licensing for this version.

The major features for all versions are listed in Table 1-1.

Feature	Starter	Home Basic	Home Premium	Business	Enterprise	Ultimate
Aero user interface			X	X	X	X
BitLocker hard drive encryption					X	X
Optional dual processors*				X	X	X
Complete PC backup				X	X	X
Encrypting File System (EFS)				X	X	X
IE parental controls	X	X	X			X
Network and Sharing Center	X	X	X	X	X	X
Scheduled and network backups			X	X	X	X

Table 1-1 Vista Versions and Their Features

Feature	Starter	Home Basic	Home Premium	Business	Enterprise	Ultimate
Tablet PC			X	X	X	X
Windows DVD Maker			X			X
Windows Media Center			X			X
Windows Movie Maker			X			X
Windows SideShow			X	X	X	X
Shadow Copy backup				X	X	X
Join a domain				X	X	X
Group Policy				X	X	X
Processor: 32-bit or 64-bit		X	X	X	X	X
Flip 3D display			X	X	X	X
Remote Desktop				X	X	X
Windows Meeting Space			X	X	X	X

*Core duo processors are allowed for all versions

Table 1-1 Vista Versions and Their Features (continued)

Here are the minimum hardware requirements for Vista. However, as you consider this list, please note that with only the limited memory and video listed in the second and third bullets, you will not be able to see the Aero user interface:

- A processor rated at least 800 MHz
- 512 MB of memory
- SVGA video
- 20 GB hard drive with at least 15 GB free space
- CD-ROM drive

Recommended hardware requirements for Vista are:

- A processor rated at least 1 GHz, which can be 32-bit or 64-bit
- 1 GB of memory
- Video card or embedded video that has at least 128 MB of graphics memory and DirectX 9 support with a Windows Display Driver Model (WDDM)
- 40 GB hard drive with at least 15 GB free space
- DVD-ROM drive
- Internet access

For best performance, a Vista system should have 2 GB of RAM or more.

INSTALLING VISTA

When you buy a brand-name new PC or laptop, the computer often comes with Vista already installed. This installation might be an Original Equipment Manufacturer (OEM) build of the OS. Just as with Windows XP, it is likely the installation files for Vista are stored on a hidden partition on the hard drive in case the Vista installation fails and needs reinstalling. The computer bundle should also include operating system recovery DVDs or CDs to be used in emergencies if the hard drive totally fails. These recovery discs will most likely include the OEM build of Vista, as well as device drivers and applications preinstalled on this computer.

When you build a computer from scratch, replace a hard drive, or need to upgrade from an older OS to Vista, you will install Vista using a single license version or a volume license version of Vista on DVD or CD (see Figure 1-14). Just as with Windows XP, you can copy the Vista installation files from the disc to a file server or to the local hard drive and install the OS from that source.

> **Notes**
>
> Vista is sold to retail customers in three ways: a single license, discounts on additional licenses after you first purchase a single license, and volume licensing. For more information, see Microsoft's Web site at *www.microsoft.com*.

Figure 1-14 Windows Vista Ultimate can be purchased only as a single license version and comes with two DVDs

This part of the chapter covers decisions you need to make before you install Vista; it also covers how to do the actual installation of the OS.

CHOOSING TO UPGRADE, CLEAN INSTALL, OR DUAL BOOT

As with previous versions of Windows, you can install Vista as a clean install, as an upgrade, or as the second OS on a computer in a dual boot configuration. The upgrade version of Vista costs less than the for-a-new-PC version. However, you can use either version to perform a clean install or an upgrade installation.

When you perform a clean install, Vista overwrites any previous OS installed and you get a fresh start. You will need to reinstall any applications, printers, and other hardware peripherals. If you format the hard drive during the installation, all data on the drive is erased. If you do not format the hard drive, user data will be saved, but you will still need to reinstall applications and peripheral devices. Before you do a clean install, be sure to back up all data on the drive and make sure you have available all the application CDs and device drivers. If you do not plan to format the hard drive, be sure to run antivirus software before you begin the installation. If you suspect a virus is present, to be safe, format the hard drive.

When you perform an upgrade to Vista, you carry forward into the Vista installation all installed applications, data, and user settings and preference. You might also carry forward problems with the previously installed OS, so only do an upgrade if your old OS installation is fairly healthy. And be sure to back up your documents and other important files and run antivirus software before you install Vista, in case there are problems. When you install Vista as the second OS in a system, called a dual boot configuration, Vista must be installed on its own hard drive partition and you must install the old OS before you install Vista. You can install Vista on a second partition on a single hard drive or on a second hard drive in the system. One good reason to use a dual boot configuration is if you are unsure if all your hardware or applications will work under Vista. After you have installed Vista and tested your hardware and software, you can then delete the old OS from the hard drive. How to delete either the old OS or the Vista installation is covered in a project at the end of Chapter 2.

UPGRADE PATHS

You can purchase and use the less expensive upgrade version of Windows Vista if you are upgrading from Windows XP or Windows 2000 to Vista. If Service Pack 2 is applied to Windows XP, you can use Windows Easy Transfer to transfer Windows XP user data and preferences to Windows Vista. Upgrade options are outlined in Table 1-2. Notice in the table that even though you can purchase the upgrade version of Vista when upgrading from Windows 2000 or Windows XP 64-bit, you must perform a clean installation of Vista on your PC. You also cannot upgrade from Windows 95/98/Me or Windows NT to Windows Vista.

Old OS	Home Basic	Home Premium	Business	Ultimate
Windows XP Professional	**Clean install**	**Clean install**	**Upgrade**	**Upgrade**
Windows XP Home	**Upgrade**	**Upgrade**	**Upgrade**	**Upgrade**
Windows XP Media Center	**Clean install**	**Upgrade**	**Clean install**	**Upgrade**
Windows XP Tablet PC	**Clean install**	**Clean install**	**Upgrade**	**Upgrade**
Windows XP x64	**Clean install**	**Clean install**	**Clean install**	**Clean install**
Windows 2000	**Clean install**	**Clean install**	**Clean install**	**Clean install**

Table 1-2 Upgrade Paths to Windows Vista

BEFORE YOU START THE INSTALLATION

Before installing Windows Vista, do the following:

- Make sure your computer qualifies for Vista. Check the minimum and recommended hardware configurations listed earlier in the chapter. Check your CPU speed, amount of installed RAM, and hard drive size and free space. Vista comes on a CD or a DVD. Know that you cannot install Vista from a DVD if you have a CD drive and not a DVD drive.
- Make sure your applications will work under Vista. If you are not sure, check the application Web sites. You might be able to download updates of the application to Vista, if necessary.
- Make sure your hardware devices will work under Vista and that you have the necessary drivers. To verify that your hardware qualifies, check out the Vista Hardware Compatibility List (HCL) at *winqual.microsoft.com/hcl*, as shown in Figure 1-15. If you are not sure that essential devices, such as a network card, will install under Vista, you can install Vista in a dual boot configuration so that, if the network card does not work under Vista, you can boot into the old OS and still have access to the network.
- Decide if you want to perform an upgrade, a clean install, or a dual boot. You cannot install Vista as a dual boot unless you have a second partition to hold Vista.

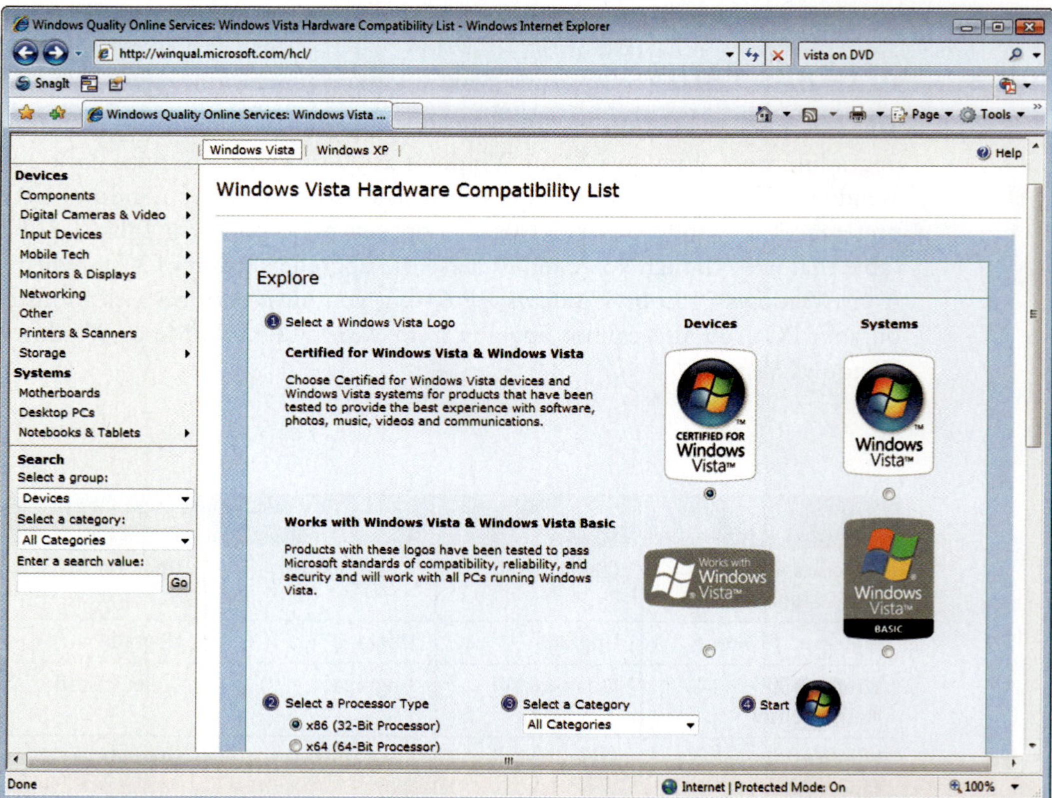

Figure 1-15 Use the Vista Hardware Compatability List to verify that your hardware qualifies for Vista

1

APPLYING CONCEPTS PERFORMING A VISTA IN-PLACE UPGRADE

To upgrade from Windows XP to Windows Vista, follow these steps:

1. From the Windows XP desktop, launch the Vista CD or DVD. The opening menu shown in Figure 1-16 appears. Click **Install now**.

Figure 1-16 Windows Vista Setup opening menu

2. On the next screen, you can choose to allow the setup program to download updates for the installation. If you have Internet access, click **Go online to get the latest updates for installation (recommended)**. Setup will download the updates as shown in Figure 1-17. When using this option, you will need to stay connected to the Internet throughout the installation.

3. Enter the Vista product key, as shown in Figure 1-18. It is printed on a sticker inside the Vista CD or DVD case.

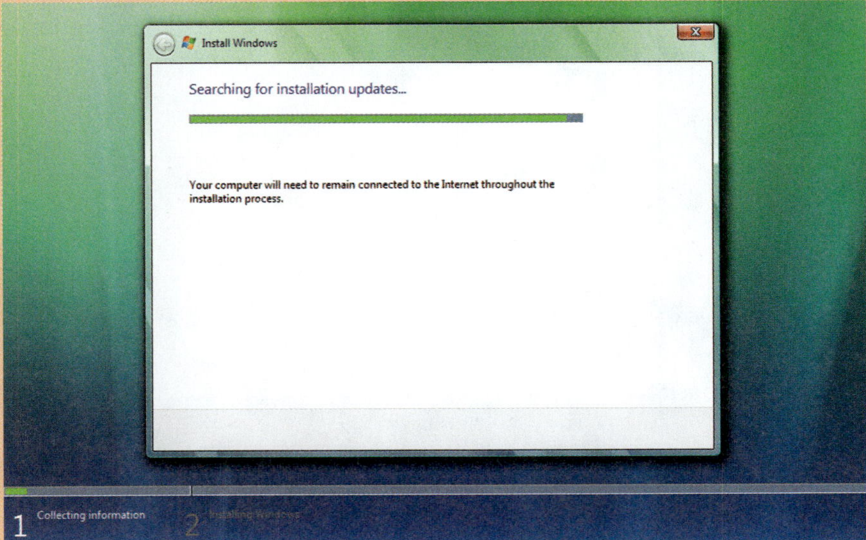

Figure 1-17 Setup uses the Internet to update the installation process

Notice in Figure 1-18 the checkbox "Automatically activate Windows when I'm online". Normally, you would leave this option checked so that Vista activates immediately. However, if you are practicing installing Vista and intend to install it several times using the same DVD, you might choose to uncheck this box and not enter the product key during the installation. When you do that, you will be prompted to select the version of Vista to install. You can later decide to enter the product key and activate Vista after the installation.

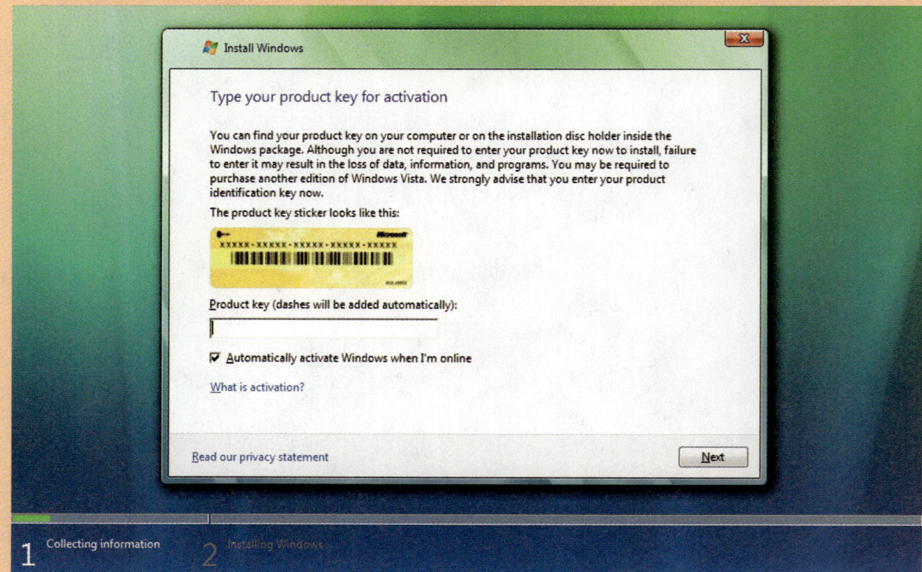

Figure 1-18 Enter the product key found inside the Vista CD or DVD case

4. On the next screen, accept the license agreement.
5. On the next screen, shown in Figure 1-19, select the type of installation you want, either an upgrade or a clean install. Select **Upgrade.**

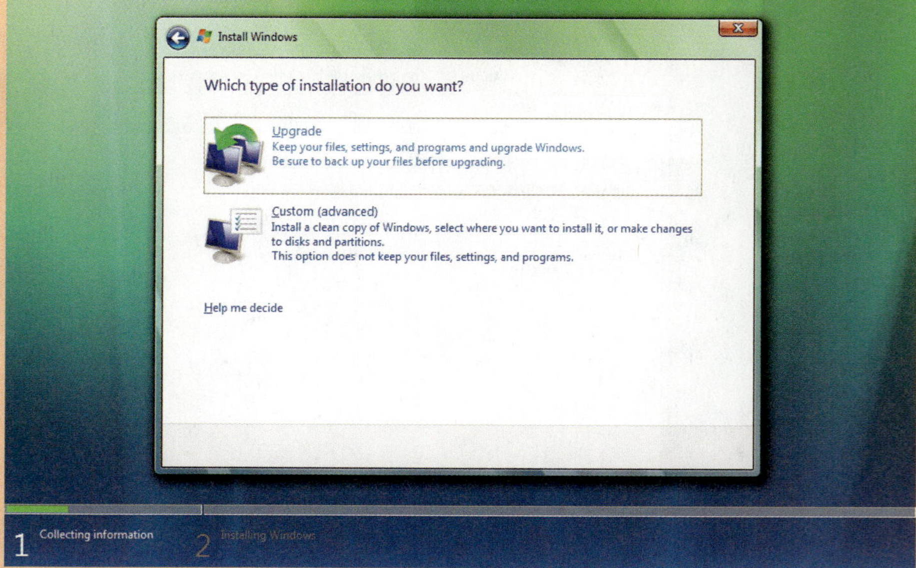

Figure 1-19 Select the type of installation you want

6. The installation is now free to move forward. The PC will reboot several times. At the end of this process, a screen appears asking for your country, time zone, currency, and keyboard layout. Make your selections and click **Next**.
7. On the following screens, you are asked to enter a user name, password, computer name, date, and time, and you are asked how you want to handle Windows updates.
8. Finally, Setup checks your computer's performance and then a logon screen appears (see Figure 1-20). After you logon, a Welcome window appears (see Figure 1-21). The installation is complete.

Figure 1-20 Vista logon screen after the installation

Figure 1-21 Vista Welcome Center appears after first logging on to Vista

Notes

If your computer is part of a Windows domain, when Vista starts up, it displays a blank screen instead of a logon screen. To log onto the domain, press Ctrl-Alt+Del to display the logon screen. If you want to log onto the local machine instead of the domain, type .\username. For example, to log onto the local machine using the local user account, Jean Andrews, type .\Jean Andrews.

PERFORMING A CLEAN INSTALL OR DUAL BOOT

To perform a clean install of Vista or a dual boot with another OS, do the following:

1. Boot directly from the Vista CD or DVD. If you have trouble booting from the disc, go into CMOS setup and verify that your first boot device is the optical drive. Select your language preference, and then the opening menu shown earlier in Figure 1-16 appears. Click **Install now**.

Notes

If your computer refuses to boot from a DVD, verify that your optical drive is a DVD drive. Perhaps it is only a CD drive. If this is the case, you can use another computer on your network that has a DVD drive to read the disc. This computer can act as your file server for the Vista installation on the first PC, or you can copy the installation files on the DVD across the network to a folder on the hard drive of your first PC and install the OS from this folder.

2. On the next screens, enter the product key and accept the license agreement.
3. On the next screen, select the type of installation you want, as shown earlier in Figure 1-19. Choose **Custom (advanced)**.
4. On the next screen, you will be shown a list of partitions on which to install the OS. For example, the computer shown in Figure 1-22 has two hard drives (Disk 0 and Disk 1), each with one partition. You can choose to install Vista on drive C (only partition on the first hard drive) or drive E (only partition on the second hard drive). For this computer, Windows XP is installed on drive C. If you choose drive C, then you will be performing a clean install on top of Windows

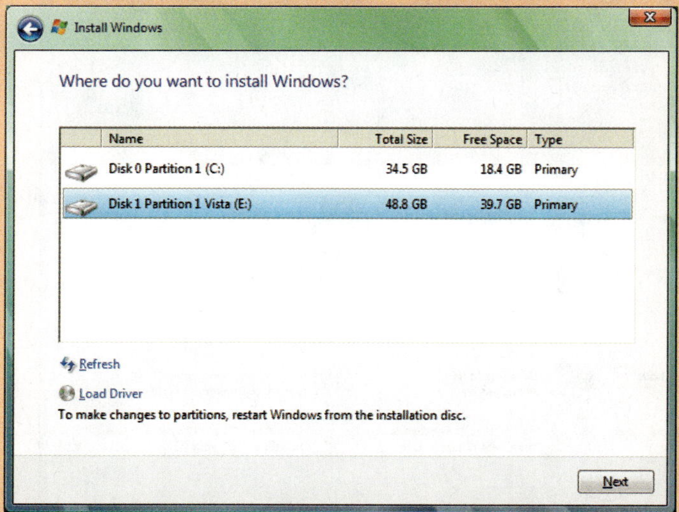

Figure 1-22 Select a partition to install Vista in a dual boot environment

1

XP, erasing XP. If you choose drive E, you will be installing Vista on the second hard drive and the system will function with a dual boot configuration. Make your selection and click **Next.**

The rest of the installation continues the same way as an upgrade installation.

PERFORM A CLEAN INSTALL USING THE VISTA UPGRADE DVD

A problem sometimes arises when you have purchased a Vista upgrade DVD or CDs but you cannot boot your Windows 2000/XP system to start the Vista installation from within Windows 2000/XP. Your only choice in this situation is to use the upgrade disc to perform a clean install. However, when you enter the product key during installation, Vista verifies that the product key is for an upgrade disc or for-a-new-PC disc. If you are using an upgrade product key for a clean install, Setup gives an error and stops the installation. The error message is, "To use the product key you entered, start the installation from your existing version of Windows." Follow these steps to get around that error:

1. Boot from the Vista DVD and start the installation. When you get to the installation window that asks you to enter your product key, do not enter the key and uncheck **Automatically activate Windows when I'm online.**
2. A message appears asking you to enter the key. Click **No** to continue. On the next screen (see Figure 1-23), select the version of Vista you have purchased, check **I have selected the edition of Windows that I purchased**, and click **Next.**
3. Complete the installation. You will not be able to activate Vista without the product key.
4. From the Vista desktop, start the installation routine again, but this time as an upgrade. If you get an error, restart the installation. Enter the product key during the installation and Vista will activate with no problems.

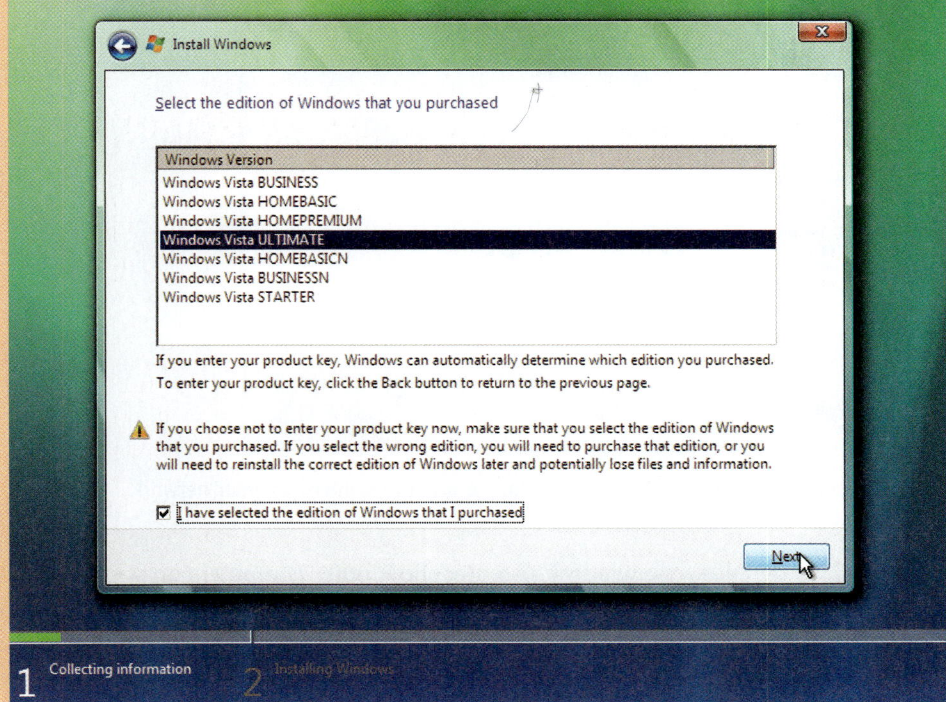

Figure 1-23 Installing Vista without entering the product key

WHAT TO DO AFTER THE INSTALLATION

After you have installed Vista, you need to do the following:

1. Verify you have network access
2. Activate and update Windows
3. Install hardware
4. Install applications
5. Create user accounts
6. Customize the Vista desktop and other settings

Let's look at each of these items in detail.

VERIFY THAT YOU HAVE NETWORK ACCESS

When you install Vista, the setup process should connect you to the network and to the Internet, if available. To verify you have network and Internet access, do the following:

1. Click **Start, Network** to open the Network window (see Figure 1-24). You should see other computers and resources on the network in the right pane and you should be able to drill down to see shared resources on these computers.

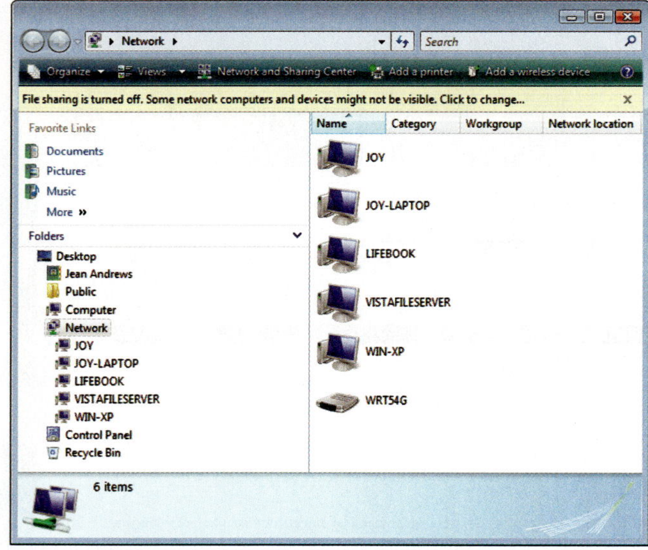

Figure 1-24 Use the Network window to access resources on your network

2. If the Network window does not show other computers on your network, first try rebooting the PC. Then verify the computer, workgroup, or domain names are correct using the System Properties dialog box: Click **Start**, right-click **Computer**, and select **Properties** from the shortcut menu. The System window appears as shown in Figure 1-25.
3. Under *Computer name, domain, and workgroup settings*, click **Change settings** and respond to the UAC box. The System Properties dialog box displays as shown in Figure 1-26.

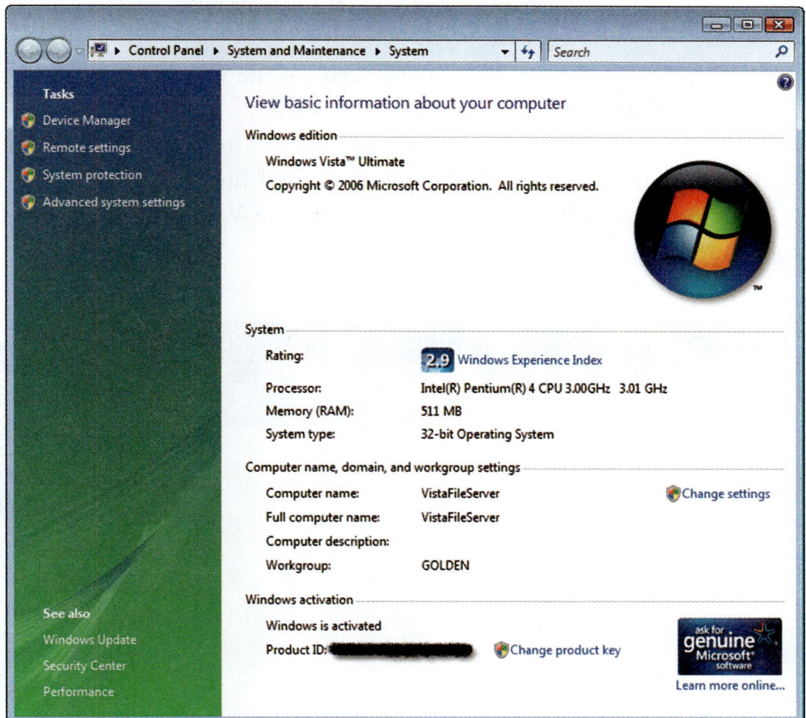

Figure 1-25 Use the System window to view or change computer settings

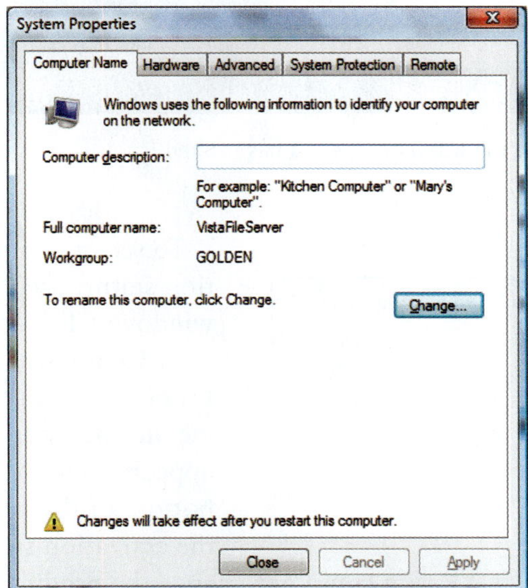

Figure 1-26 Use the System Properties window to change the workgroup name, domain name, or computer name

4. To verify you have Internet access, open **Internet Explorer** and try to navigate to a couple of Web sites.

If you have problems with accessing the network or the Internet, you will need to dig a little deeper into Vista networking, which is covered later in the chapter in the "Vista Networking Tools" section.

ACTIVATE WINDOWS VISTA AND INSTALL UPDATES

After you install Vista, you have 30 days to activate the OS. If you do not activate within the given time, the screen in Figure 1-27 displays forcing you to activate Windows, enter or purchase a new product key for the activation, or convert Vista to Reduced Functionality Mode (RFM), which greatly limits what you can do in Windows. After you are in RFM mode, if you activate Vista, it will return to the fully functioning mode.

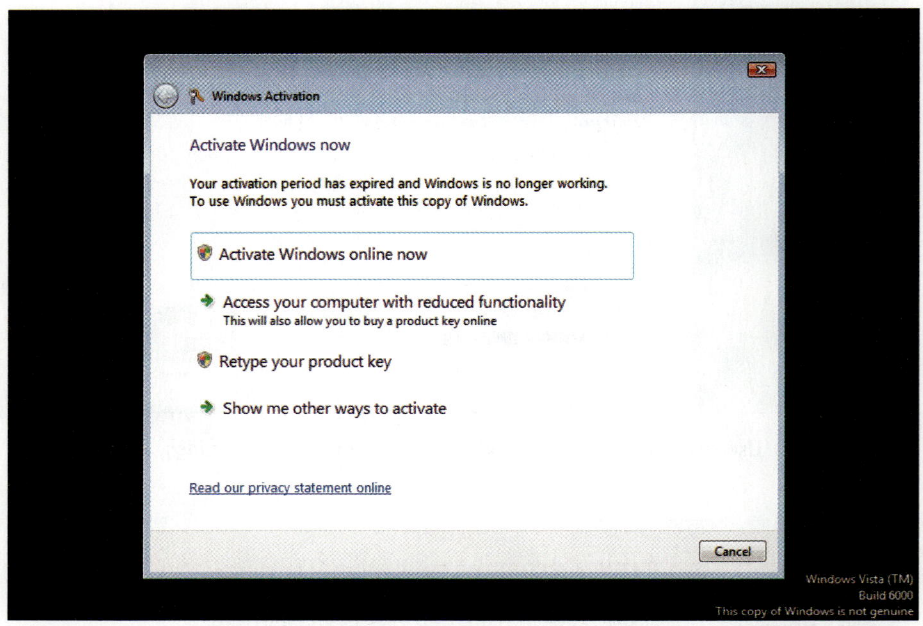

Figure 1-27 Vista informs the user when the activation period has expired

> **Notes**
>
> If you need more than 30 days before you activate Windows, you can use this command in a command prompt window: `slmgr - rearm`. Your activation period will be extended an additional 30 days from the day you issue the command. You can use the command three times, at which time Vista will revert to RFM mode.

To see or change the activation status, use the System window: Click Start, right-click Computer, and select Properties from the shortcut menu. The System window appears. Scroll down to the bottom of the window to see the activation status (refer back to Figure 1-25). Using Windows XP, you could not change the product key unless you were in the process of activating XP, but with Vista, the product key can be changed at any time. For example, if you discover your product key is a pirated key, you can change it before you activate Vista. If you change the key after Vista is activated, you must activate Vista again, because the activation is tied to the product key and the system hardware. Incidentally, if

> **Notes**
>
> The Vista DVD includes the Windows Anytime Upgrade feature. Using this feature, if you have purchased Vista Home Basic, Home Premium, or Business versions, you can upgrade them to Vista Ultimate using the same DVD. To do that, go to the Microsoft Web site (*www.microsoft.com*), purchase the upgrade, and download an upgrade program file which includes a new product key. You use the downloaded file and the Vista DVD to install the new version of Vista.

you replace the motherboard or replace the hard drive and memory at the same time, you must also reactivate Vista.

After Vista is activated, the next step is to update Vista. To download and apply Vista updates, click Start, All Programs, and Windows Update. The Windows Update window appears as shown in Figure 1-28. Click Install updates and follow directions on screen.

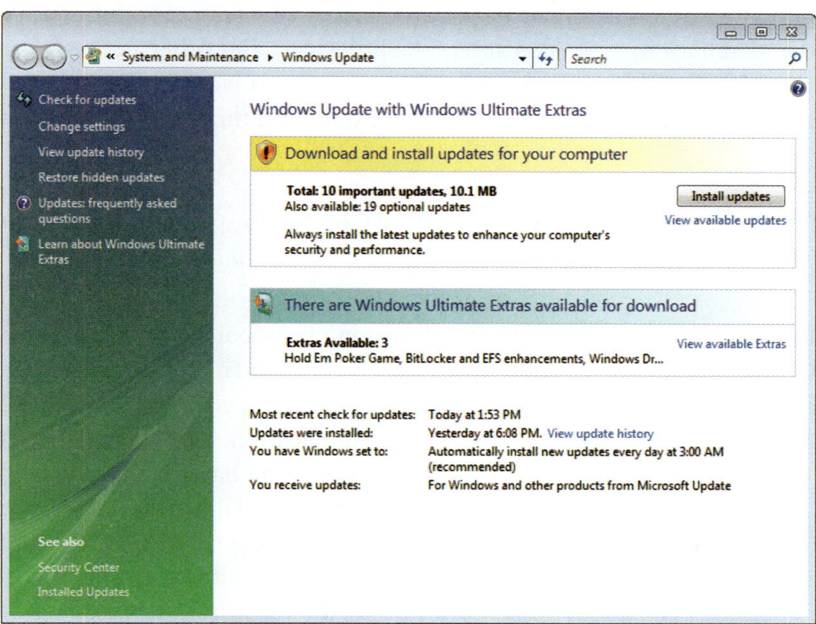

Figure 1-28 Windows Update allows you to download and install updates for your computer

During the Vista installation, you were asked how you want to handle Vista updates. To verify or change this setting, in the left pane of the Windows Update window, click Change settings. From the Change settings window, shown in Figure 1-29, you can decide how often, when, and how you want Vista to install updates. The recommended setting is to

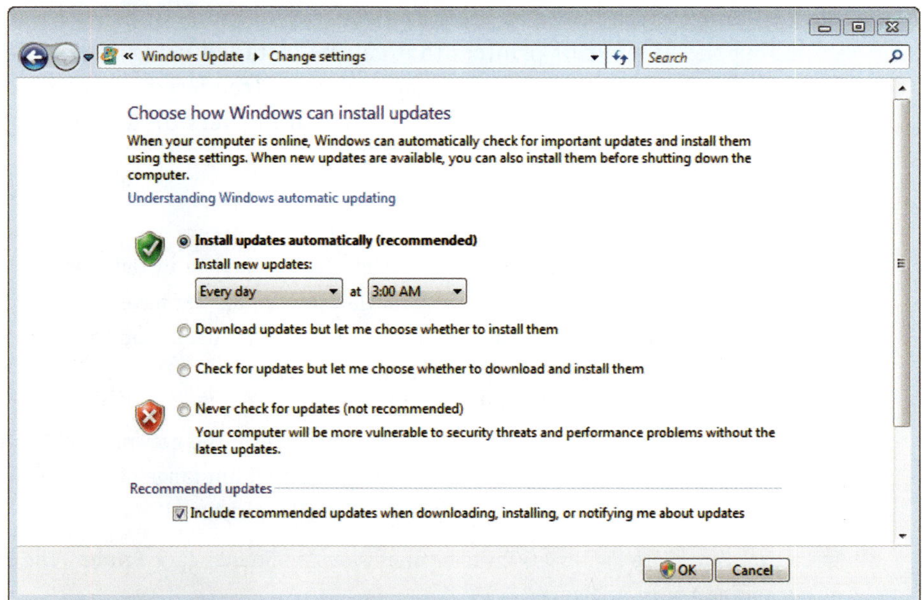

Figure 1-29 Manage how and when Vista is updated

allow Vista to automatically download and install updates daily. However, if you are not always connected to the Internet or your connection is very slow, you might want to manage the updates differently.

INSTALL HARDWARE

You are now ready to install the hardware devices that were not automatically installed during the installation, such as printers, USB devices, and other peripherals. As you install each device, reboot and verify the software or device is working before you move on to the next item. Let's look at how to install printers and then we will turn our attention to USB devices.

INSTALLING AND CONFIGURING PRINTERS

Four significant changes in the way Vista handles printing are as follows:

- Vista supports a new and improved printing protocol called XML Paper Specification (XPS). This protocol specifies how a page is formatted (called rendering the page) before the print job is spooled to the printer, and is written using the XML programming language. When you print from an application, Vista uses either GDI or XPS for rendering based on the type of printer driver installed. Recall that GDI (Graphics Device Interface) is the rendering protocol supported by Windows XP and earlier versions of Windows.
- Local, network, and wireless (including Bluetooth) printers can be installed using the Add Printer Wizard, which is accessed from Control Panel.
- Printers connected to print servers on an enterprise network are managed using the Network Printer Installation Wizard (to install one of these remote network printers) and the Print Management console together with the Printer Migrator utility (to manage print servers). How to use these tools when supporting print servers is not covered in this book.
- Group Policy can be used to limit and control all kinds of printer-related tasks including the number of printers that can be installed using the Add Printer Wizard, how print jobs are sent to print servers (rendered or not rendered), which print servers the computer can use, and which printers on a network the computer can use.

> **Notes**
>
> Windows Vista and Windows XP also support two other printer protocols, PostScript and PCL, that both require the printer to format or render a page before printing.

APPLYING CONCEPTS

Now let's look at how to install a printer. To install a local USB printer, all you have to do is plug in the USB printer and Vista installs the printer automatically. On the other hand, you will need to follow these steps to install a non-USB local printer or a network printer:

1. For a network printer, make sure the printer is connected to the network and turned on. For a wireless printer, turn on the printer and set the printer within range of the PC. For a parallel port or serial port printer, connect the printer to the PC and turn it on.
2. In Control Panel (see Figure 1-30), under Hardware and Sound, click **Printer**. The Printers window opens as shown in Figure 1-31.

Figure 1-30 To install and manage printers, use the Control Panel to access the Printers window

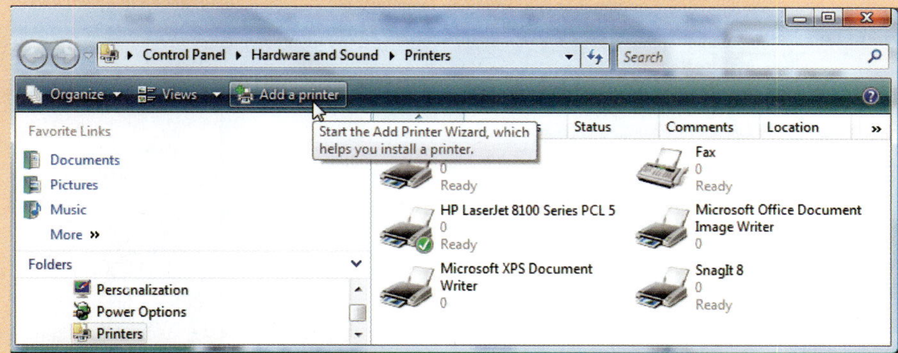

Figure 1-31 Use the Printers window to install a new printer

> **Notes**
>
> Notice in Figure 1-31 that Vista includes the Microsoft **XPS Document Writer** as an installed printer. If you write to this printer, you will create an .xps file that can then be viewed in Internet Explorer. The file is similar to a .pdf file and can be viewed, edited, printed, faxed, emailed, or posted on Web sites.

3. Click **Add a printer**. In the Add Printer window that appears (see Figure 1-32), select the type of printer.
4. If you select a local printer, the next step is to select the local printer port. You are then asked to select the printer from a list of supported printers or provide the printer drivers from CD or some other location. If you select a network printer, Vista searches for available printers and lists them. Select the printer from the list and click **Next**. If your printer is not listed,

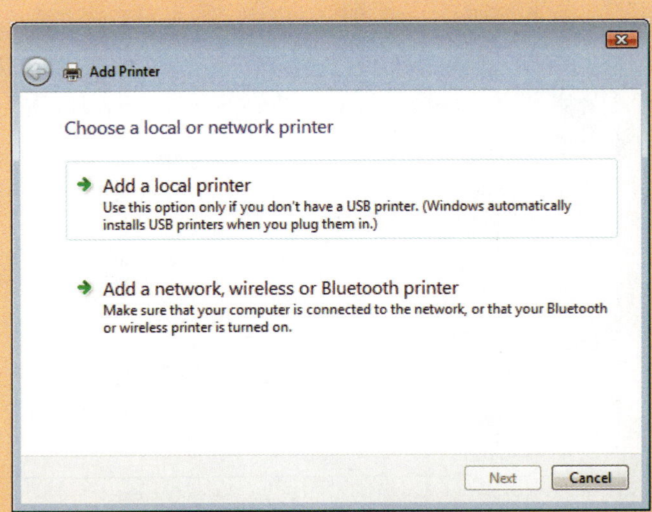

Figure 1-32 Select the type of printer to install

click **The printer that I want isn't listed.** You will then be able to point to the port or IP address of the printer. In Figure 1-33, we are installing a network printer identified by its IP address, which is 192.168.1.109.

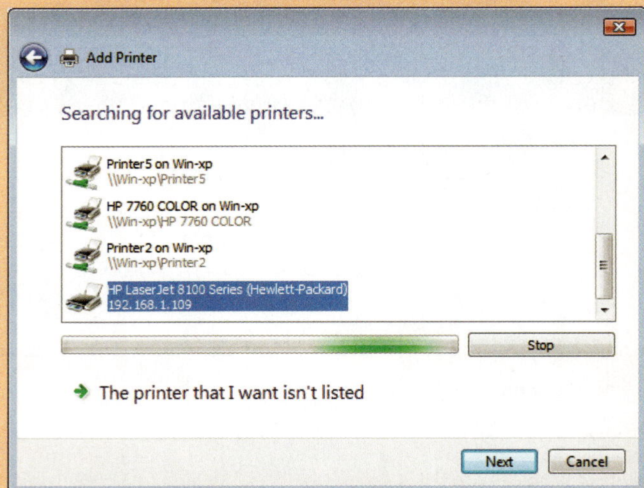

Figure 1-33 Select the printer from the list of available printers

5. In the next window, shown in Figure 1-34, you can change the name of the printer, such as "John's Office Printer," or leave the printer name as is. If this printer will be your default printer, check **Set as the default printer.** Click **Next** to continue.
6. To test the printer, in the next window, click **Print a test page.** Click **Finish** to complete the installation.

Just as with Windows XP, configuring add-on devices for a printer and setting printer preferences is done using the printer properties window. To access the window, open the Printers window and

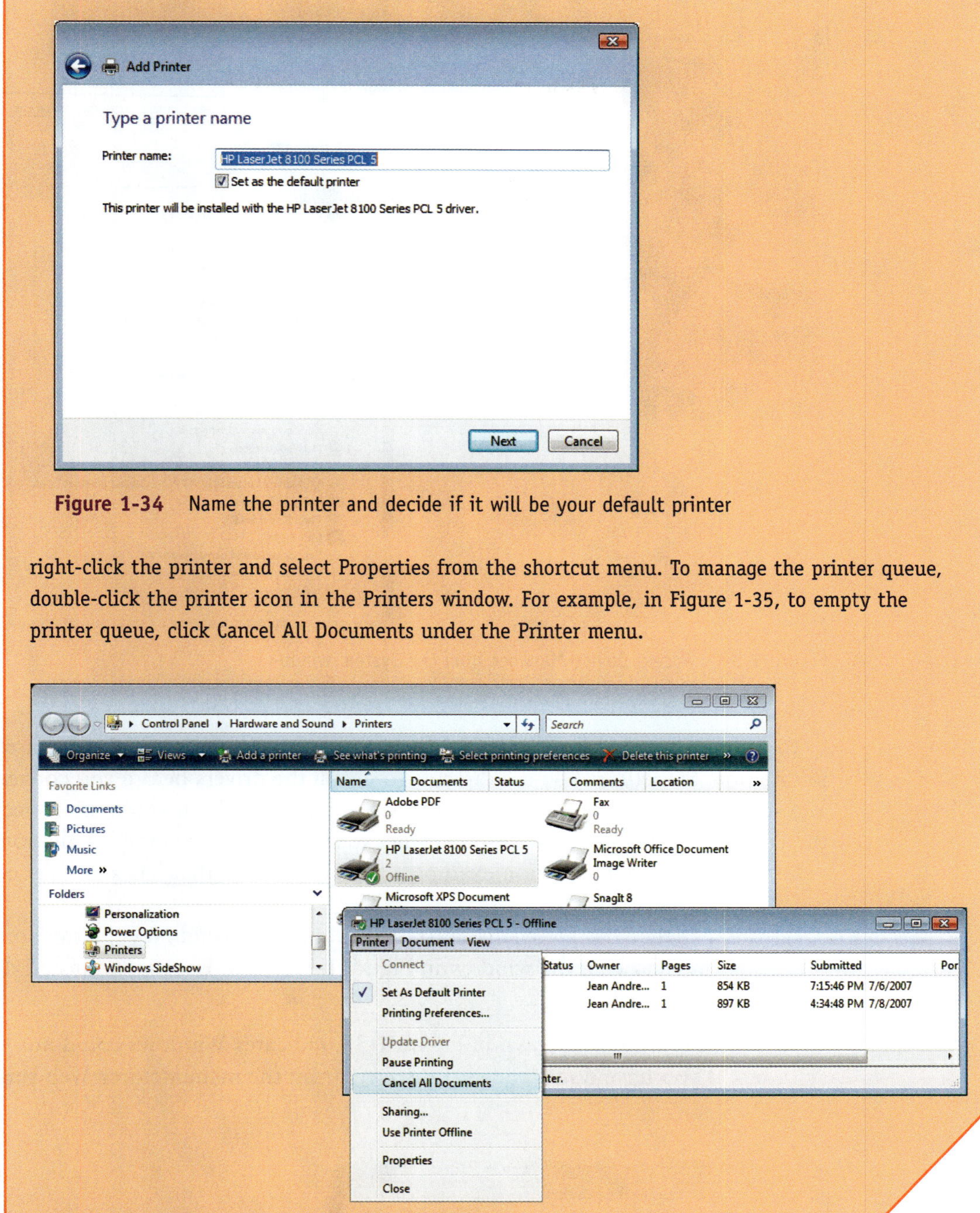

Figure 1-34 Name the printer and decide if it will be your default printer

right-click the printer and select Properties from the shortcut menu. To manage the printer queue, double-click the printer icon in the Printers window. For example, in Figure 1-35, to empty the printer queue, click Cancel All Documents under the Printer menu.

Figure 1-35 Clear the printer's queue

INSTALLING OTHER HARDWARE DEVICES

Just as with Windows XP, the primary tool for managing hardware in Vista is Device Manager. To access Device Manager, click Start, right-click Computer and click Properties on the shortcut menu. In the System window that appears, in the left pane, click Device Manager (see Figure 1-36). Device Manager looks and works about the same way as it does in Windows XP. Use it to uninstall devices, update drivers, and troubleshoot problems with devices.

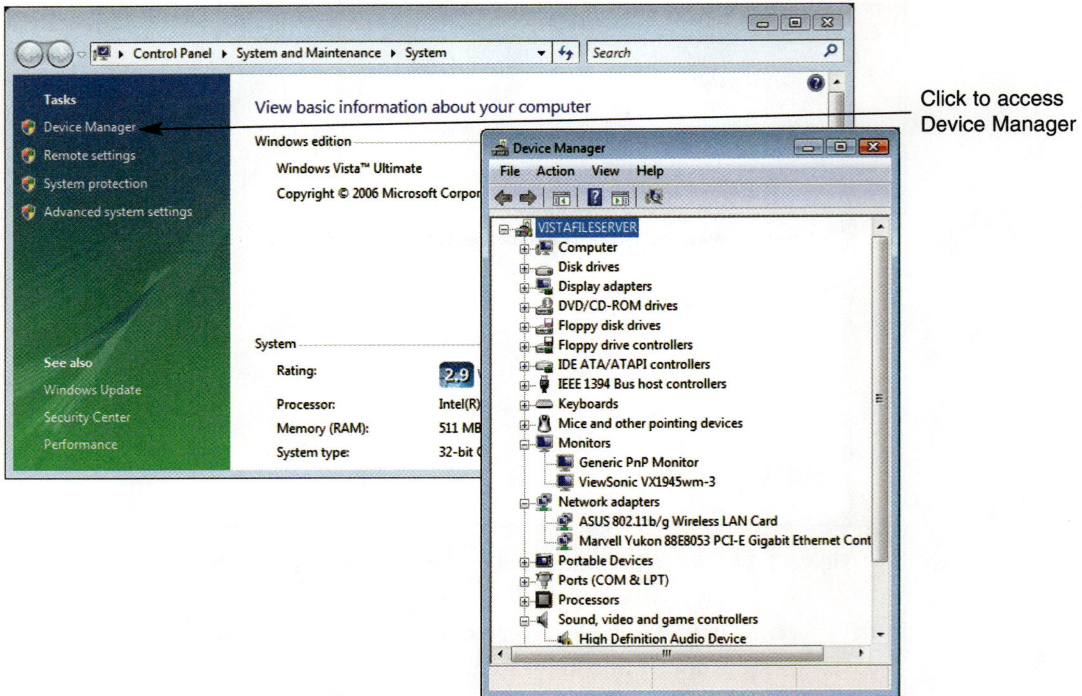

Figure 1-36 Access Device Manager from the System window

To install a new hardware device, always read and follow manufacturer directions for the installation. Sometimes you are directed to install the drivers before you connect the device, and sometimes you will need to first connect the device. When you first connect a new device, the Found New Hardware wizard launches to step you through the installation.

Let's look at one installation example of a Web camera that has a problem:

1. Connect the USB Web camera to the PC and the Found New Hardware wizard launches showing the window in Figure 1-37. Click **Locate and install driver software (recommended)**.
2. The next window, shown in Figure 1-38, indicates Windows could not locate the drivers. If you have downloaded the drivers from the manufacturer Web site or have the

Figure 1-37 Opening window of the Found New Hardware wizard

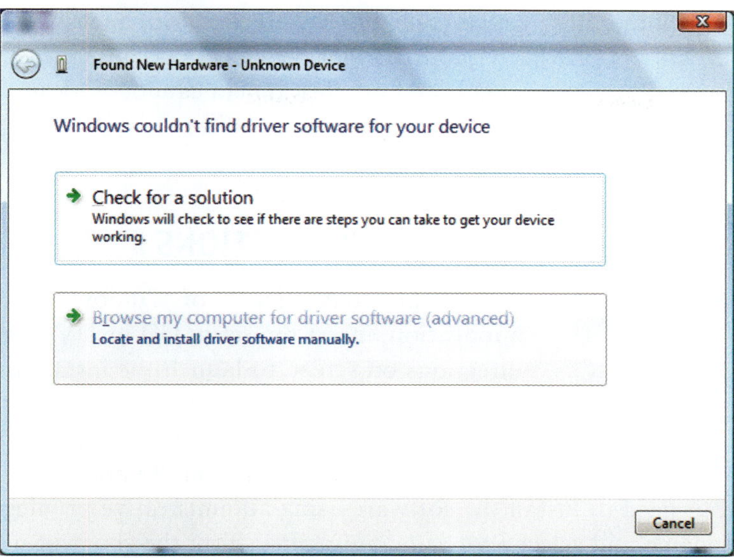

Figure 1-38 Windows could not find drivers for the device

drivers on CD, click **Browse my computer for driver software (advanced)**. Locate the drivers and continue with the installation.

3. If you do not have the drivers, click **Check for a solution**. Vista will attempt to help you find the drivers. In Figure 1-39, Vista has correctly identified the device and provided a link to the driver download page of Creative Technology, LTD—the camera manufacturer.

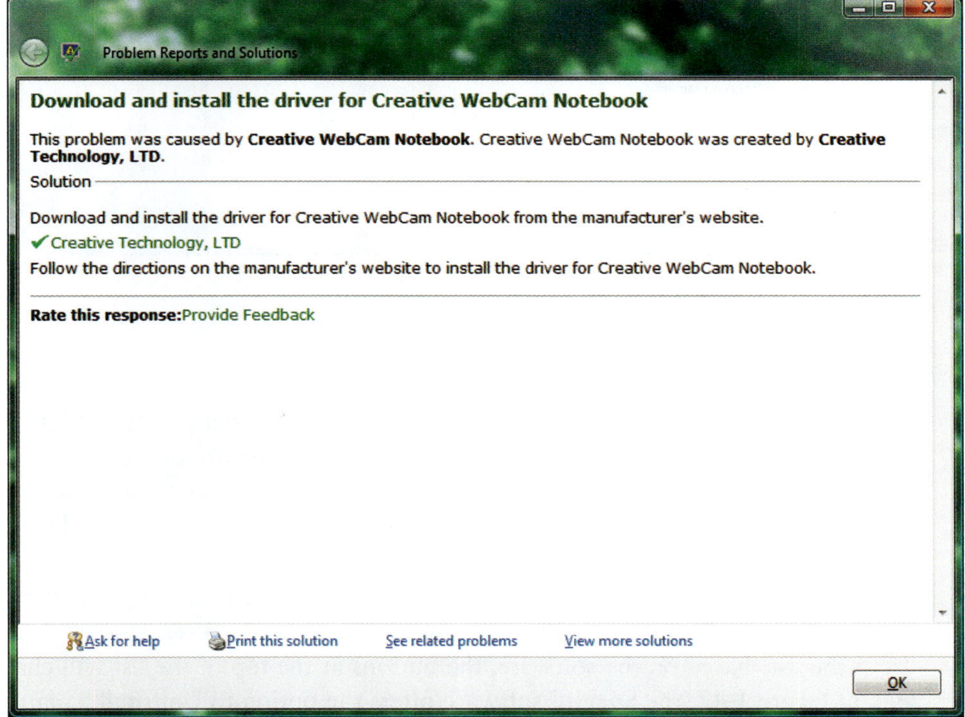

Figure 1-39 The Problem Reports and Solutions window helps to find device drivers

4. When you click that link, you are taken to a Web page with a message from Creative saying they will not provide Vista drivers for the camera because the camera is too old. Therefore, this camera cannot work under Vista. (Too bad—it was only a year old.)

Notes

To avoid the problems just described, even though Vista will try to help you locate drivers, always make sure you have the device drivers for Vista on CD or downloaded to the hard drive before you begin an installation.

INSTALL APPLICATIONS

As with previous versions of Windows, to install an application, insert the setup CD or DVD and follow directions on screen to launch the installation routine. For software downloaded from the Internet using Windows Explorer, double-click the program filename to begin the installation. If you are not logged in as an administrator, but need to install the software using administrative privileges, right-click the program filename and select *Run as administrator* from the shortcut menu (see Figure 1-40).

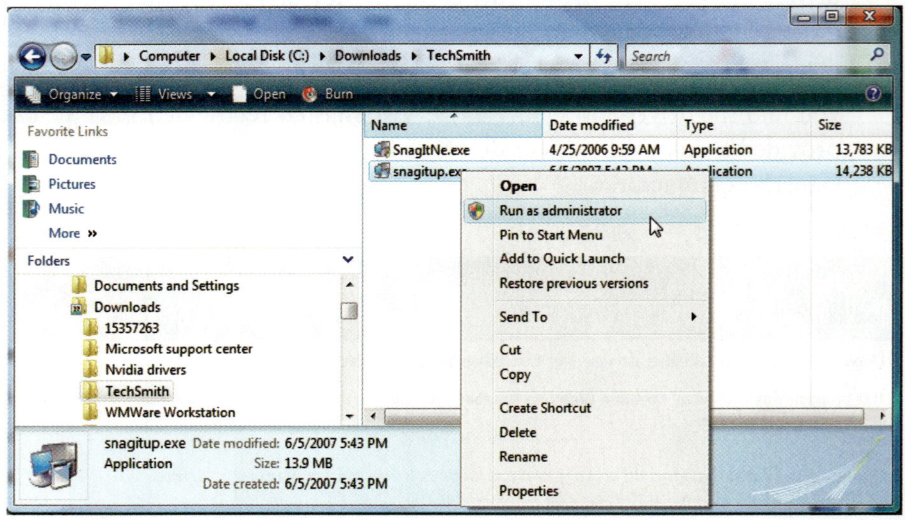

Figure 1-40 Execute a program using administrative privileges

In Windows Vista, the Windows XP Add or Remove Programs applet has been replaced with the Programs and Features window. To manage software on your Vista PC, from Control Panel, click Programs (see Figure 1-30 earlier in the chapter). The list of tools to manage installed programs appears in the left pane of the Programs window shown in Figure 1-41.

To see a list of installed programs, under Programs and Features, click *Uninstall a program*. The Programs and Features window shown in Figure 1-42 appears. Select a program from the list. Based on the software, the buttons at the top of the list will change. For example, in Figure 1-42, the SnagIt8 software offers the option to Uninstall, Change, or Repair the software.

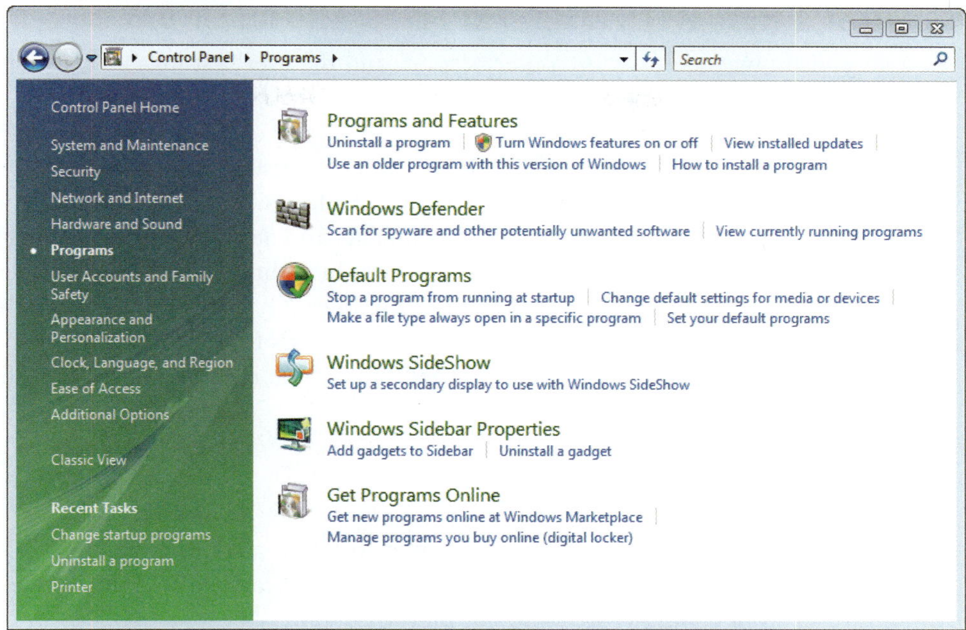

Figure 1-41 Manage software on your PC using the Programs window

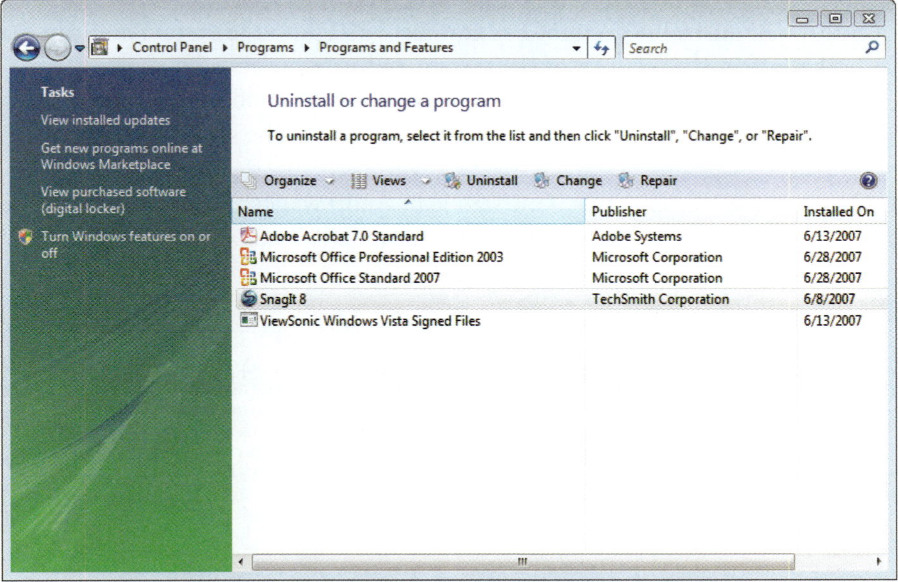

Figure 1-42 Select a program from the list to view your options for managing the software

CREATE USER ACCOUNTS

When Vista is first installed, it creates one user account with administrative privileges and the all-powerful Administrator account. (The Administrator account is disabled by default.) Even if you are the single user for a computer, be sure to create at least one other user account for your normal work that has limited power. Malicious software can sometimes take advantage of an administrator account when it is active so it is best to not log in as an administrator for normal day-to-day activities.

In the following sections, you will learn about new features in Vista for managing user profiles and user data, how to set up a new user account, and how to transfer user data and preferences from another computer to a Vista computer.

WHAT'S NEW WITH USER PROFILES AND USER DATA

Using Vista, when you set up a user account and the user first logs in, a user profile is created that consists of two general items:

- A folder together with its subfolders, which is created under the %SystemDrive% \Users folder, for example, C:\Users\Jean Andrews. Under Windows XP, this folder was under the %SystemDrive%\Documents and Settings folder, for example, C:\Documents and Settings\Jean Andrews. In addition, the user subfolders under Vista are organized differently than under Windows XP.
- A registry hive file named Ntuser.dat in the user's folder contains user settings and maps to the HKEY_CURRENT_USER key of the registry. This works the same way as it did in Windows XP.

Using Vista, there are two types of user profiles:

- **Local user profiles** are created and used solely on a single computer.
- **Roaming user profiles** are stored in the Active Directory on a domain and follow a user from computer to computer on the domain.

Using Vista, there are two levels of user accounts:

- An **administrator account** has complete access to the system and can make changes that affect the security of the system and other users.
- A **standard user** can use software and hardware and make some system changes, but cannot make changes that affect the security of the system or other users.

The user folder (for example, C:\Users\Jean Andrews) contains a group of subfolders organized differently than the group under Windows XP. Take a look at Figure 1-43 to see the

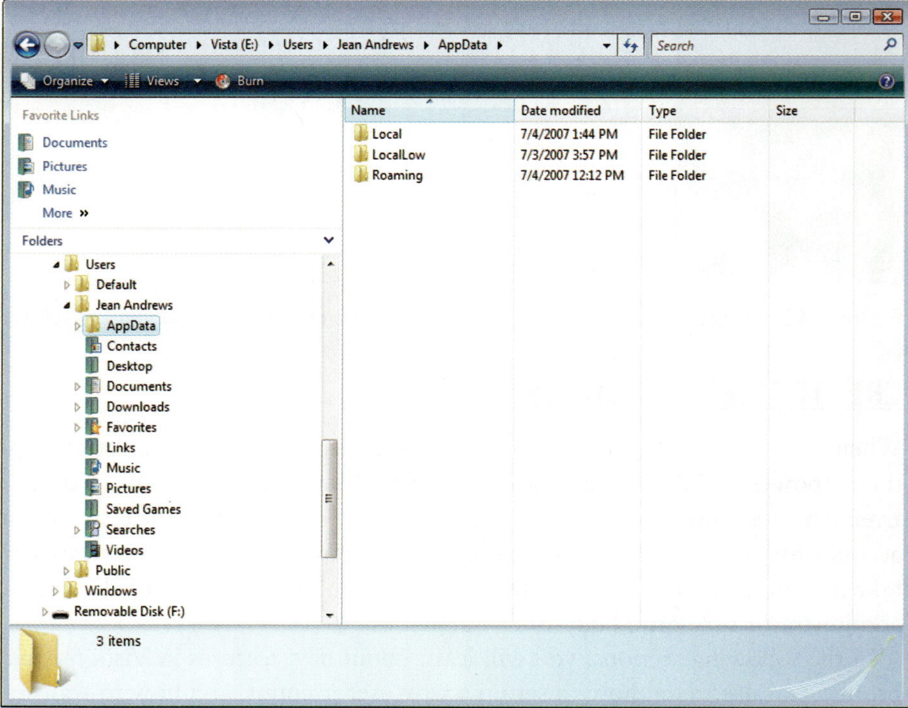

Figure 1-43 A user profile contains a folder and subfolders to hold user and application data

new Vista organization. This group of folders and subfolders is called the user profile namespace. The organization of these subfolders under Vista is cleaner and easier to manage than the organization under Windows XP.

Also notice in Figure 1-43, the \Users\Public folder. Microsoft encourages you to put files in this Public folder that will be shared on the network so that your private user data folders are better protected.

APPLYING CONCEPTS

SETTING UP A NEW USER ACCOUNT

To set up a new user account, follow these steps:

1. From Control Panel, under User Accounts and Family Safety, click **Add or remove user accounts** and respond to the UAC box. The Manage Accounts window appears, as shown in Figure 1-44.

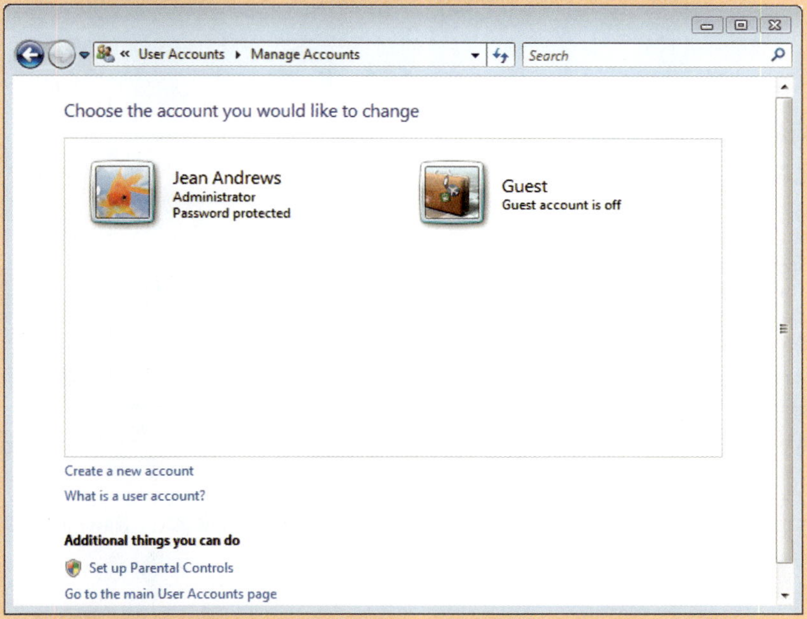

Figure 1-44 Use the Manage Accounts window to create accounts and set parental controls

2. Click **Create a new account.** On the Create New Account window shown in Figure 1-45, enter the account name and select the type of account (Standard user or Administrator). Then click **Create Account.**

3. The account now displays in the Manage Accounts window. Click the account to see a list of changes you can make to the account. The Change an Account window appears, as shown in Figure 1-46. If you want to set a password for the new account, click **Create a password** and enter the password on the next screen.

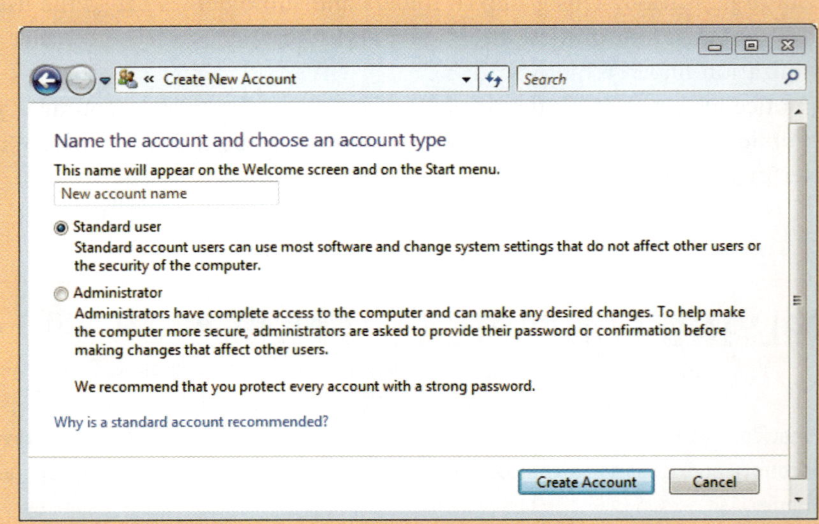

Figure 1-45 Name the account and select the account type

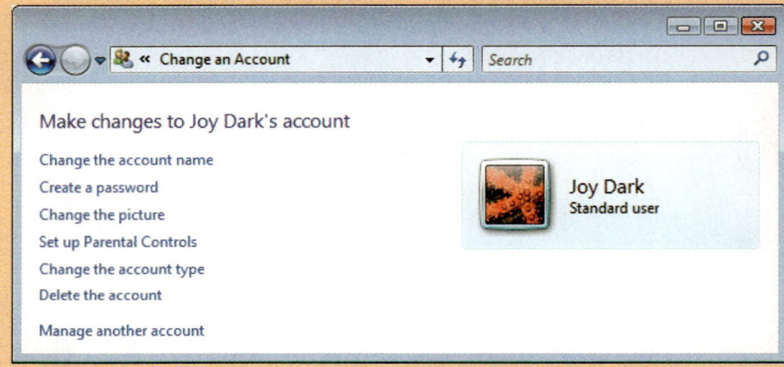

Figure 1-46 Make changes to an account

Another way to create and manage accounts is to use the Computer Management console. Follow these steps:

1. To open the console, click **Start**, right-click **Computer**, select **Manage** from the shortcut window, and respond to the UAC box. In the console window, under System Tools, Local Users and Groups, right-click **Users** and select **New User** from the shortcut menu. The New User dialog box appears as shown on the right side of Figure 1-47.
2. Fill in the appropriate information and click **Create**. The new Standard account is now listed under Users.
3. To change an account, right-click the account and select **Properties** from the shortcut menu. Using the properties window (see Figure 1-48), you can control the password, which user groups the account belongs to, and the path to the user's profile. Incidentally, if you want to give Administrator privileges to a Standard account, add the account to the Administrators group.

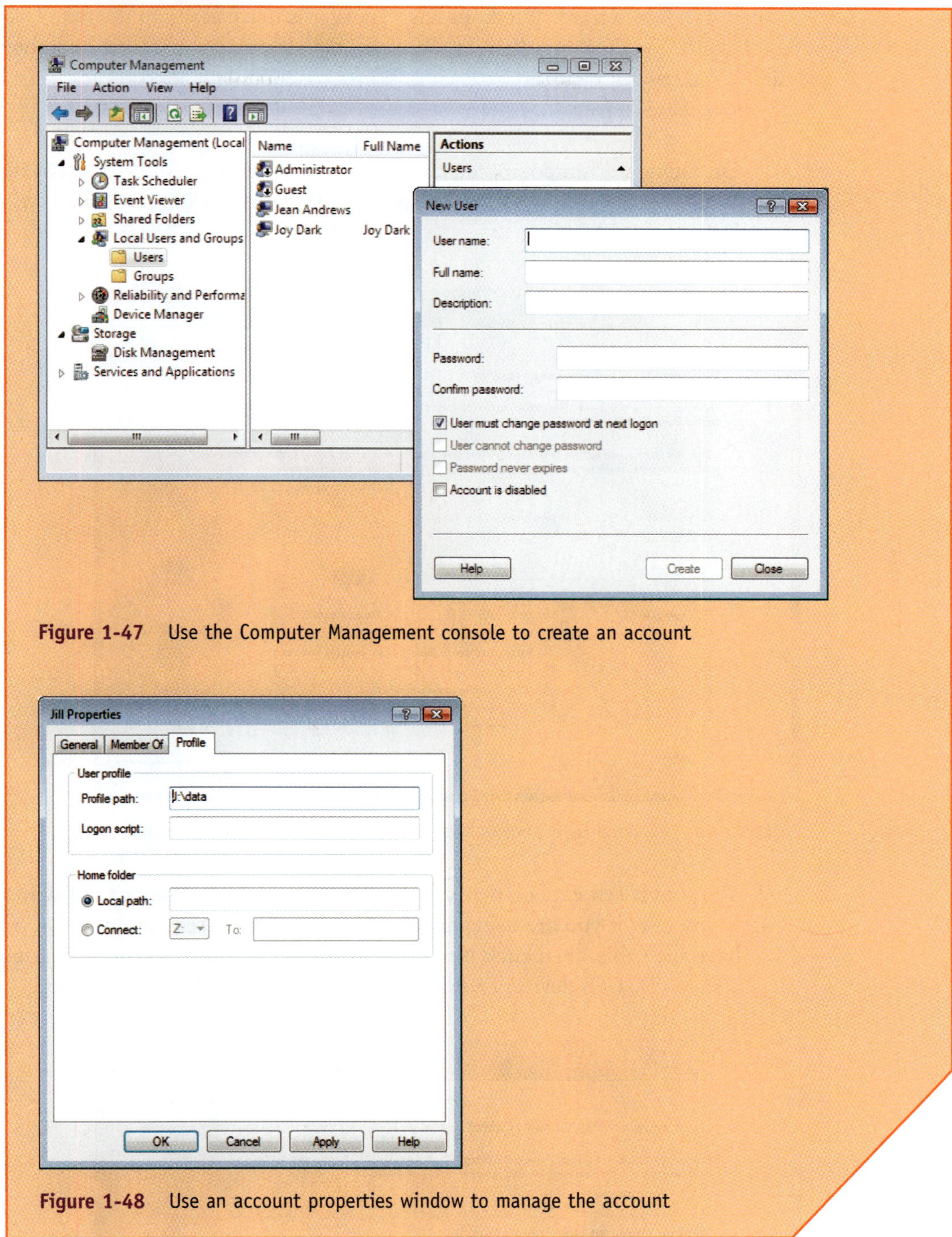

Figure 1-47 Use the Computer Management console to create an account

Figure 1-48 Use an account properties window to manage the account

In the next chapter, you will learn more about managing and securing user accounts, including controlling which files and folders a user can access.

TRANSFERRING USER DATA AND PREFERENCES

When you first install Vista on a new computer, you might need to transfer user data and preferences from an old computer to the new computer. Two tools used for this purpose are the User State Migration Tool (USMT) and Windows Easy Transfer.

USMT is an automated tool used in large organizations when Vista is being deployed to multiple computers. Windows Easy Transfer is a manual tool similar to Windows XP Files and

Settings Transfer Wizard. Windows Easy Transfer is much easier to use than USMT and the better choice for a few installations. To use it, the old computer (source computer) must be using Windows XP with Service Pack 2, Windows 2000 with Service Pack 4, or Windows Vista.

Follow these steps:

1. On the new Vista computer, click **Start, All Programs, Accessories, System Tools,** Windows Easy Transfer, and respond to the UAC box. The opening window is shown in Figure 1-49.

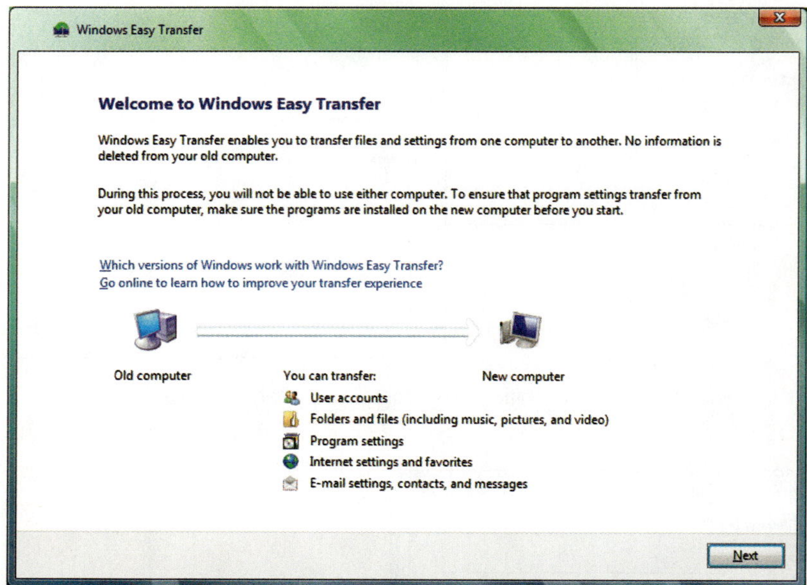

Figure 1-49 Windows Easy Transfer lists the type of data that can be transferred

2. The tool is self explanatory and easy to follow. As you work your way through, the utility asks if you are using an Easy Transfer Cable (see Figure 1-50). If you do not have the cable, then click **No, show me more options** to transfer data using a network, CD, DVD, USB device, or external hard disk.

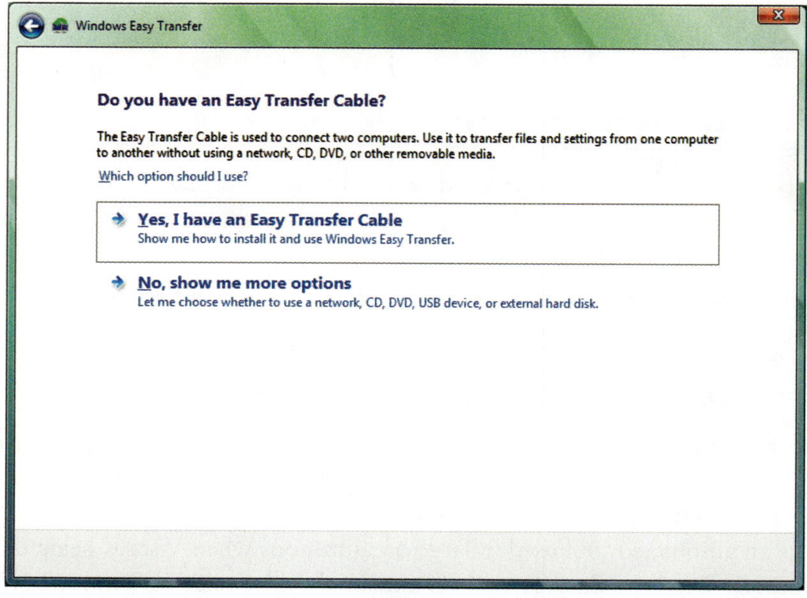

Figure 1-50 Tell Windows Easy Transfer which device will be used for the transfer

3. The next window is shown in Figure 1-51. If your old computer is running Windows XP or Windows 2000, you will need to install the Windows Easy Transfer software. In this situation, choose **No, I need to install it now.**

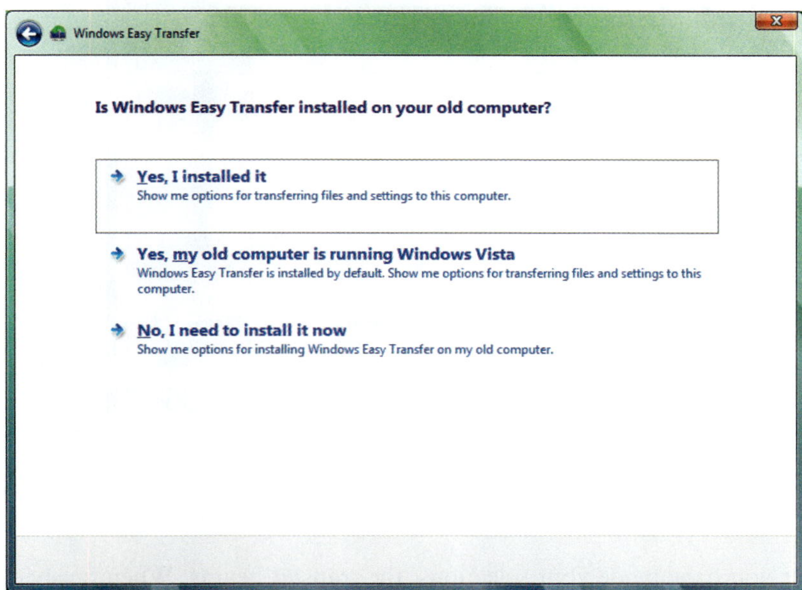

Figure 1-51 Is Windows Easy Transfer installed on your old computer?

4. The next window (see Figure 1-52) asks how you will install the software. If the two computers are on the same network, select **External hard disk or shared network folder.**

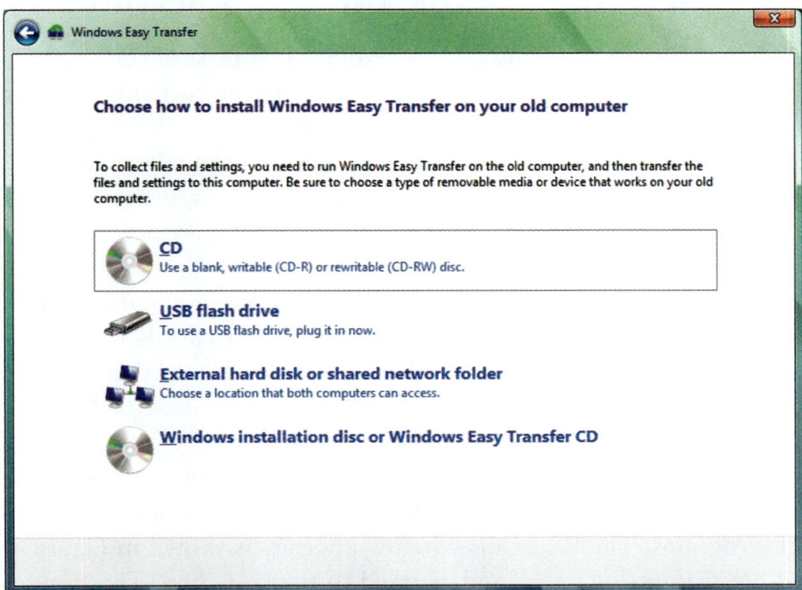

Figure 1-52 Choose how you will install the Windows Easy Transfer software on the old computer

5. After the software is installed and running on the old computer, the two computers will be communicating. The next step is to select the files, folders, and other items on the old computer that you want to transfer. The window that appears on the old computer for you to make your selections is shown in Figure 1-53.

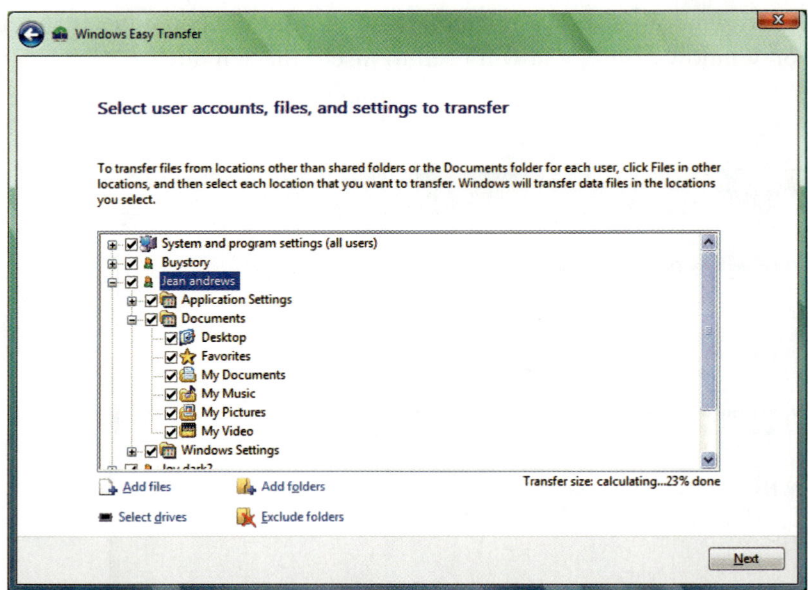

Figure 1-53 Select folders, files, and settings to transfer

6. After you have made your selections, the transfer begins. When finished, be sure to verify that everything is safely transferred before you delete the data on the old computer. In fact, it is a good idea to keep the old computer intact until the user has worked on the new computer for about a month, just in case the user left something important behind.

CUSTOMIZE THE VISTA DESKTOP AND OTHER SETTINGS

To customize the Vista desktop and display settings, first be sure you are logged on under the correct user account, because these settings apply to the currently logged-on user. Then in the Control Panel, click Appearance and Personalization. In the Appearance and Personalization window shown in Figure 1-54, you can make selections to change the desktop background, color scheme, screen resolution, screen saver, desktop theme, taskbar, Start menu, folder options, fonts, and sidebar gadgets so that Windows will look and work the way you want it.

You can also configure the Start menu using the Taskbar and Start Menu Properties dialog box or from Group Policy. To use the dialog box, right-click Start and select Properties from the shortcut menu. Notice in Figure 1-55 the two new tabs that were not available under Windows XP—Notification Area and Toolbars. Using these tabs, you can control when icons and toolbars appear in the taskbar.

When Vista is first installed, by default, it turns certain software components on and others off. To see how these features are set and change these settings, from the Control Panel, click Programs. The Programs window appears as shown in Figure 1-56. Click *Turn Windows features on or off* and respond to the UAC box. The Windows Features dialog box opens. To expand groups of items, click the plus sign beside a checkbox. Generally, the features are set as they should be. However, to meet specific user needs, you might need to turn on Telnet client, Telnet server, FTP server, or some similar seldom-ly-used Windows feature. To get more information about an item, search for it in Windows Help and Support. Check or uncheck a feature to turn it on or off. Click OK when you are done.

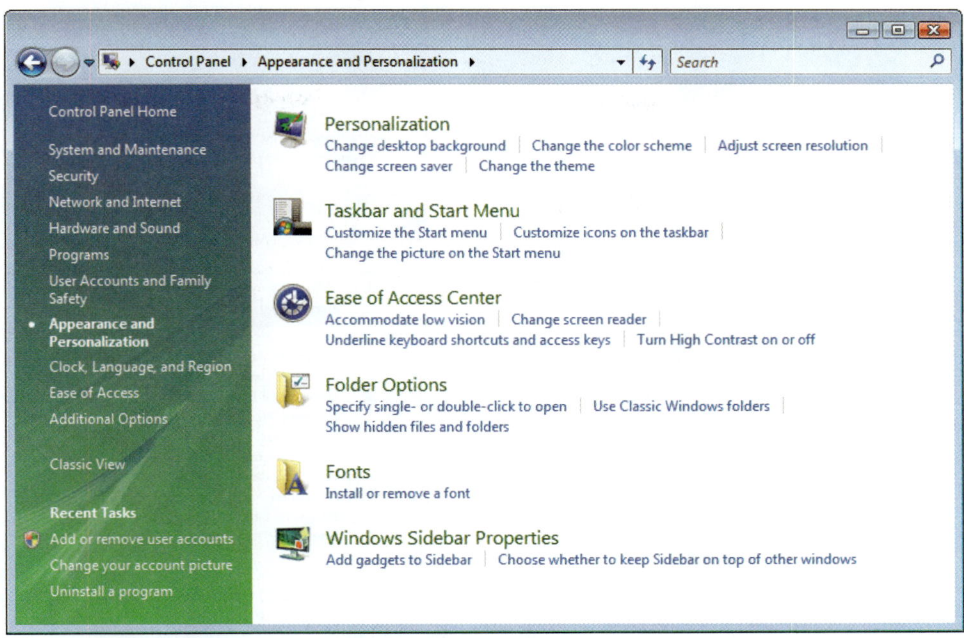

Figure 1-54 Use the Appearance and Personalization window to customize the Vista desktop

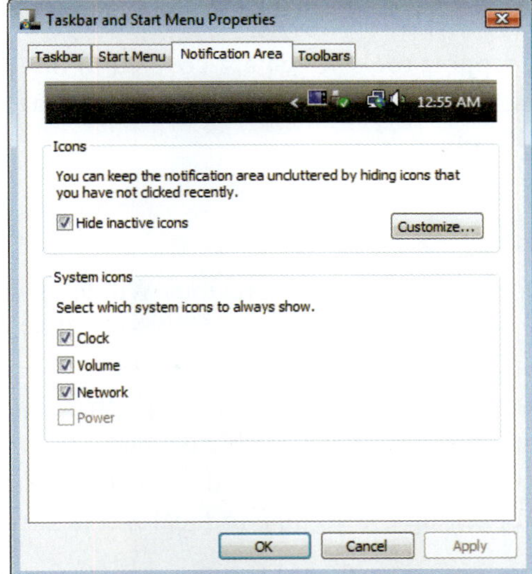

Figure 1-55 Manage the taskbar using the Taskbar and Start Menu Properties box

You should now have Vista configured and functioning as you want it. To finish up, do one last restart and verify everything is working and looking good. After you have verified everything, it is a good idea to back up the entire volume on which Vista is installed. How to perform Windows backups is covered in the section, "Backups Using Windows Vista," later in the chapter.

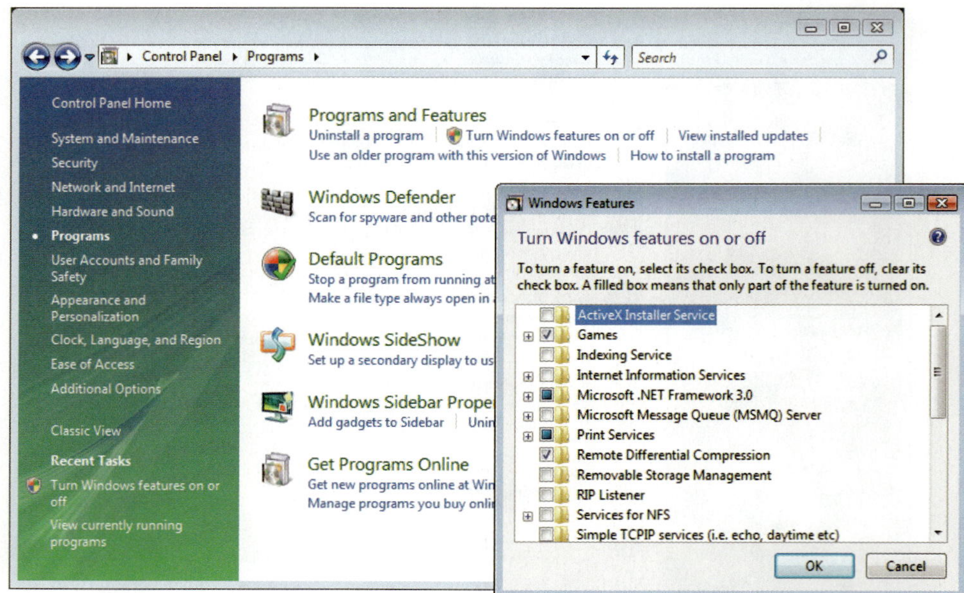

Figure 1-56 Control what Windows features are available

VISTA SUPPORT TOOLS

Vista offers many new and improved support tools which are covered in this section. This includes backups using Vista, Windows Memory Diagnostics, tools to manage a hard drive, networking tools, Group Policy, and Resource Monitor.

BACKUPS USING WINDOWS VISTA

The Vista backup utility is greatly improved over that of previous Windows versions. Here are key improvements and features:

- When Vista backs up files, it uses a feature called shadow copy that takes a snapshot of a file so that you can back up a file even when the file is open.
- Complete PC backup will back up entire volumes. The data is compressed so that it takes up less space, and you can back up the volume to local media such as a removable hard drive or DVDs.
- Files and folders are compressed into .zip files as they are backed up and can be backed up to local media or to a network drive. After the initial backup is performed, later automatic backups are done incrementally. The initial backup creates a folder for the backup and incremental backups are stored in subfolders. Multiple copies of these incremental backups are kept so that you can retrieve a backup from several generations back. Because the backed-up files are Zip files, you can easily search for old backups, and you can even use a different operating system to search and recover backed up files.

First let's look at how to perform a Complete PC backup and restore from that backup, and then we will look at how to backup and restore files and folders.

COMPLETE PC BACKUP

A Complete PC backup makes a backup of the entire volume on which Vista is installed and can also back up other volumes. The best practice to protect a Vista system is to make a

Complete PC backup after you have installed Vista, all hardware devices, and all applications. This backup works similar to recovery DVDs that come with a brand name computer used to recover from a failed hard drive to return the system to its original state at the time of purchase.

> **Notes**
>
> Recall that Complete PC backup is not available in Vista Starter or Vista Home versions.

The Complete PC backup must be saved to a local device, such as an external hard drive or DVDs. Do not back up the volume to another partition on the same hard drive. After the initial backup is made, Vista will automatically keep this backup current by making incremental backups. Vista does not keep multiple copies of Complete PC backups, as it does with files and folders.

To decide how much space you will need on your backup device, follow these steps to find out the size of the volume or volumes you are backing up:

1. To open Windows Explorer, right-click **Start** and click **Explore** from the shortcut menu. Then right-click the Vista volume and select **Properties** from the shortcut menu.
2. In the properties window, find the capacity and used space on the volume. For example, in Figure 1-57, you will see drive C is 64 GB and the used space on the drive is about 9 GB.

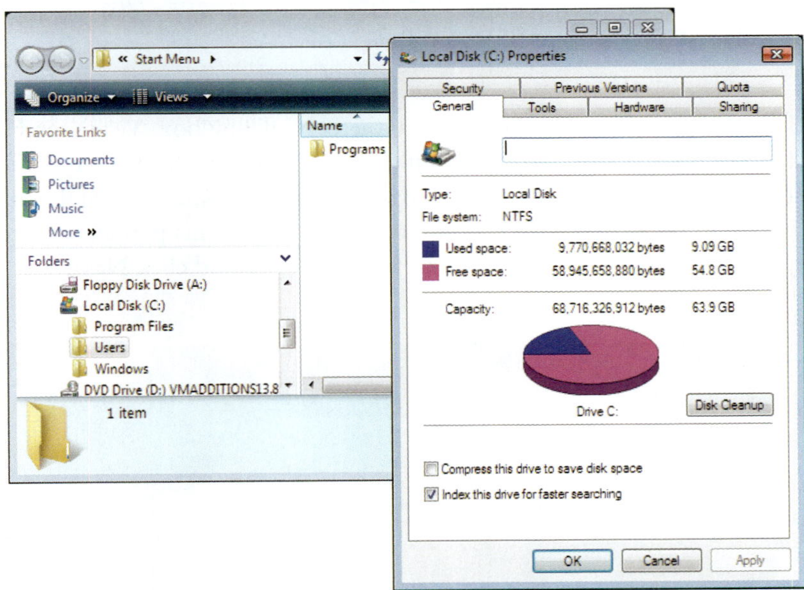

Figure 1-57 Use Windows Explorer to find out the capacity and used space for each volume you are backing up

Complete PC backup will compress the data, so the backup will not be as large as the used space, but, to be on the safe side, allow that much space for the backup and then plenty of room to grow for future backups. How much growing room? The most backup space you will ever need is the total size of all volumes being backed up. If you are backing up to DVDs, know that one single-layer DVD holds about 4.5 GB.

Follow these steps to create the initial Complete PC backup:

1. Connect your backup device to your PC. If you are using an external hard drive, use Windows Explorer to verify you can access the drive.
2. From Control Panel, under System and Maintenance, click **Back up your computer.** The Backup and Restore Center window appears as shown in Figure 1-58.

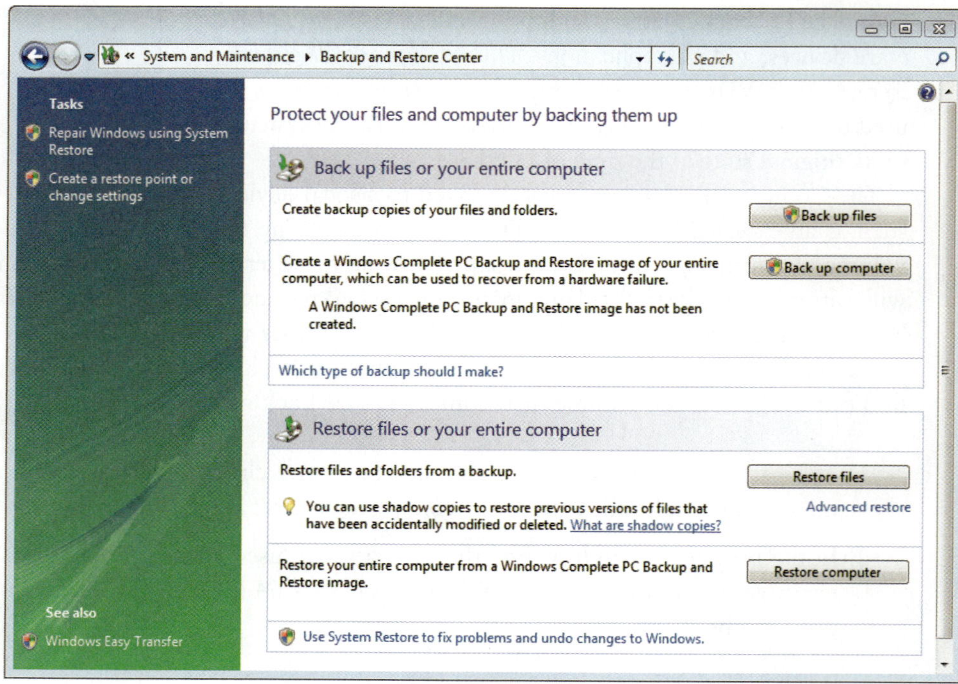

Figure 1-58 Windows Vista Backup and Restore Center

3. Click **Back up computer** and respond to the UAC dialog box. Vista searches for available backup devices and then displays a window similar to the one shown in Figure 1-59. The choices displayed depend on the available backup devices. For example, in Figure 1-60, the option to back up to DVDs is not available because this particular system does not have a writeable DVD drive. Select the backup device and click **Next.**

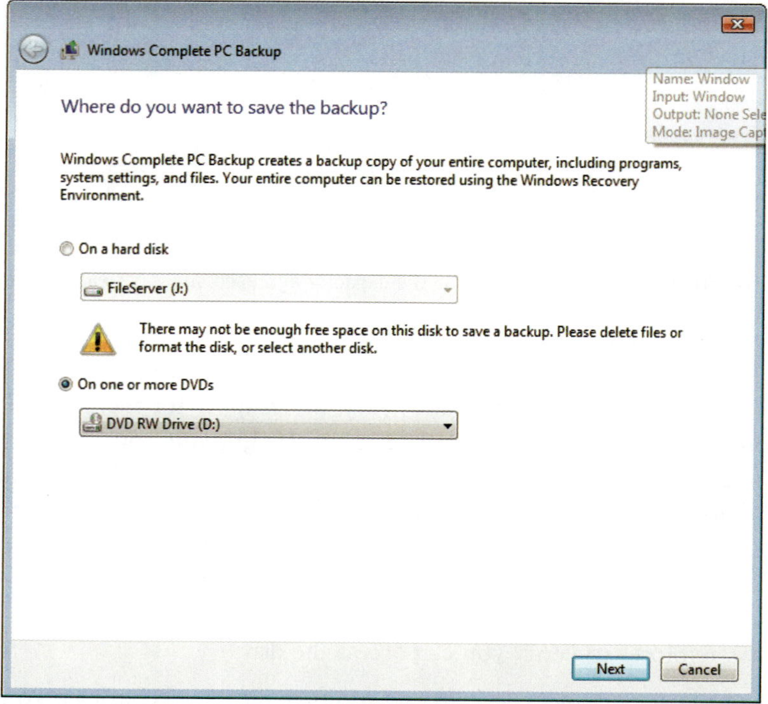

Figure 1-59 Vista Backup asks where you want to save the backup

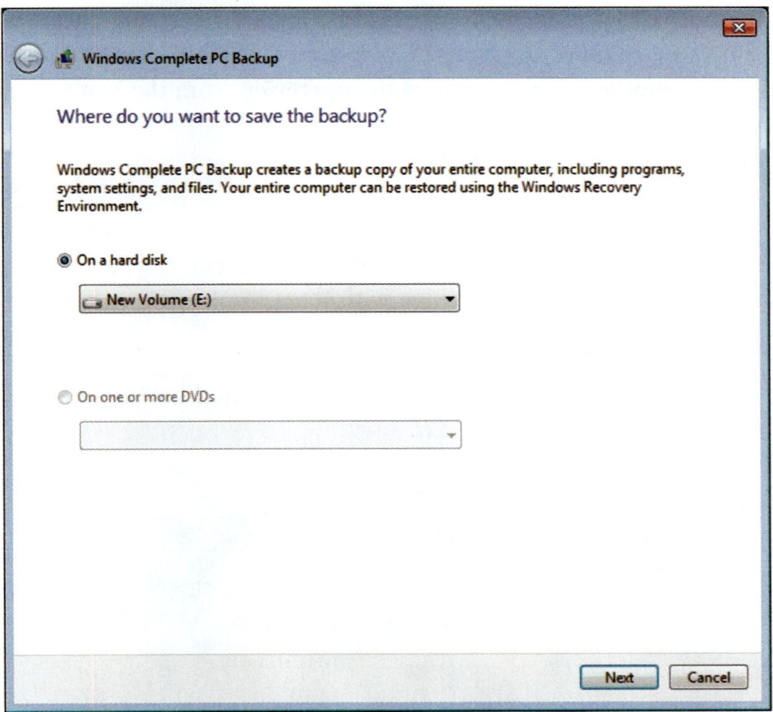

Figure 1-60 Options to hold the backup depend on available hardware

4. If the system contains multiple volumes, Vista displays a window asking if you want to back up additional volumes. Make your selections and click **Next.**
5. On the next window (see Figure 1-61), the backup tells you the maximum amount of space expected for the backup, assuming no compression as well as room for house-keeping. If you are backing up to DVDs, the backup tells you about how many DVDs are required. Click **Start backup** to begin the backup.

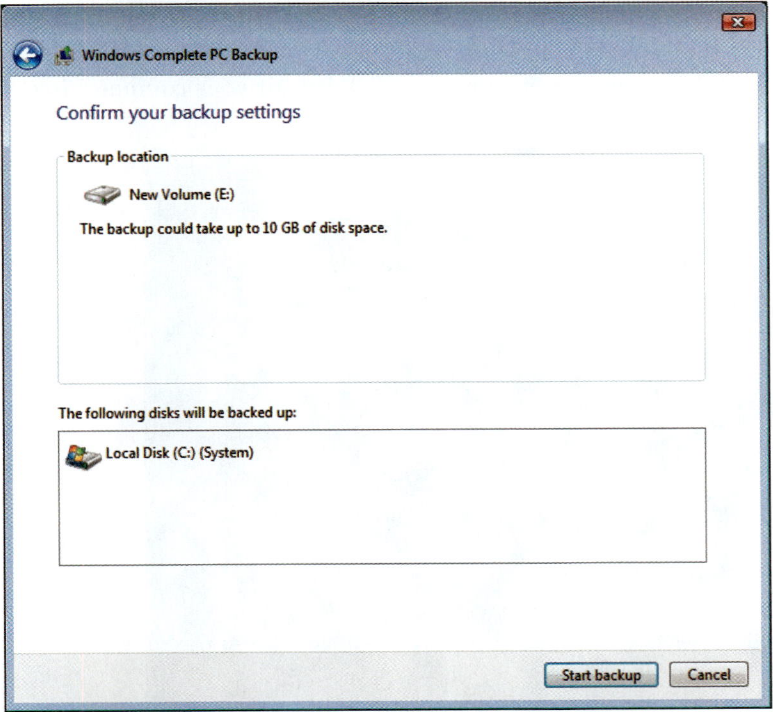

Figure 1-61 Confirm your backup settings and begin the backup

In the event your hard drive fails or Vista is so corrupted you cannot recover it, you can restore the volume or volumes from your Complete PC backup. Because the entire Vista volume will be overwritten, you must perform the operation from the Vista setup DVD using the Windows Recovery Environment (Windows RE).

Follow these steps to recover the system from backup:

1. Because this process will erase everything on the Vista volume and any other volumes included in the Complete PC backup, make every attempt to save any important data on these volumes before you continue with these steps.
2. Connect the backup device to your computer.
3. Boot from the Vista DVD and select your language and keyboard layout preferences, as shown in Figure 1-62. Click **Next.**

Figure 1-62 Select language and keyboard preferences

4. The Install Windows screen appears. Click **Repair your computer** (see Figure 1-63).

Figure 1-63 Opening menu when you boot from the Vista DVD

5. System Recovery searches for an installed OS. If it finds one, select it and click **Next.** If it does not find an installed OS, just click **Next.**
6. If System Recovery presents a logon dialog box, log into the system using an administrator account and password.
7. The System Recovery Options window shown in Figure 1-64 appears. Click **Windows Complete PC Restore,** and follow directions on screen to restore the system from backup.

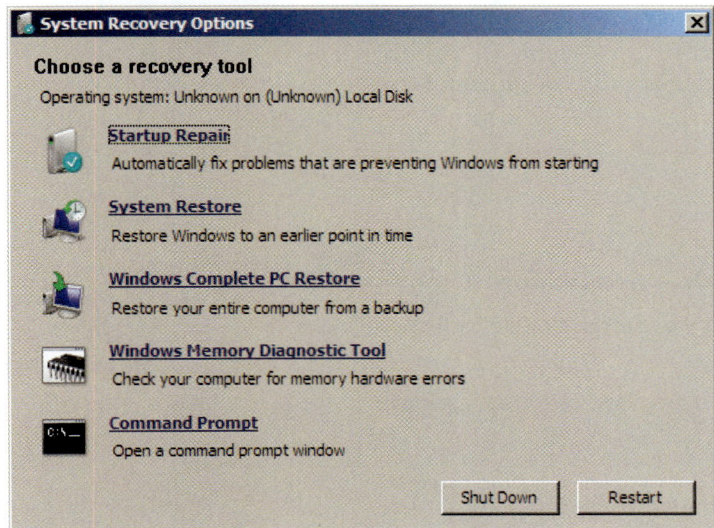

Figure 1-64 Restore the system to a previous Complete PC backup

In the next chapter, you will learn more about the Windows Recovery Environment including how to use all the options shown in Figure 1-64 and what you can do to recover from a failed Vista system without having to revert back to the last Complete PC backup.

BACK UP FILES AND FOLDERS

As part of routine maintenance of a system, you need to schedule routine backups of all user data folders. Follow these steps to back up files and folders:

1. On the Backup and Restore Center window shown earlier in Figure 1-58, click **Back up files** and respond to the UAC box. On the next window (see Figure 1-65), select where you want to save your backup and click **Next.**
2. On the next window, select the volumes on your computer that contain folders or files you want to back up and click **Next.**
3. On the next window, shown in Figure 1-66, select the type of files you want to back up and click **Next.**
4. The next window lets you select how often (daily, weekly, or monthly), what day (day of week or day of month), and what time of day to schedule automatic incremental backups of today's full backup. Make your selections and click **Save settings and start backup.**

To see the status of the last file and folder backup or the last Complete PC backup, click Start, All Programs, Accessories, System Tools, Backup Status and Configuration.

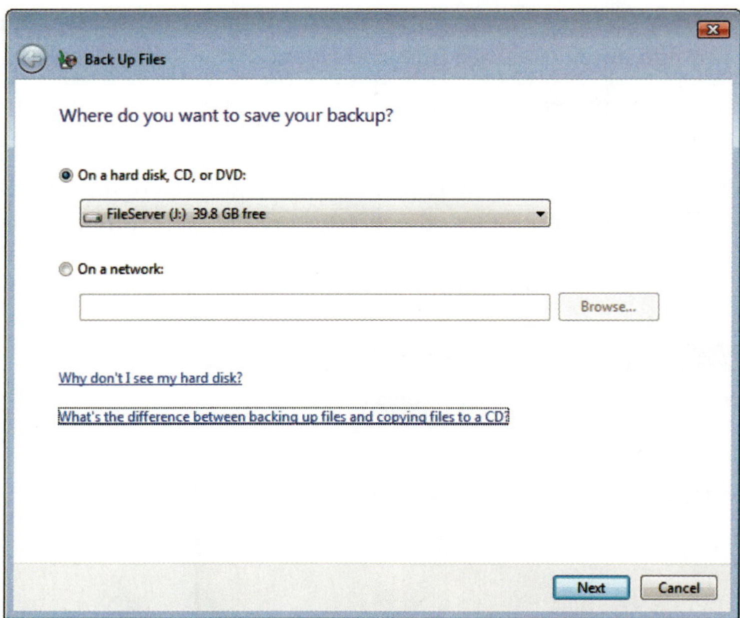

Figure 1-65 Select your backup location for files and folders

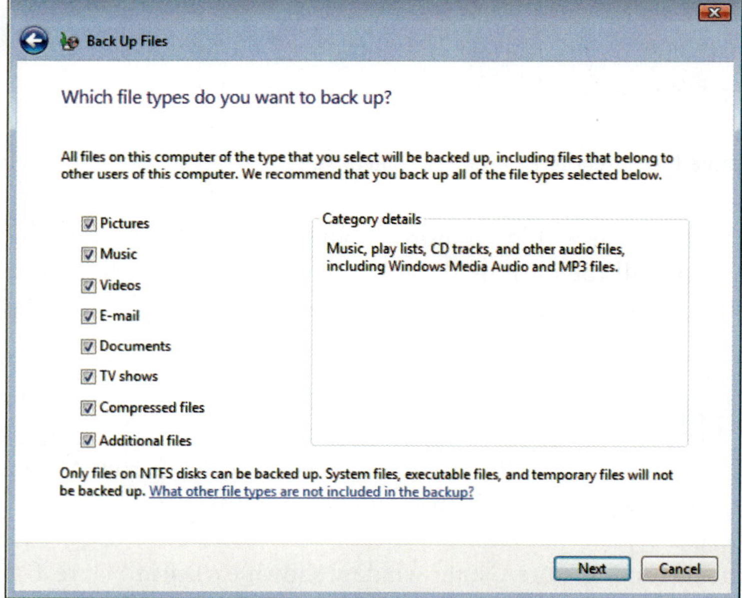

Figure 1-66 Select the types of files to back up

The Backup Status and Configuration window opens as shown in Figure 1-67. Using this window, you can change the backup settings. When you change the settings, a new, full backup is created.

To restore files from backup, on the Backup Status and Configuration window, click Restore Files and follow directions on screen to select a specific backup and specific folders or files to restore.

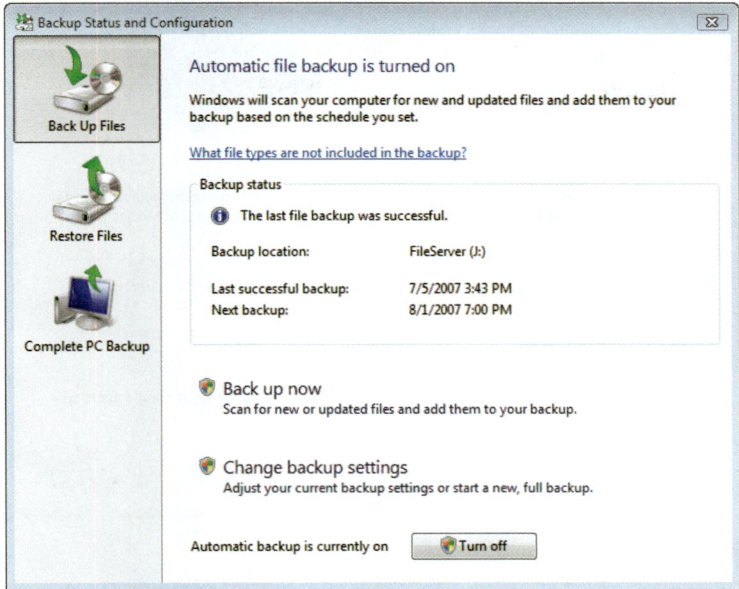

Figure 1-67 Backup Status and Configuration window

WINDOWS MEMORY DIAGNOSTICS

Windows Memory Diagnostics tests memory for errors and works before Windows Vista is loaded. The diagnostic test can be initiated using one of these methods:

- If Windows Error Reporting (WER) or Microsoft Online Crash Analysis (MOCA) detects that memory might be failing, the utility will prompt the user to test memory on the next reboot. If the user agrees by clicking *Check for problems the next time you start your computer*, then diagnostic tests are run on the next restart. After Windows desktop loads, a bubble message appears giving the test results. If the test shows that memory is giving errors, replace the memory modules.
- You can test memory at any time using the command prompt. To do so, click Start, All Programs, Accessories, Command Prompt. The Command Prompt window opens. Type `mdsched` and press Enter, as shown in Figure 1-68, and respond to the UAC box. This executes the program file, mdsched.exe. In the dialog box that appears, also shown in the figure, you can choose to run the test now or on the next restart.
- When troubleshooting a failed system, if the Vista desktop cannot load, you can run the memory diagnostic test from the Vista boot menu. This menu normally displays with a dual boot configuration so you can select the OS to load. If you are not using a dual boot machine, you can force the menu to display by pressing the space bar during the boot. The resulting menu appears as shown in Figure 1-69. Use the Tab key to highlight the option Windows Memory Diagnostic and press Enter.
- For any computer that has a DVD drive, you can run the test using the Vista DVD even if the computer is using a different OS than Vista:

  1. Boot from the Vista DVD. On the window that appears, select your language preference and click **Next**.
  2. On the opening menu of the Vista DVD, click **Repair your computer**, as shown earlier in Figure 1-63.

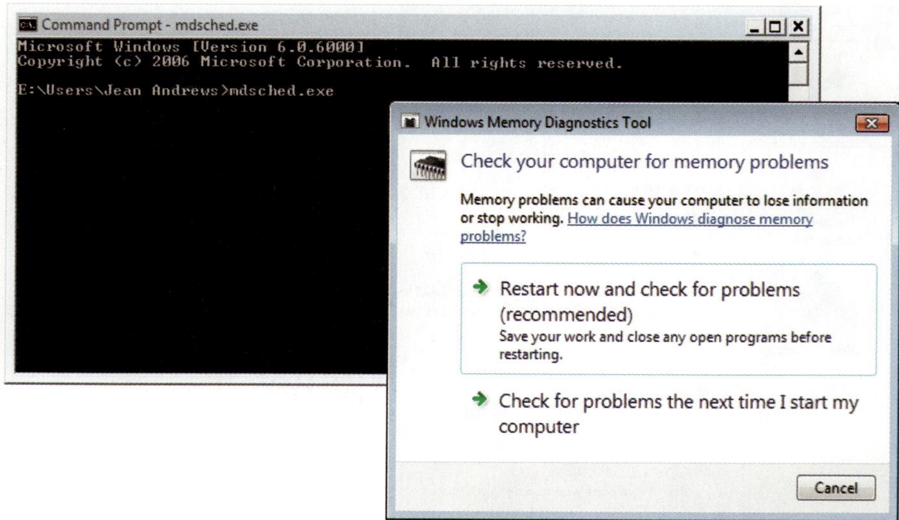

Figure 1-68 Use the mdsched command to test memory

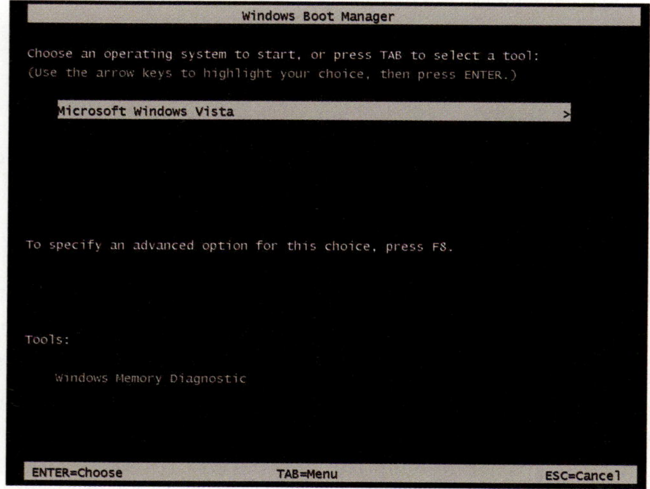

Figure 1-69 Force the Windows Boot Manager menu to display by pressing the space bar during the boot

3. The System Recovery Options window, shown earlier in Figure 1-64, appears. Click **Windows Memory Diagnostic Tool.**
4. On the next window, click **Restart now and check for problems (recommended).** The system will reboot and the memory test will start.

TOOLS TO MANAGE A HARD DRIVE

Just as with Windows XP and Windows 2000, Vista uses the `Chkdsk` and `Defrag` commands, the Disk Management utility, and Windows Explorer to manage hard drives. In this section, we will look at how Vista Disk Management is an improvement over the Windows XP version and discuss Windows ReadyBoost. In the next chapter, you will learn about new hard drive security features under Vista.

WINDOWS VISTA DISK MANAGEMENT

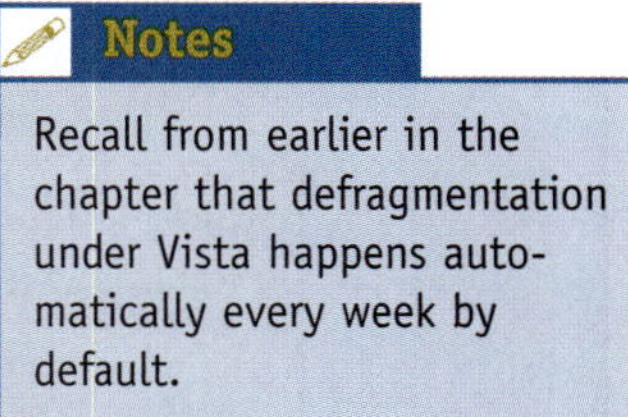

Notes

Recall from earlier in the chapter that defragmentation under Vista happens automatically every week by default.

Using Vista Disk Management, you can resize a hard drive partition without losing data on the partition. To access Disk Management, click Start, right-click Computer, select Manage from the shortcut menu, and respond to the UAC box. In the left pane of the Computer Management window, click Disk Management. The Disk Management pane appears on the right side of the window, similar to the one in Figure 1-70. (You can also access the window from Control Panel by way of System and Maintenance, Administrative Tools, Computer Management, and Disk Management.) To shrink, extend, or delete a partition, right-click the partition and make your selection from the shortcut menu which is showing in the figure.

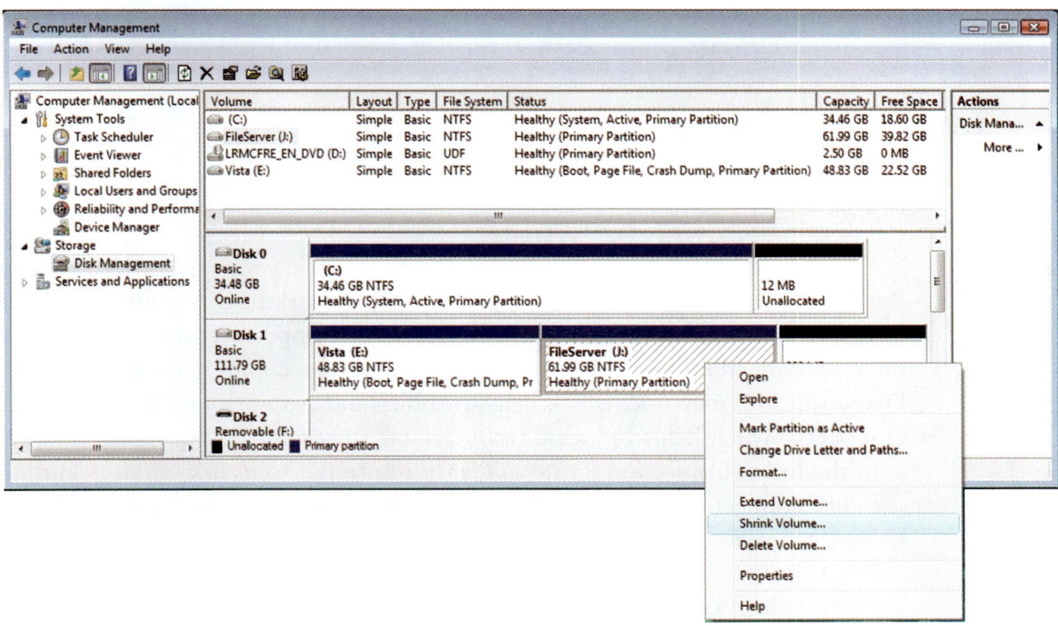

Figure 1-70 Using Vista Disk Management, you can dynamically resize a partition

WINDOWS READYBOOST

Windows ReadyBoost uses a flash drive or secure digital (SD) memory card to boost hard drive performance. The faster flash memory is used as a buffer to speed up hard drive access time. When you first connect the drive, Windows will automatically test it to see if it qualifies for ReadyBoost. To qualify, it must have a capacity of 256 MB to 4 GB with at least 256 MB of free space, and run at about 2 MB/sec of throughput. If the device qualifies, Windows will ask your permission to use the device for ReadyBoost, which will tie up at least 256 MB of free space. You can manually have Windows test a memory card or flash drive for ReadyBoost by right-clicking on the device and selecting Properties from the shortcut menu. On the device properties window, click the ReadyBoost tab, as shown in Figure 1-71.

The best flash devices to use for ReadyBoost are the ones that use the faster buses. For example, an onboard memory card reader in a laptop will be faster than a USB 1.1 external memory card reader. You see the greatest performance increase using ReadyBoost when you have a slow hard drive (running at less than 7200 RPM). When you remove the device, no data is lost because the device only holds a copy of the data.

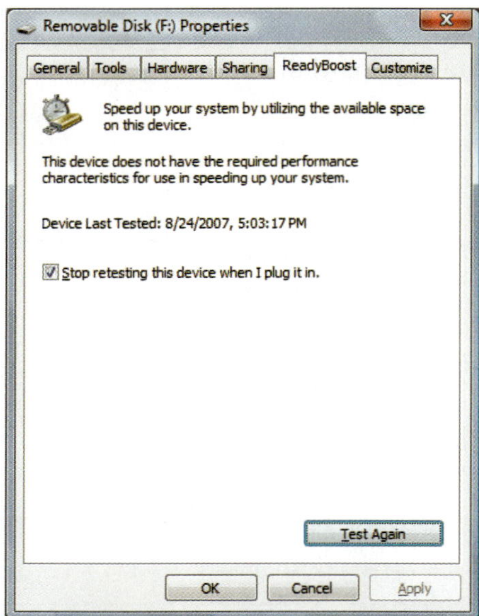

Figure 1-71 Offer a device for Windows to use for ReadyBoost

VISTA NETWORKING TOOLS

Both the networking tools and the underlying networking components of Windows Vista have changed from Windows XP, and these new components should make Vista work better on a network than its predecessor. Two of these new components are the Network Diagnostics Framework, which helps troubleshoot network problems, and Network Discovery, which helps to locate resources on a network.

In the following sections, you will learn to use the Network window and how to manage network connections, including the special concerns of wireless network connections. So, let's get started.

USING THE NETWORK WINDOW

The Windows XP My Network Places window has been replaced by Windows Vista Network window, but the two tools work pretty much the same way to view network connections. You can access the Network window from Windows Explorer (click Network) or from the Start menu (click Start, Network). Either way, the Network window appears similar to the left window in Figure 1-72. Use it to find resources on your network. Just as with Windows XP, to map a network drive to a folder on the network, right-click the folder and select Map Network Drive from the shortcut menu. The Map Network Drive dialog box appears as shown in the right window of Figure 1-72.

MANAGING NETWORK CONNECTIONS

The Network and Sharing Center and the Network Connections windows together replace the Network Connections window of Windows XP and offer new functionality to manage network connections. Follow these steps to explore how both windows work:

1. To open the Network and Sharing Center, use one of these two methods: Click **Start**, right-click **Network**, and select **Properties** from the shortcut menu. Another method is from Control Panel, click **View network status and tasks.** Either way the Network and Sharing Center window opens as shown in Figure 1-73.

1

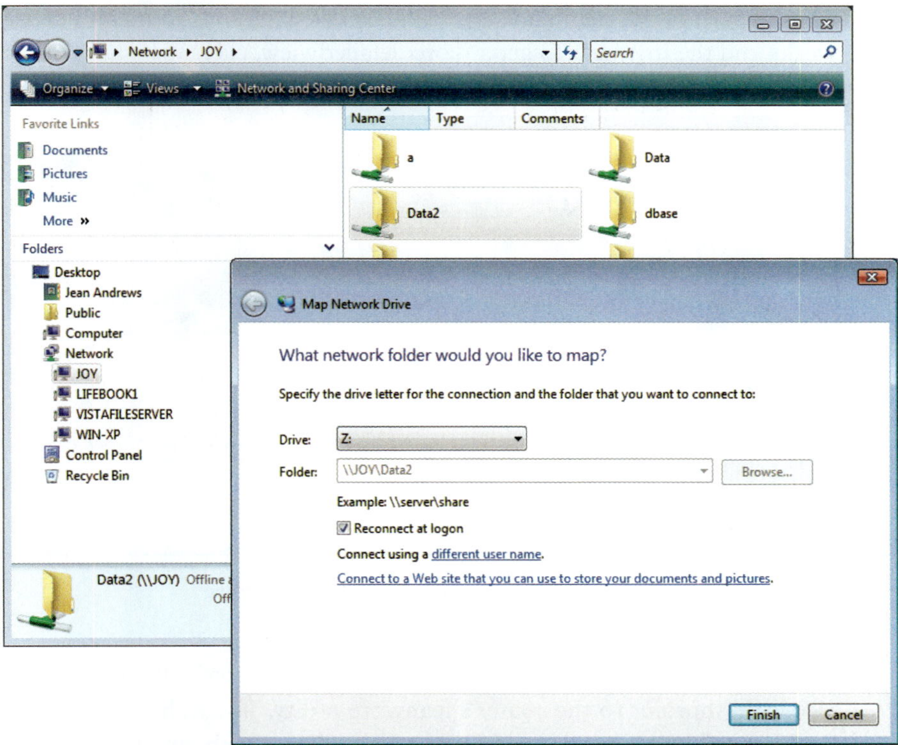

Figure 1-72 Dialog box used to map a network drive

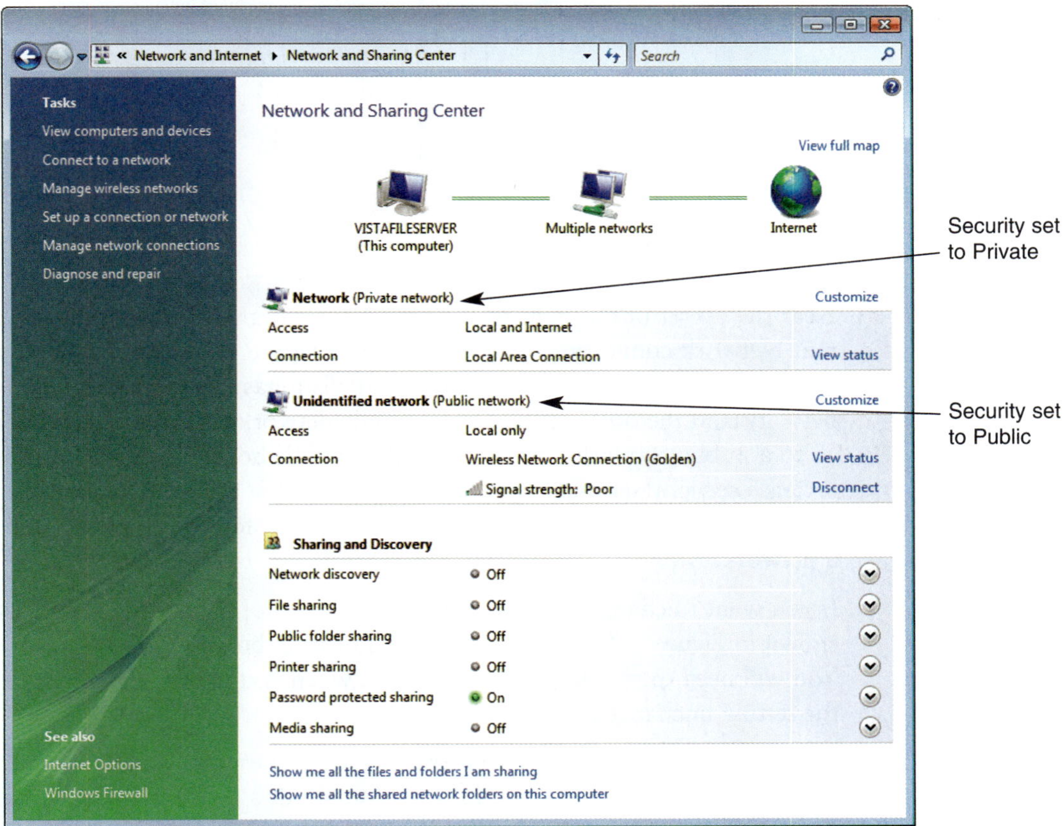

Figure 1-73 Use the Network and Sharing Center to manage Vista networking

2. Near the top of the right pane is a high-level view of how your computer connects to networks and the Internet. To get a more detailed view, click **View full map**. The Network Map window appears (see Figure 1-74) showing a diagram of networked devices.

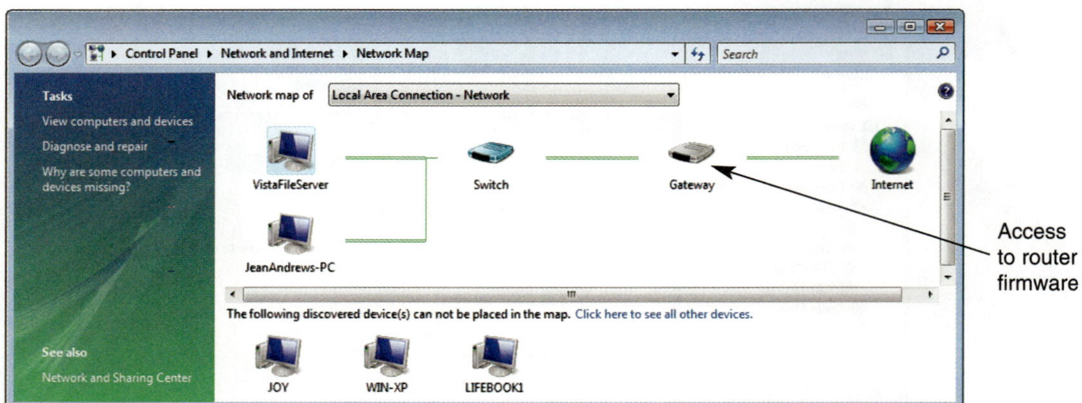

Figure 1-74 Use the Network Map to see how a network is configured

3. Ever needed to configure a router but forgot the router's IP address? Vista gives you a nice little shortcut to the router's firmware utility. Just right-click the **Gateway** icon in the Network Map window and select **View device webpage** from the shortcut menu (see Figure 1-75).

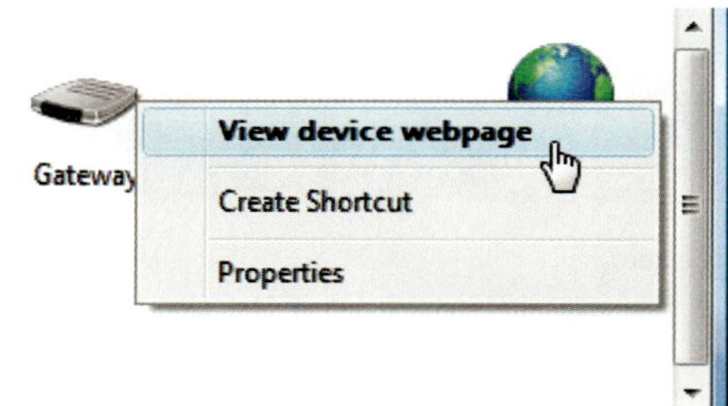

Figure 1-75 Use the Network Map to access router firmware

4. Near the center of the right pane of the Network and Sharing Center is a list of current Network connections. The computer in Figure 1-73 has two active network connections (wired and wireless). Notice that Vista has identified one network as a private network and the other network as a public network. If Vista believes you are connected to a public network (such as a wireless public hotspot at a coffee shop), it will increase security settings for your computer so that others are not able to access your computer. These settings can also make it difficult for you to access some resources on a network.

5. If you want to change the Public or Private status of a network, click **Customize**, shown in Figure 1-73. The Set Network Location box appears as shown in Figure 1-76. You will need to respond to the UAC box when you change the setting. For now, leave the setting unchanged.

6. In the Network and Sharing Center, click **View status** for a network connection to see a status dialog box giving you information about a connection and options to manage the connection. Figure 1-77 shows a status box for a wired network, and Figure 1-78 shows a wireless network status box.

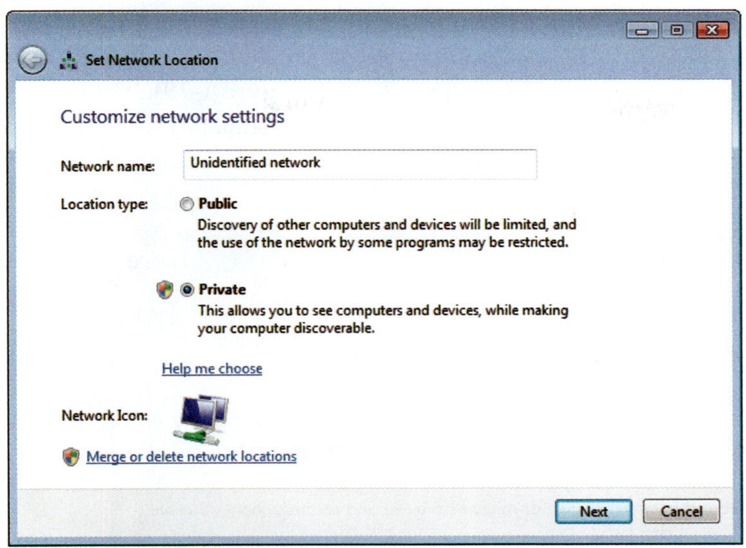

Figure 1-76 Change the public or private setting for a network

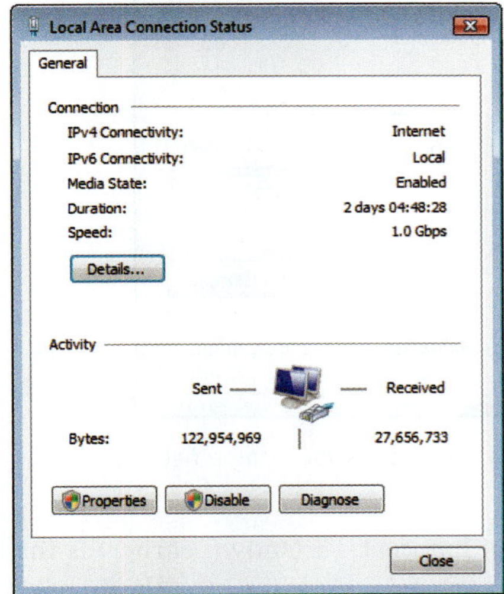

Figure 1-77 Use the Connection Status box for a network to view the connection status and diagnose problems with the connection

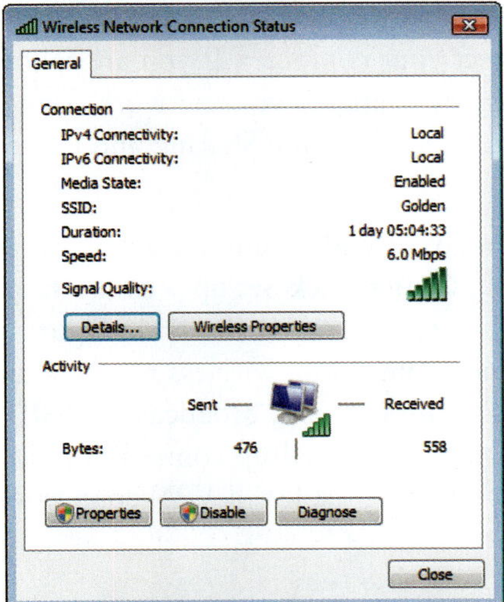

Figure 1-78 Status of a wireless network connection

7. If you click **Diagnose** in the status box for the wireless network in Figure 1-77, Windows Network Diagnostics reports what might be wrong with the connection and offers suggestions to fix the problem (see Figure 1-79). The report is generated by the Network Diagnostics Framework, which sometimes puts more details about the problem in the system event log that you can view using Event Viewer.

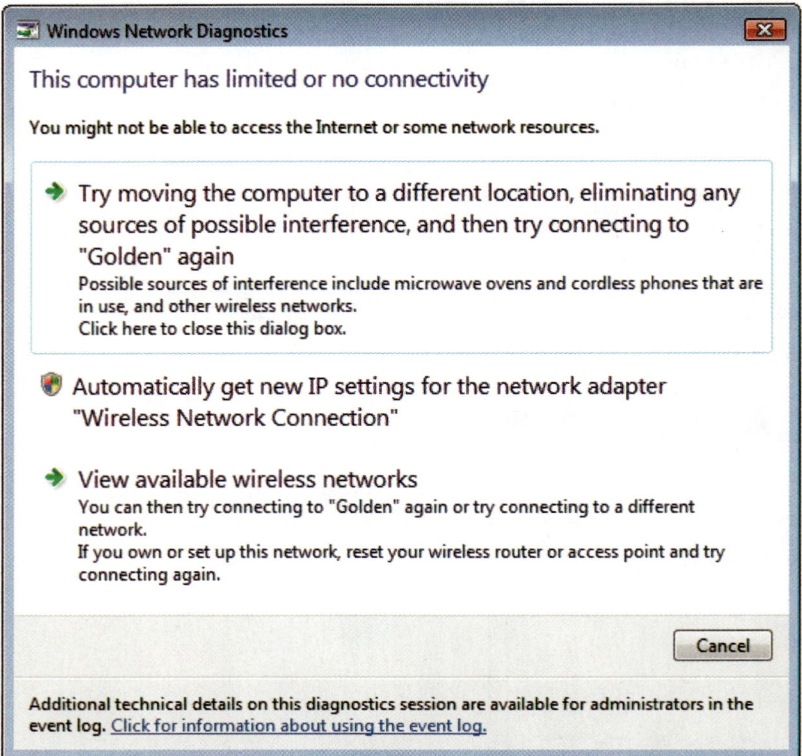

Figure 1-79 Windows Network Diagnostics makes suggestions for fixing a network problem

8. Near the bottom of the right pane in Figure 1-73 (shown earlier) is the Sharing and Discovery area, which lists current security settings for sharing and discovering resources on the network. Click the down arrow to the right of each item to see more information about the setting and change the setting. For example, in Figure 1-80, you can see information about the Network discovery and File sharing settings. When connected to a public network, network discovery and file sharing are automatically turned off to protect your computer. If you are following along at a Vista computer as you read this, try changing your network connection from private to public and back to private to see how the Sharing and Discovery settings respond to your changes.

9. To initially create a wireless, broadband, or dial-up connection to the Internet, in the left pane of the Network and Sharing Center, click **Set up a connection or network.** The Set up a connection or network wizard opens as shown in Figure 1-81. Notice in Figure 1-81 you can set up an Internet connection, wireless router, a hidden wireless connection (when the wireless access point does not broadcast its SSID), a wireless ad hoc connection (computer to computer), and a dial-up connection. Not showing in the window is a final choice at the bottom of the list: a VPN connection to your workplace.

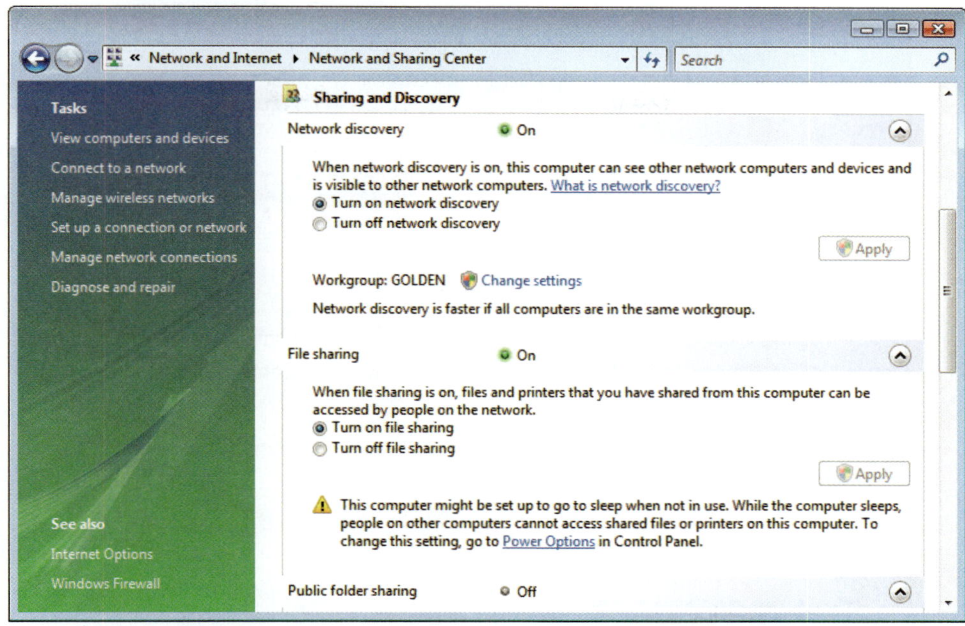

Figure 1-80 Sharing and Discovery settings control how your computer works on the network

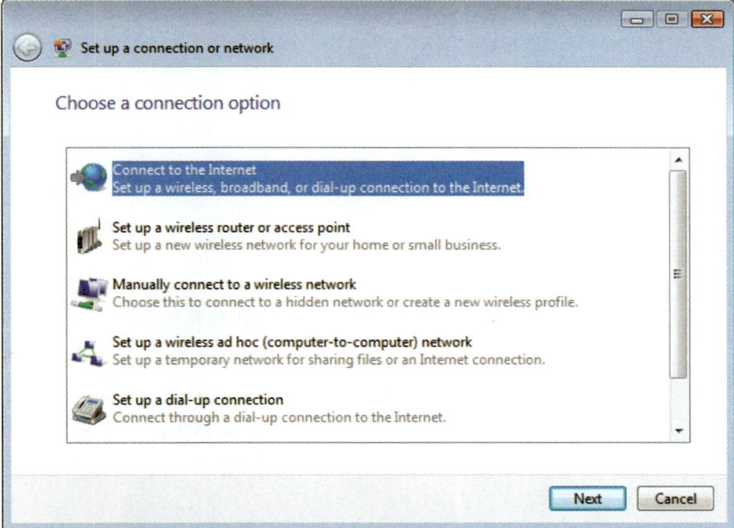

Figure 1-81 Set up a new network connection

10. Select the type of connection, click **Next**, and follow directions on screen to make the connection.

11. To manage your network devices, in the left pane of the Network and Sharing Center, click **Manage network connections.** The Network Connections window shown in Figure 1-82 opens. Select a device and the list of tasks appears in the menu bar.

12. To allow other computers to use the Internet connection on this computer (Internet Connection Sharing), right-click the network device, select **Properties** from the shortcut menu, and respond to the UAC box. In the properties box, click the **Sharing** tab. Then check **Allow other network users to connect through this computer's Internet connection** (see Figure 1-83). When you click **Settings**, you can control which Internet services other users have access to when they are using this connection.

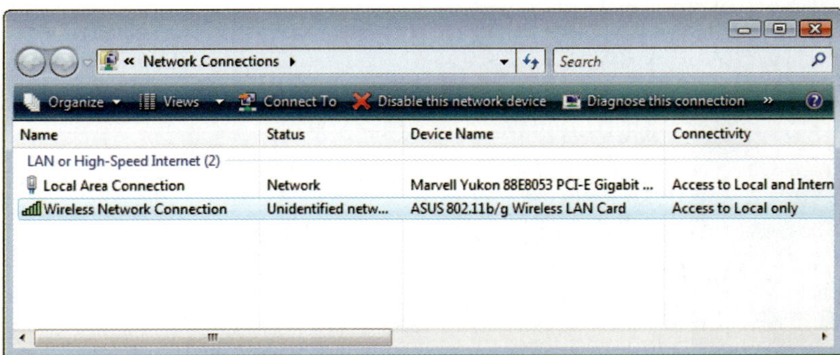

Figure 1-82 Manage your network devices from the Network Connections window

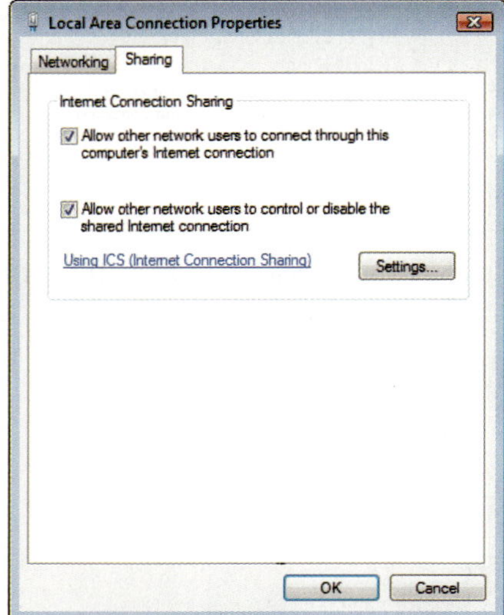

Figure 1-83 Configure Internet Connection Sharing

CONNECT TO AND MANAGE WIRELESS NETWORKS

Follow these steps to connect to a wireless network:

1. In the left pane of the Network and Sharing Center window, click **Connect to a network.** The Connect to a network window opens as shown in Figure 1-84.

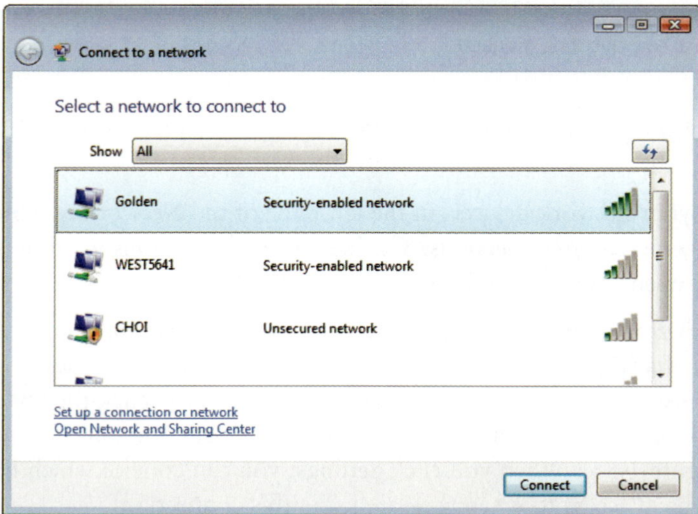

Figure 1-84 Select a wireless network

2. Select the wireless network you want to connect to and click **Connect**. If Windows sees the wireless network is secured, you will be asked for the passphrase and the passphrase setting will be saved. The connection is made and appears in the Network list.

To see the settings for a wireless network, in the Network and Sharing Center window, click View status. In the status box, click Wireless Properties. The properties box as shown in Figure 1-85 appears. Using the Connection tab, you can decide when to use this network. To see the security settings for this wireless connection, click the Security tab (see Figure 1-86). The correct security settings for the wireless network were sensed by Vista when you initially made the connection to the wireless access point.

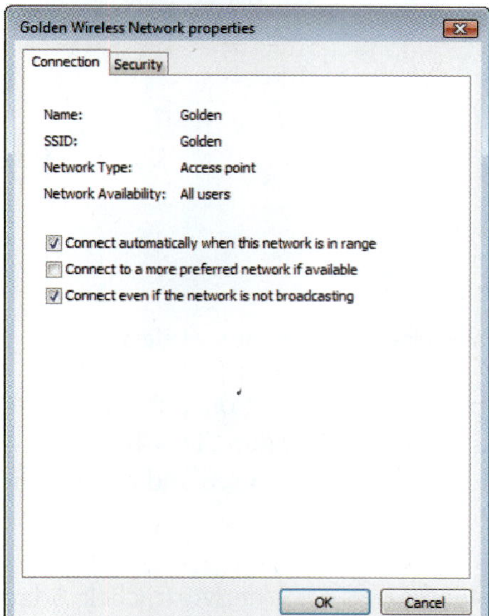

Figure 1-85 Properties of the wireless connection

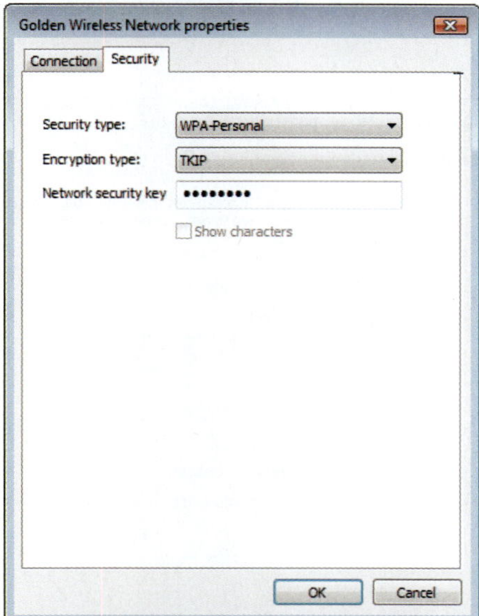

Figure 1-86 Security settings for the wireless connection

If you travel with a notebook computer, you might find it necessary to control which networks you connect to, and sometimes it is useful to control which users can connect to a wireless network. All this can be done using the Network and Sharing Center. In the left pane, click *Manage wireless networks*. The Manage Wireless Networks window appears as shown in Figure 1-87.

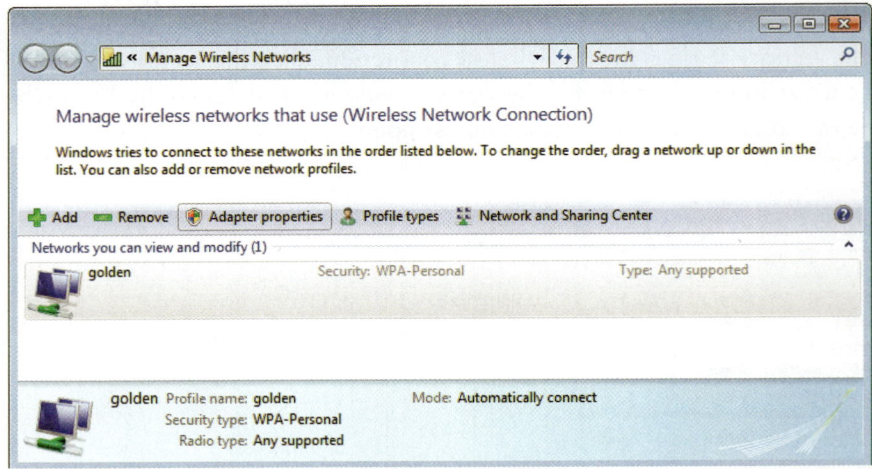

Figure 1-87 Use the Manage Wireless Networks window to control how wireless networking can be used

You can add a new wireless network, remove an existing one, change the order that will be used when Vista connects to a wireless network, configure TCP/IP settings, and control user access to a network. For example, do the following to see and change the TCP/IP settings for a network:

1. In the Manage Wireless Networks window, select a network, click **Adapter properties**, and respond to the UAC box. The Wireless Network Connection Properties box appears as shown on the left in Figure 1-88.

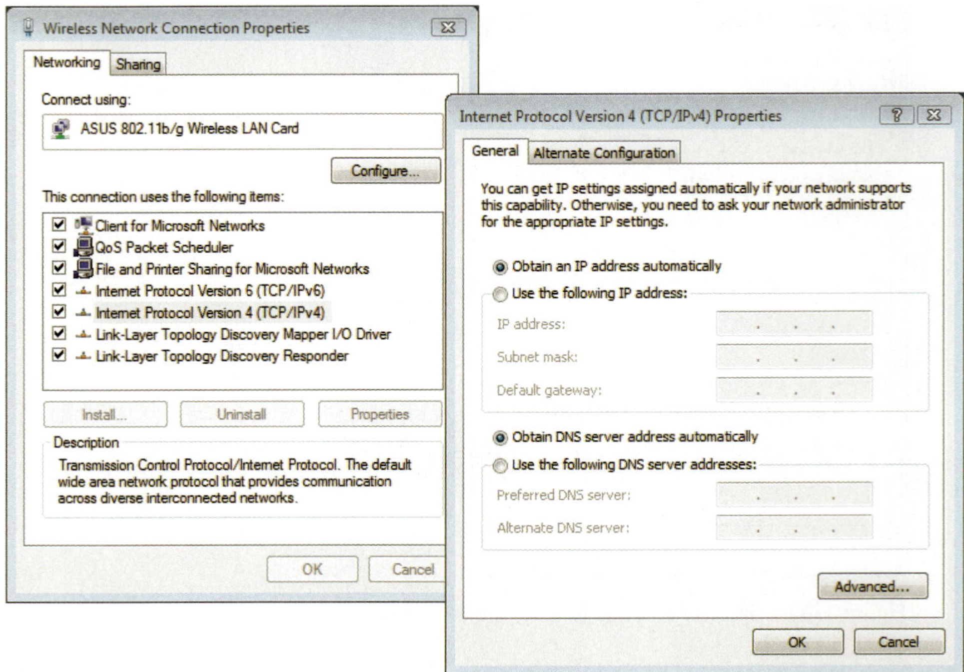

Figure 1-88 Change the TCP/IP properties for a network

2. Select **Internet Protocol Version 4 (TCP/IPv4)** and click **Properties** to see the TCP/IP properties window on the right side of Figure 1-88. Here you can configure static and dynamic IP address settings and click the Alternate Configuration tab to enter an alternate setting for this network.

These TCP/IP settings apply only to this one network connection because each network connection maintains its own TCP/IP settings.

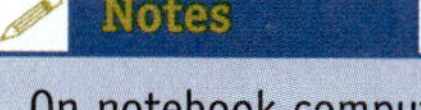

Notes

On notebook computers, be sure your wireless adapter is turned on. You might have a wireless switch on the keyboard or on the rear of the notebook case. In Windows, from Control Panel, click Mobile PC, and then click Windows Mobility Center. Then click Turn wireless on (see Figure 1-89).

As you work with the new Vista networking tools, you will find more than one way to do a task, but what you have just learned is more than adequate to get you going when supporting a small secured wired or wireless network.

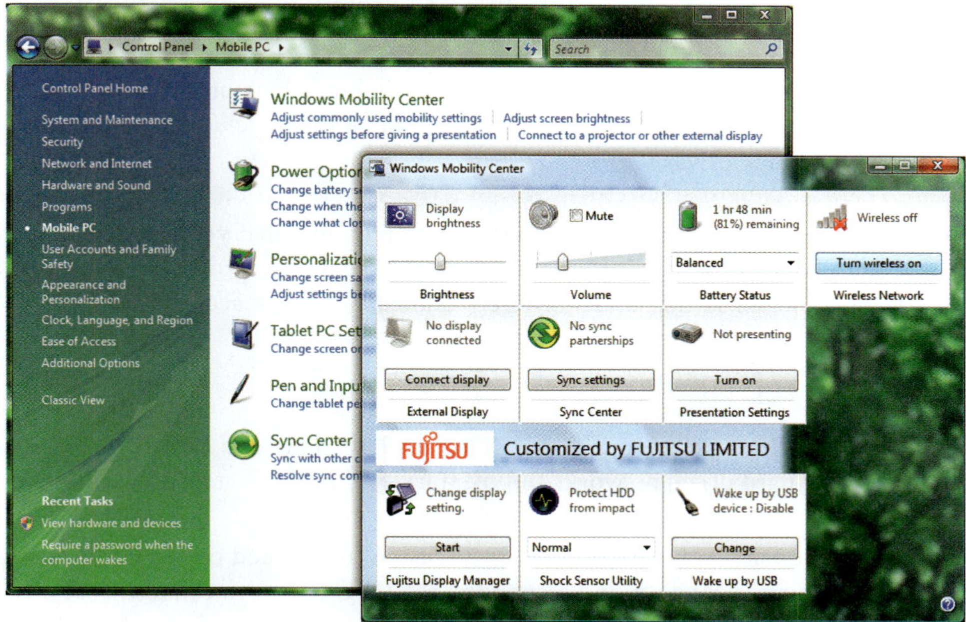

Figure 1-89 For a notebook computer, use the Windows Mobility Center to configure Vista notebook settings

GROUP POLICY

Vista gives much more power and authority to Group Policy than previous Windows operating systems. To access the Group Policy console, click Start, enter Gpedit.msc in the Search box, and respond to the UAC box. The console that appears is shown in Figure 1-90.

Using Group Policy, an administrator can control these tasks and more:

- Power management policies on desktop and notebook computers including sleep settings and hard drive settings
- File and data management polices including disk quotas, System Restore, and offline files and synchronization
- Access and connectivity policies including network connections, dial-up connections, and Remote Assistance

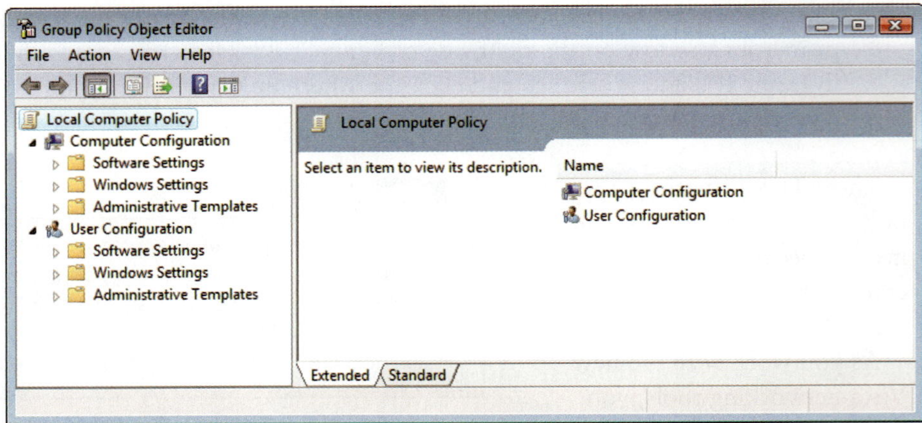

Figure 1-90 Windows Vista Group Policy includes many new policies

- Printer policies including who can add and use a printer
- Device installations including how digitally signed drivers are handled, who can install devices, and how devices are installed
- Computer startup and shutdown scripts and user logon and logoff scripts
- What happens when a user logs on including which programs will launch
- How all types of removable storage can be used, including CDs, DVDs, and floppy and tape drives

This list is not complete. The best way to find out what you can and cannot do with Group Policy is to poke around in the menu tree. Using Group Policy, it is possible to lock down a system so that users have very limited control or access.

RESOURCE MONITOR

The Vista **Resource Monitor**, also called the **Reliability and Performance Monitor**, monitors the CPU, hard drive, network, and memory. Follow these steps to use Resource Monitor:

1. To open Resource Monitor, open **Task Manager** and on the **Performance** tab, click **Resource Monitor** and respond to the UAC box. You can also access Resource Monitor from the Computer Management console by doing the following: Click Start, right-click Computer, select Manage from the shortcut menu, respond to the UAC box, and click Reliability and Performance. Either way, the Resource Monitor window appears as shown in Figure 1-91.
2. One useful purpose of Resource Monitor is to identify a process that is using the network or other resource excessively. For example, click the down arrow to the right of Network to see a list of processes using the network, as shown in Figure 1-91. If you click the **Total** column, the processes will be sorted so that the one at the top is using the most bandwidth. If you do not recognize the process, consider that it might be malware, but if the process is svchost.exe, know that this is a Windows component.
3. To end a suspicious process, note the process PID (Process Identifier) and return to Task Manager. In the Task Manager window, click the **Processes** tab (see the right side of Figure 1-92).
4. To add the PID to the window, click **View** and **Select Columns.** Check **PID (Process Identifier)** and click **OK.** You can now identify the process in the list of running processes.
5. To end the process, select it and click **End Process.**

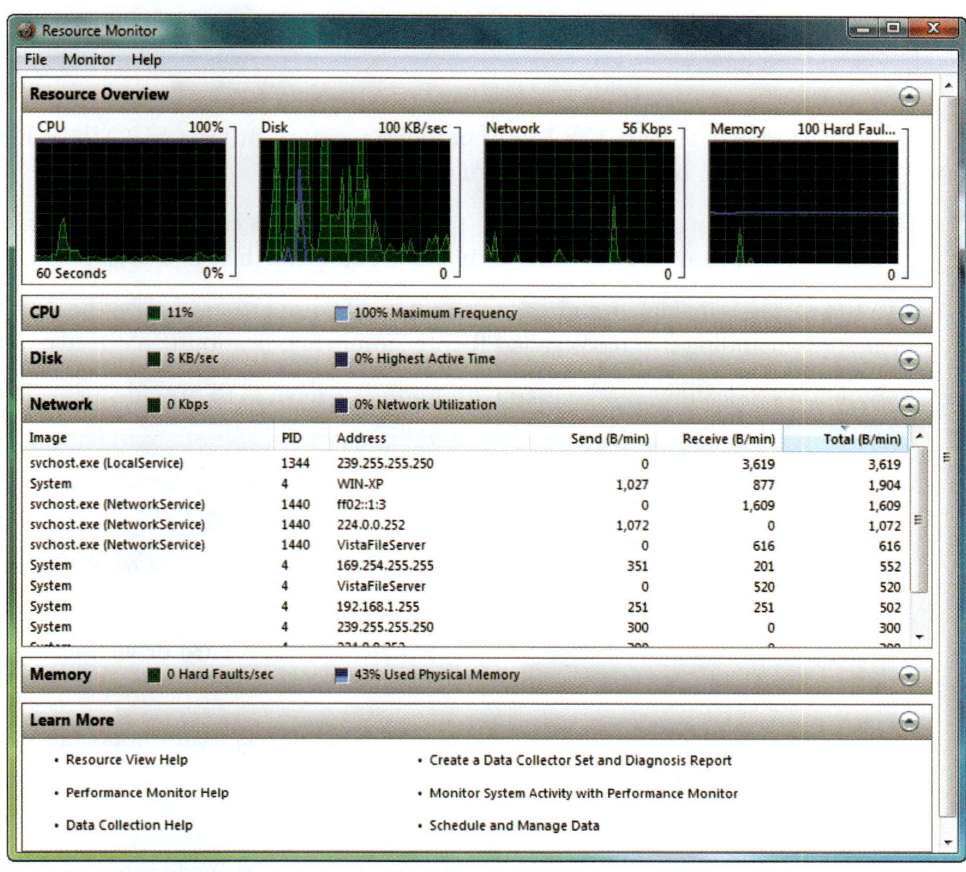

Figure 1-91 Use Resource Monitor to monitor CPU, disk, memory, and network activity

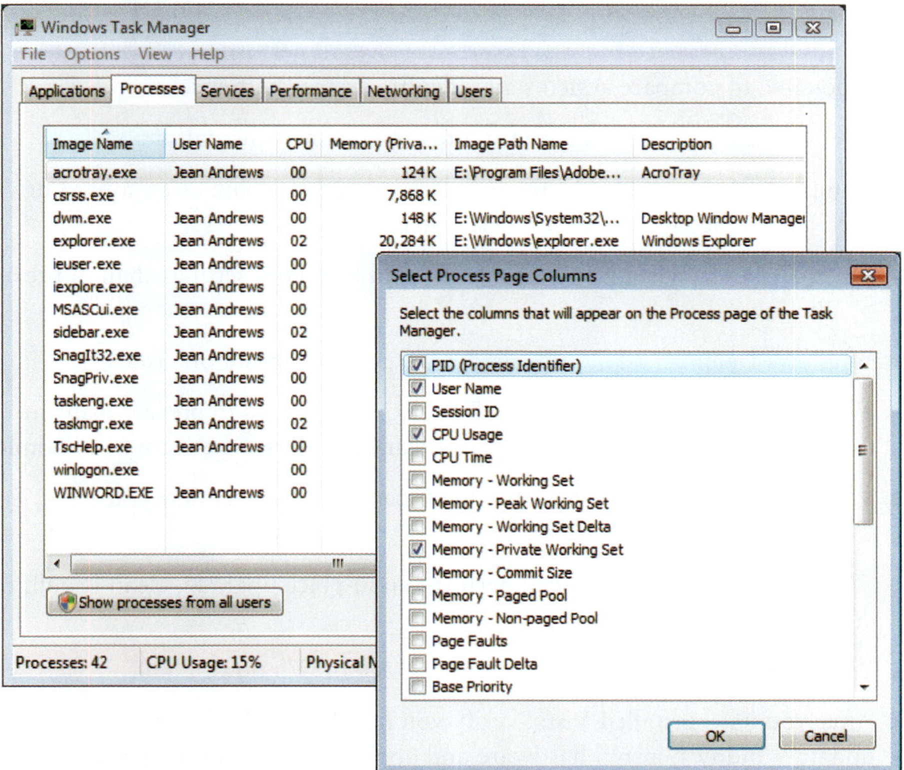

Figure 1-92 Select the columns that appear in Task Manager

>> CHAPTER SUMMARY

- The Windows Vista Aero user interface requires you have a video card that supports the technology, at least 128 MB of graphics memory, at least 512 MB of RAM, and the Home Premium or higher version of Vista.
- The Vista start menu is reorganized to help make items easier to find and includes a Search box that can be used to execute commands and locate files and Web pages.
- Vista includes a sidebar and gadgets that can be used to customize the desktop with information including live feeds called Really Simple Syndication (RSS) feeds.
- Windows SideShow can be used with hardware devices to provide a small secondary display that works even when the computer is turned off.
- Internet Explorer 7 uses tabs instead of separate windows, an integrated search box, and many new security features.
- ReadyBoost can use a flash memory device or SD memory card to buffer hard drive data to improve hard drive performance.
- ReadyDrive works with flash memory installed inside a hard drive housing to improve the drive's performance.
- The Network and Sharing Center is new to Vista and is used to manage, support, and troubleshoot network connections.
- Vista supports IPv6, a new generation of TCP/IP that uses 128-bit IP addresses.
- Disk defragmentation automatically happens weekly on Wednesdays at 1:00AM.
- BitLocker Drive Encryption encrypts an entire volume on a hard drive to protect data on the drive in the event the drive is stolen.
- Windows Experience Index measures the overall performance rating of a system, making it possible to compare systems and identify system bottlenecks.
- Sleep mode is a hybrid between standby mode and hibernation.
- Complete PC backup backs up an entire volume or volumes on a hard drive and can be used to completely recover a failed system.
- Group Policy in Vista is more powerful and has more settings than in previous versions of Windows.
- Windows Defender is an integrated anti-spyware feature of Vista.
- The User Account Control (UAC) dialog box is intended to prevent malware from being able to hack into a system and also to allow Standard users to perform some administrative tasks.
- Versions of Vista include Starter, Home Basic, Home Premium, Business, Enterprise, and Ultimate.
- When installing Vista, you can perform an in-place upgrade, clean install, or dual boot configuration.
- You can upgrade to Vista from Windows XP or Windows 2000.
- After you have installed Vista, verify you have network and Internet access, activate and update Windows, install hardware and applications, set up user accounts, and customize Vista user settings.

- You have 30 days to activate Vista after it is installed.
- Vista supports the XML Paper Specification (XPS) protocol to render pages before they are sent to a printer. XPS documents can be created by Vista and used similarly to PDF files.
- Non-USB printers are installed from the Printers window accessed from Control Panel. USB printers install automatically.
- During the hardware installation process, if Vista cannot locate drivers, it searches the Internet for help.
- Applications are managed from the Programs and Features window of Vista accessed from the Control Panel.
- The user profile namespace is created in the %SystemDrive%\Users folder. User settings are stored in the Ntuser.dat drive of the registry.
- Two kinds of user profiles are local user profiles and roaming user profiles.
- Two types of user accounts are administrator accounts and standard user accounts.
- The Public folder is intended to be used for files shared on the network.
- User accounts can be managed from the Computer Management console or the Manage Accounts window accessed from the Control Panel.
- Two tools used to transfer user data and preferences from an older computer to a Vista computer are the User State Migration Tool (USMT) and Windows Easy Transfer. The latter tool is easier to use and appropriate for a few transfers.
- Use the Windows Features dialog box to turn Vista features on or off.
- Two types of backups are Complete PC and file and folder backups. Windows file and folder backups are kept in .zip files.
- Windows Memory Diagnostics can test memory during the boot and identify faulty memory modules.
- Disk Management can be used to dynamically resize a partition on a hard drive.
- Resource Monitor, also called the Reliability and Performance Monitor, monitors the CPU, hard drive, network, and memory.

>> KEY TERMS

administrator account – A type of user account that has complete access to the system and can make changes that affect the security of the system and other users.

Aero user interface – The graphical interface for Vista that provides a 3D appearance and requires a graphics card that supports the technology. The graphics card has to support DirectX 9 graphics. The interface is not available on Vista Home Basic.

BitLocker Drive Encryption – A Vista feature that locks down a hard drive if it is stolen from a notebook or desktop computer. It encrypts the entire system volume and is designed to be used in conjunction with EFS for high security requirements.

Complete PC backup – A Vista backup option that creates a backup of the entire system volume and other volumes on the computer. The backup can later be used to recover from a failed hard drive, restoring the drive to the time of the last incremental Complete PC backup.

local user profile – A user profile created and used solely on a single computer.

Network Connections – Together with the Network and Sharing Center window, replaces the Network Connections window of Windows XP and offers new functionality to manage network connections.

Network and Sharing Center – Together with the Network Connections window, replaces the Network Connections window of Windows XP and offers new functionality to manage network connections.

Public folder – The folder in the %SystemDrive%\Users folder that is intended to hold data that users share on a network.

ReadyBoost – A Vista feature designed to improve hard drive performance that uses a USB flash memory device or secure digital (SD) memory card to buffer data on the drive.

ReadyDrive – A Vista feature that makes use of the flash memory installed inside hybrid hard drives to speed up startup time and resume time from hibernation.

Really Simple Syndication (RSS) feed – Using either a gadget in your sidebar or the Feed tab in the IE window, this Windows feature gives you an easy method of subscribing to periodic downloaded feeds.

roaming user profiles – A user profile stored in the Active Directory on a server that follows a user from computer to computer on the domain.

shadow copy – A Vista feature that takes a snapshot of a file so that Windows Backup can back up a file even when the file is open.

sleep mode – A hybrid of standby mode and hibernation. After a period of inactivity, the PC first enters standby mode and then, after longer inactivity, enters hibernation.

standard user – A type of user account that can use software and hardware and make some system changes, but cannot make changes that affect the security of the system or other users.

User Account Control (UAC) dialog box – A dialog box that appears each time a user attempts to perform an action that can be done only with administrative privileges. The box is intended to prevent malware from hacking a system and allow a Standard user to perform administrative tasks.

user profile namespace – The folder and its subfolders where user data and preferences are kept. The folder is stored in the %SystemDrive%\Users folder.

Windows Anytime Upgrade – A Vista feature that allows a user to purchase an upgrade to Vista Ultimate after having already purchased a Vista Home edition. A new product key is issued from Microsoft, while the additional features are installed from the user's original CD or DVD.

Windows Defender – Anti-spyware software that is integrated into Windows Vista.

Windows Easy Transfer – A Vista feature that allows user data and preferences to be transferred from an old PC to a Vista PC.

Windows Experience Index – A Vista summary index designed to measure the overall performance of a system so that you can compare systems and identify performance bottlenecks in a particular system.

Windows Vista Business – A version of Vista intended for business users, which includes support for joining a domain, Group Policy, and Encrypted File System, but does not support Windows Media Center, Movie Maker, DVD Maker, and parental controls.

Windows Vista Enterprise – A version of Vista that includes additional features over Windows Vista Business including BitLocker.

Windows Vista Home Basic – A version of Vista designed for low-cost home systems that do not require full security and networking features.

Windows Vista Home Premium – A version of Vista similar to Windows Vista Home Basic that includes additional features.

Windows Vista Starter – A version of Vista with limited features intended to be used in developing nations.

Windows Vista Ultimate – A version of Vista that includes every Vista feature.

XML Paper Specification (XPS) – A printing protocol by Microsoft used to render a page before it is sent to the printer. It is expected to replace GDI, an earlier rendering protocol.

XPS Document Writer – A Vista feature that creates a .xps document file that works similarly to an Adobe .pdf file. When printing from an application, the writer appears in the list of printers.

>> REVIEWING THE BASICS

1. How much video memory must be on a graphics card before Vista supports the Aero user interface?
2. What keys do you press to cause Vista to display open application windows in a flip 3D view?
3. The Run dialog box in Windows XP has been replaced with which box in Windows Vista?
4. An RSS feed can be used in which two Windows components?
5. Which Vista feature lets you use an SD memory card to boost hard drive performance?
6. How many bits are there in an IP address using IPv6?
7. By default, how often does Vista automatically defrag a hard drive?
8. Which Vista feature lets you encrypt an entire volume of a hard drive?
9. When a user logged in under a Standard account attempts to open Device Manager, what dialog box appears?
10. Which Vista version includes all features of Vista?
11. What is the minimum amount of RAM necessary to run Vista?
12. After you have installed Vista, how many days do you have before it needs activating?
13. Using Vista, what page formatting protocol replaces GDI?
14. Using Vista, how do you create an .XPS document file?
15. When you first install Vista, what two user accounts are created?
16. What type of user profile is used solely on a single computer?
17. Which folder is the preferred folder to hold user data to be shared on the network?
18. Which two tools can be used to create user accounts?
19. Which two tools can be used to transfer user data and preferences from an old PC to a Vista PC?
20. Can a Complete PC backup be created on a network drive?
21. Can you use Windows Backup to back up folders to a network drive?
22. When Vista backs up a file, what is the file extension of the backup file?
23. What is the command to schedule a Windows Memory Diagnostics test?
24. Which four resources does Resource Monitor track?
25. How many bits are in an IP address that follows the IPv4 standard?

>> THINKING CRITICALLY

1. When Vista configures a network as a public network, what must you do before you can share files on the network?
   a. Make the network a private network.
   b. Manually turn on file sharing.

c. Disconnect and reconnect to the network.

d. Either a or b.

2. You have purchased an Upgrade version of Windows Vista Ultimate. You are planning to install Vista on a computer that has Windows XP installed, but the Windows XP installation is seriously corrupted and you cannot boot from the hard drive. What can you do?

   a. Reinstall Windows XP and then install Windows Vista as an upgrade.

   b. Boot from the Vista DVD and perform a clean installation of Vista and then install Vista a second time as an upgrade.

   c. Either a or b will work.

   d. Neither a or b will work. You must purchase For-a-new-PC version of Windows Vista.

3. A Vista computer hangs at odd times and sometimes gives errors during startup. What is a likely problem and which Windows tool is best to use?

   a. The registry might be corrupted; use Regedit to check the registry.

   b. The Vista installation might be corrupted; use a Complete PC backup to restore the hard drive.

   c. Memory might be faulty; use Windows Memory Diagnostics to test memory.

   d. A network connection is not working; use the Network and Sharing Center to run diagnostics on the network.

>> HANDS-ON PROJECTS

PROJECT 1-1: Test Memory

On a Vista computer, boot to the Windows Boot Manager menu to test memory. Answer these questions:

1. How did you launch the Windows Boot Manager menu?
2. What messages did you see while the memory test was in progress?
3. What message did you see about the test after the Windows desktop loaded?

PROJECT 1-2: Create User Accounts

On a Vista computer, do the following to explore user accounts:

1. Create a standard account named Jane Doe and an administrator account named Tom Jones.
2. Log onto the system as Tom Jones and then log onto the system as Jane Doe.
3. Logged on as Jane Doe, try to view the folders in the Tom Jones user profile namespace. What error message do you see? Print the screen showing the error message.
4. Now try to open Device Manager. Print the screen showing the UAC box.

PROJECT 1-3: Use ReadyBoost

Some flash memory devices qualify for ReadyBoost on a Vista computer and some do not. If you have access to a USB flash drive, try the device. Does it qualify for ReadyBoost? If you have access to an SD memory card and your computer has an SD card reader, try that device. The SD memory card installed in an internal SD card reader should qualify. Reboot the Vista computer with and without the card installed. Can you notice a difference in the boot time? Can you notice a difference in the overall performance of the computer with and without the ReadyBoost memory card installed?

PROJECT 1-4: Use Wireless Networking

Using a Vista computer with wireless capability, connect to a wireless network. What is your IP address on the network? List the steps you used to find out your IP address.

>> REAL PROBLEMS, REAL SOLUTIONS

REAL PROBLEM 1-1: Investigate and Use Windows Meeting Space

Using the Windows Help and Support window, search for information on Windows Meeting Space. What is the tool? When would you want to use it? What can you do with Windows Meeting Space? Test the tool with a friend on a network connection.

REAL PROBLEM 1-2: Installing Windows Vista

Perform either an in-place upgrade or a clean install of Vista. As you perform the installation, follow all appropriate instructions in the chapter and keep notes as you go. Then answer these questions:

1. For which hardware devices did you need to provide drivers in Windows Vista?
2. Did you encounter any errors during the installation? If so, how did you resolve these errors?
3. How did you install Windows updates after the installation was finished?
4. How long did the installation take?

CHAPTER

2

Securing and Troubleshooting Windows Vista

In this chapter, you will learn:

- **About the new security features of the different versions of Windows Vista and how to configure these features**
- **About tools for troubleshooting hardware and software problems under Windows Vista and strategies to apply when troubleshooting**
- **How the Vista startup process differs from that of Windows XP, about the new Vista Recovery Environment, and about strategies to use when troubleshooting Vista startup problems**

When a new Windows OS comes on the market, PC support technicians must quickly learn how to support, maintain, and troubleshoot it. This chapter helps you do just that, as it is chock-full of information and procedures for supporting, maintaining, and troubleshooting Windows Vista. So fasten your seat belt and hang on, because a lot of learning is going to happen!

Windows Vista has been hailed by Microsoft as the most secure operating system it has produced to date. In this chapter you'll learn how Microsoft changed the underlying architecture of the OS and how Vista works to better secure the OS from an outside attack over the network or by careless or malicious users of the OS. You will learn how to configure several of these security features. Then we will turn our attention to troubleshooting hardware and software using Vista, understanding Vista startup, and troubleshooting Vista startup problems.

SECURITY IMPROVEMENTS IN WINDOWS VISTA

The improvements in Windows Vista security hinge on taking more control over what users and processes can and cannot do. One strategy is to give administrators more control over the rights and privileges given to regular users. Another strategy is to improve the Vista infrastructure so that behind-the-scenes malware attacks are thwarted or, at the least, users are given the opportunity to "just say no."

Here is a quick rundown of key security improvements in Vista:

- Administrators can use Group Policy settings to lock down many more features in Vista than in earlier operating systems. Here are a few examples:
    - Administrators can control wireless network settings on a notebook computer so users cannot use unsecured networks.
    - Administrators can make Windows Firewall work the way they want it to so that users cannot use a public network any way they want to.
    - To protect data, Encrypting File System (EFS) can be implemented across an entire domain or on a local computer.
    - To prevent data theft, policies can be set to limit the use of removable media.
- Internet Explorer 7 can be secured so that it cannot install software or write files outside the Temporary Internet Files folder unless the user gives permission.
- Other ways unwanted software is kept from being installed on a PC are the User Account Control (UAC) dialog box and Windows Defender. The UAC box requires that an administrator confirm the action before software can be installed, and Windows Defender notifies the user when a process attempts to install itself or add a process to startup.
- To prevent data theft, Vista includes BitLocker Drive Encryption for the entire system volume on a notebook's hard drive.
- Smart cards can be implemented more easily and used to control access to a system.
- Windows Firewall has an expanded user interface, can monitor both incoming and outgoing traffic, and filters traffic by more criteria, including user groups, IP addresses, ports, service names, and interface type.
- EFS has been improved to store encryption keys on smart cards and to encrypt the system page file.
- Using Windows Vista 64-bit editions, all drivers must be digitally signed.
- To help prevent programs that might do damage from being accidentally or maliciously launched, two levels of access are assigned to a command prompt window. An **elevated command prompt** can only be attained by an administrator after he or she has responded to a UAC box.

Now that you have a general idea what to expect from Vista's improved security, let's see how some of these features work and how you can use them. In the following sections, you will learn about Mandatory Integrity Control levels, the User Account Control box, the elevated command prompt, Windows Firewall, Windows Defender, Internet Explorer 7 security features, BitLocker Encryption, and securing shared files and folders.

MANDATORY INTEGRITY CONTROL LEVELS

A new Windows Vista feature is **Mandatory Integrity Control (MIC)**. MIC is invisible to users and you cannot configure it, but, as a smart support technician, you still need to understand how it works so that you can better understand why one process has more privileges than another. MIC is like a security guard who gives out security badges (or integrity levels) to those entering a building (or OS) based on how, when, or where a visitor enters.

Based on the trustworthiness of the process, as determined by how, when, or where the process was started, MIC assigns one of four integrity levels to a process:

- Low-integrity access level (also called untrusted level). Processes can write only to those folders that have little effect on the system. An example of such a folder is the Temporary Internet Files folder. Internet Explorer 7 runs at this level when it is running in Protected Mode. When running in Protected Mode, any process started by IE 7, such as an add-on downloaded from the Internet, is assigned the low-integrity access level. You will learn more about Protected Mode later in the chapter.
- Medium-integrity access level (also called user level). Processes working at this level have access to the user's Documents folder and can write to certain areas of the registry considered user specific, such as HKEY_CURRENT_USER. The Vista desktop runs at this level. Any process that has not already been assigned an integrity level is assigned this medium-integrity access level, which is why it is the most used level.
- High-integrity access level (also called administrative level). At this level, a process can install files in the Program Files folder and write to areas of the registry that affect the entire system, such as the HKEY_LOCAL_MACHINE key. When administrators start a process, the process works at this level.
- System-integrity access level. System processes run at this level.

USER ACCOUNT CONTROL (UAC) DIALOG BOX

Recall from Chapter 1 that the User Account Control (UAC) dialog box is intended to prevent background tasks from getting too much control of a system and to encourage careless administrators to "think before you click" when using processes or tools powerful enough to damage something. The UAC box can also be used to allow standard users access to certain administrative tools.

Whenever someone logged on as an administrator attempts to launch a process that requires administrative privilege, the UAC box appears as shown in Figure 2-1. The administrator clicks Continue. If a standard user attempts to launch a process that requires administrative privileges, the UAC box in Figure 2-2 appears. To continue, the standard user must enter an administrator's password. In the figure, notice the box gives the name of an administrator, in this case, Jean Andrews.

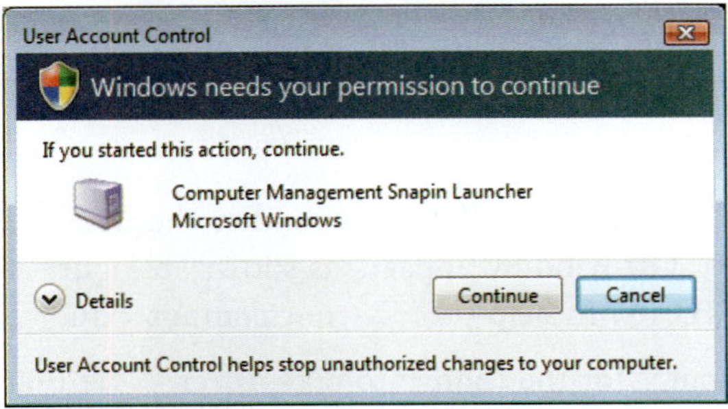

Figure 2-1 The User Account Control box presented to an administrator

Figure 2-2 The User Account Control Box presented to a standard user

The recommended best practice is for an administrator to limit the use of the elevated administrative account, using it only for such activities as installing new software or hardware, and to use a less privileged standard account for day-to-day work, such as sending email or writing documents. Using the standard account, he or she can respond with his administrative password when he or she occasionally needs to perform an administrative task.

The UAC box is an important Vista security feature, but some administrators find it annoying (if not down-right condescending) because, in effect, it's asking the question, "Are you sure you really want to do this?" Although not recommended, there are several ways you can disable this box. Here is one way:

1. From Control Panel, click **User Accounts and Family Safety**. On the next window, click **User Accounts**. The User Accounts window appears as shown in Figure 2-3.

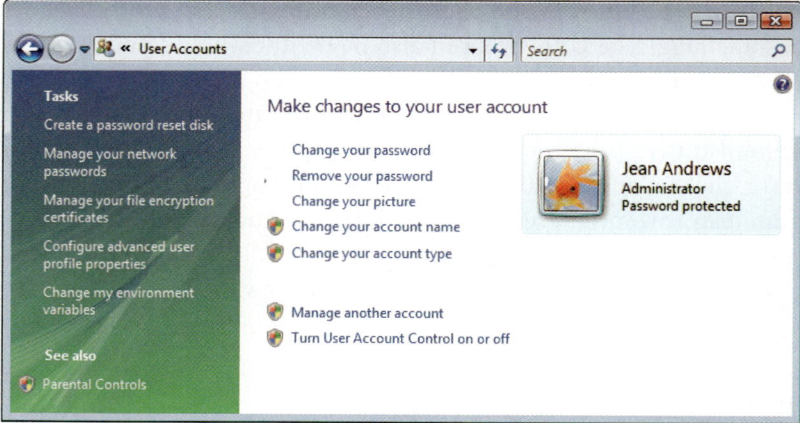

Figure 2-3 Manage your administrator account

2. Click **Turn User Account Control on or off** and respond to the UAC box. The Turn User Account Control On or Off window appears as shown in Figure 2-4. Uncheck **Use User Account Control** (UAC) **to help protect your computer** and click **OK**.
3. You must restart your computer for the change to take affect. Note that the change applies to all users of this computer. If you want to turn the UAC box back on, return to the window in Figure 2-4, and check the feature.

Figure 2-4 Turn the UAC dialog box on or off

ELEVATED COMMAND PROMPT

Windows Vista has two levels of command prompt windows: a standard window and an elevated window. To open a standard command prompt window in Vista, you can click Start, type cmd.exe in the Search box, and press Enter, or you can click Start, All Programs, Accessories, and Command Prompt. Either way, the command prompt window in Figure 2-5 appears. In this window, you can enter Vista commands. Notice in the figure that the default directory is the currently logged on user's folder.

```
Command Prompt
Microsoft Windows [Version 6.0.6000]
Copyright (c) 2006 Microsoft Corporation.  All rights reserved.

E:\Users\Jean Andrews>ipconfig /release
The requested operation requires elevation.

E:\Users\Jean Andrews>_
```

Figure 2-5 A command prompt window with standard rights

Commands that require administrative privileges will not work from this standard command prompt window. To get an elevated command prompt window, click Start, All Programs, Accessories, and right-click Command Prompt. Then select *Run as administrator* from the shortcut window and respond to the UAC box. The resulting command prompt window is shown in Figure 2-6. Notice the word "Administrator" in the title bar, which indicates the elevated window, and the default directory, which is the *%systemdrive%* \Windows\system32 folder.

```
Administrator: Command Prompt
Microsoft Windows [Version 6.0.6000]
Copyright (c) 2006 Microsoft Corporation.  All rights reserved.

E:\Windows\system32>
```

Figure 2-6 An elevated command prompt window

WINDOWS FIREWALL

Vista's Windows Firewall is an improvement over the original Windows Firewall first introduced with Windows XP Service Pack 2. One change with Vista's Windows Firewall is that the firewall recognizes three profiles to use when making security settings:

- The **domain profile** uses the least level of security and is used when the firewall recognizes the computer is logged onto a domain. The assumption is that network administrators have put in place security measures for the entire domain, so that individual PCs can relax a bit on security and more freely trust their neighbors.
- The **private profile** offers more security and is used when the computer is not logged onto a domain and all active networks (wired and wireless, including Bluetooth) are configured as private networks. Recall from the last chapter that a network is configured as a private or public network using the Network and Sharing Center.
- The **public profile** offers the most security and is used when the firewall recognizes the computer is connected to a public network. Time for shields up!

The firewall monitors network connects and disconnects and proactively reconfigures itself as needed. In addition, you can manually configure firewall settings at any time using the Windows Firewall window or using Group Policy. The firewall settings affect many Windows components and activities including Windows Meeting Space, Remote Desktop, Remote Assistance, using a network projector, Network Discovery, and so forth.

To view and change Windows Firewall settings, follow these steps:

1. Click **Start**, right-click **Network** and click **Properties**. The Network and Sharing Center window opens. In the lower-left pane, click **Windows Firewall**. The Windows Firewall window opens, as shown on the left side of Figure 2-7.
2. Click **Change settings** and respond to the UAC box. The Windows Firewall Settings dialog box appears, as shown in the right side of Figure 2-7.

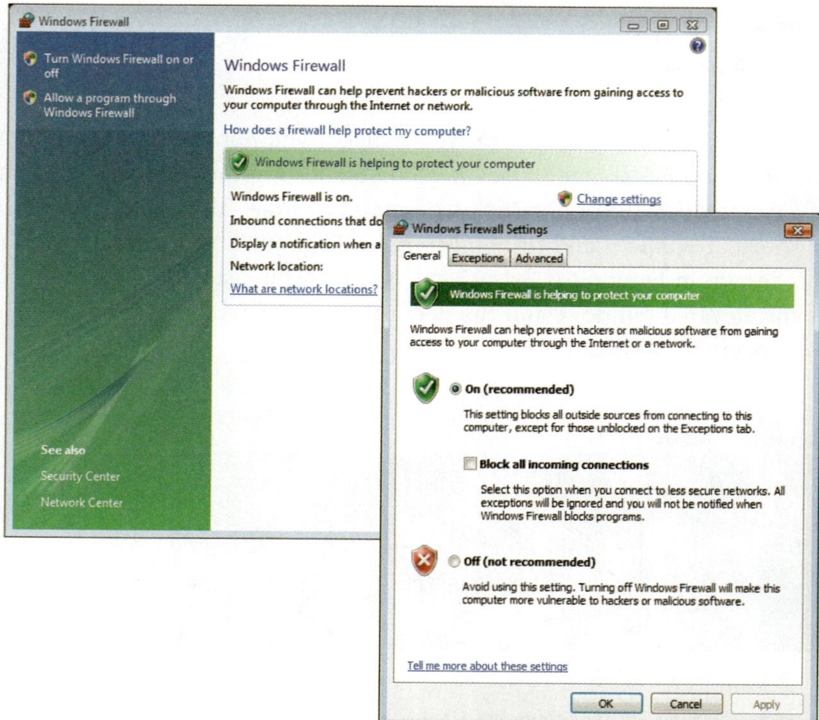

Figure 2-7 Use the Windows Firewall Settings dialog box to change firewall settings

3. Notice in the figure you can turn the firewall on and off and block all incoming connections. Click the **Exceptions** tab to see the list of programs and activities that are affected by the firewall (see Figure 2-8). Notice this list includes more items than were included in the Windows XP firewall.

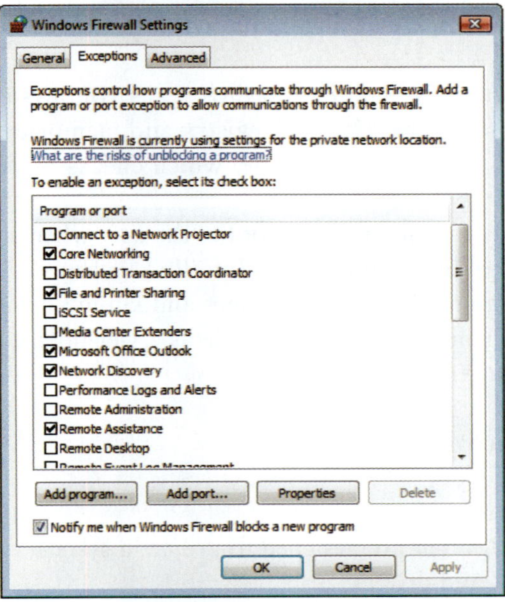

Figure 2-8 Exceptions that can be allowed to communicate through the firewall

A feature new to Vista is the Windows Firewall with Advanced Security console that can be used to configure the firewall on a local or remote computer. To use the console, from Control Panel, click System and Maintenance and then click Administrative Tools. In the Administrative Tools window, double-click Windows Firewall with Advanced Security and respond to the UAC box. The console window in Figure 2-9 appears, which is used to control and monitor inbound and outbound activity at a detailed level.

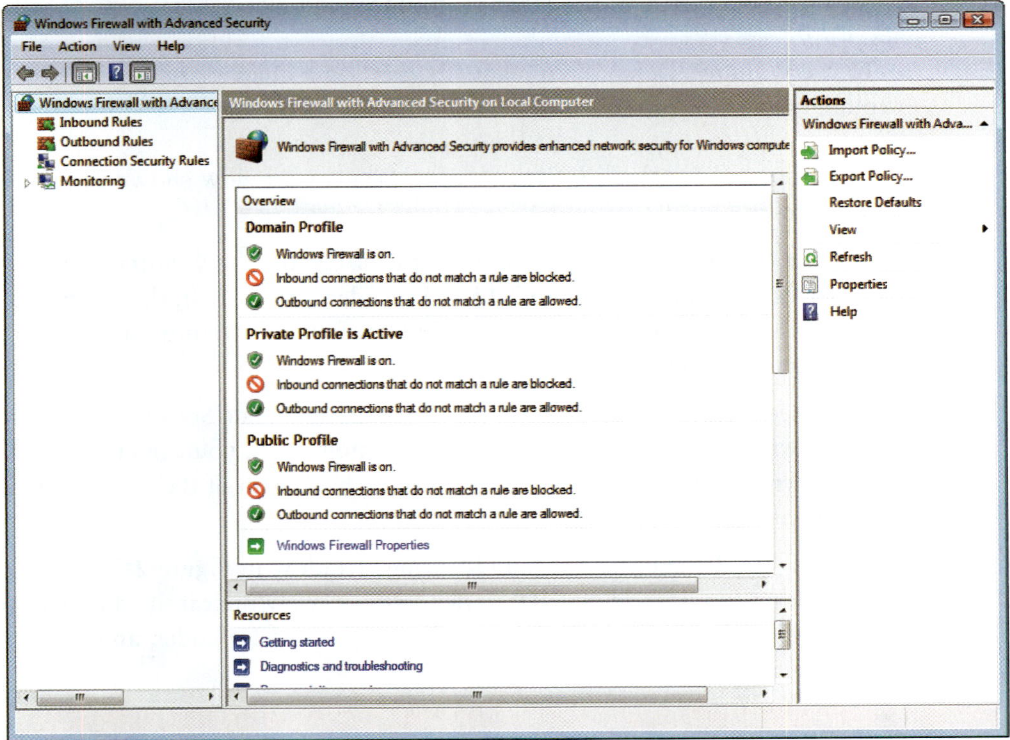

Figure 2-9 Windows Firewall with Advanced Security console

WINDOWS DEFENDER

Windows Defender, first introduced by Microsoft as stand-alone anti-adware and anti-spyware software, is an integrated part of Windows Vista. In Vista, its chief job is to act as a police officer, constantly watching for malicious software trying to install itself on your PC without your knowledge. By default, it is configured to work in two ways:

- Defender automatically downloads updates and then scans your system every day at 2:00AM. It does a quick scan, checking the registry and memory. However, you can manually perform a full scan at any time, which checks all files on the computer.
- Defender continually monitors a computer and notifies the user when a process is attempting to make changes to the system or install itself. As a support technician, you need to train users to recognize the Defender messages and know how to respond to them, because sometimes malware tries to masquerade as a Defender window so it can trick users into accepting changes.

Overall, Defender monitors these activities:

- Any changes to startup processes
- Any changes to security settings that are designed to protect a system against malware
- Suspicious activity by services and drivers
- Suspicious activity when an application is launched
- When an application registers itself to automatically start at any time
- When attempts are made to install Windows add-ons or background utilities
- Attempts to install an add-on to Internet Explorer; sometimes when you click a link on a Web site, the site attempts to install an add-on without your knowledge.
- Changes to Internet Explorer security settings; malware sometimes attempts to change these settings without your knowledge.
- When Internet Explorer attempts to download files

To use Windows Defender to manually perform a quick or full scan of your system and explore other tools provided by Defender, do the following:

1. In Control Panel, click **Security**. The Security window shown in Figure 2-10 appears.
2. Click **Windows Defender**. If Defender is turned on, the Windows Defender window appears as shown in Figure 2-11. If Defender is turned off, the dialog box in Figure 2-12 appears; click **Turn on and open Windows Defender** to turn on Defender and open the window in Figure 2-11.
3. To see scanning options, click the down arrow beside **Scan** to see the drop-down menu shown in the figure. When you select **Custom Scan**, you can choose which drives or folders to scan. Alternately, to perform a quick scan of the system, simply click **Scan** in the menu bar of Figure 2-11.
4. Click **Tools**, and the Tools and Settings window in Figure 2-13 appears. Using this window, you can change Defender settings, view quarantined and allowed items, access online information and options regarding Defender, and use Software Explorer.

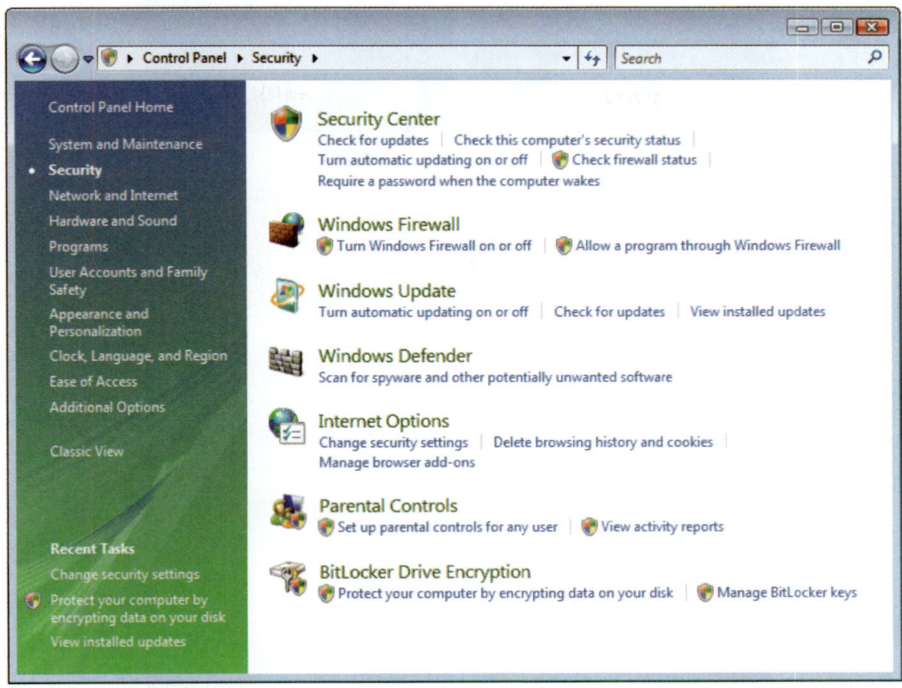

Figure 2-10 Use the Security window to manage many of Vista's security features

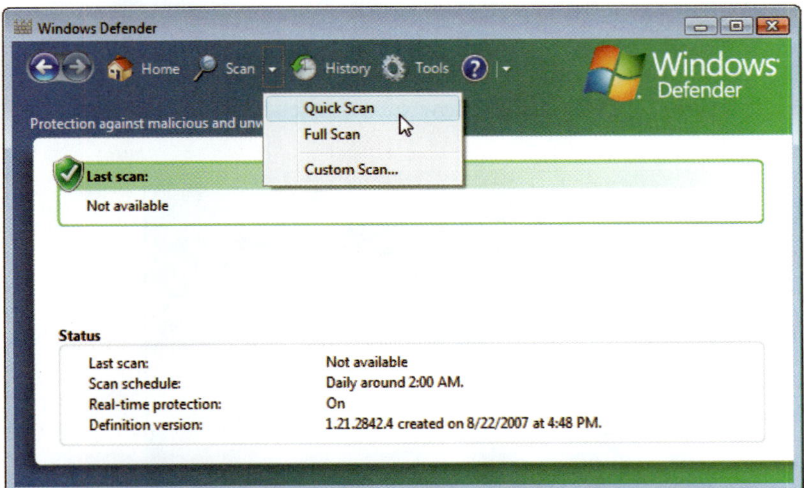

Figure 2-11 Three ways to scan a system using Windows Defender

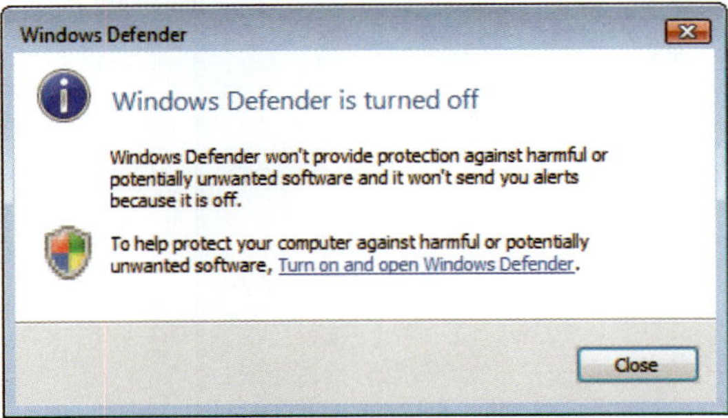

Figure 2-12 Defender is asking to be turned on

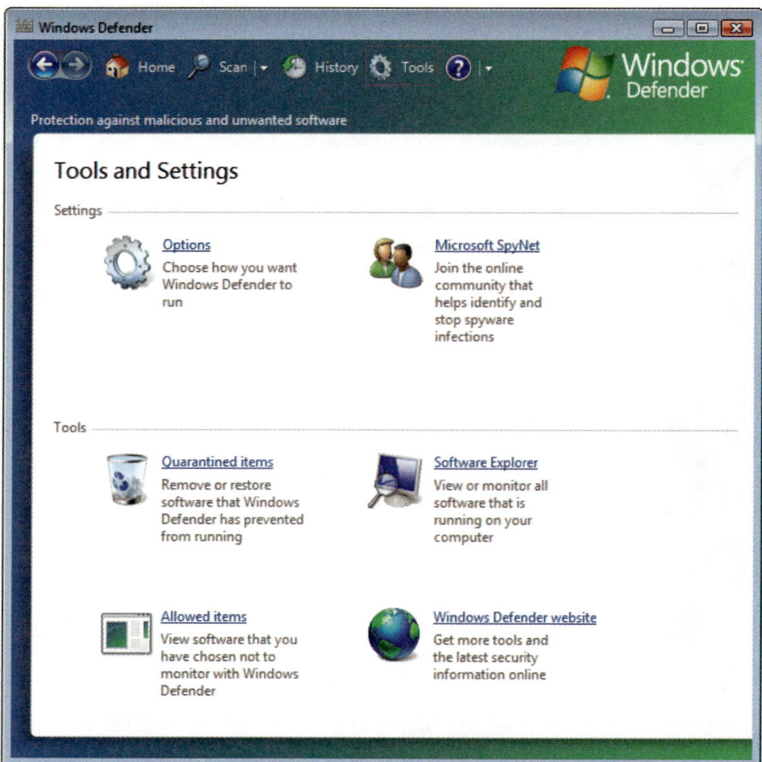

Figure 2-13 Windows Defender Tools and Settings window

5. To change Defender settings, click **Options** and the window in Figure 2-14 opens. Using this window, you can set how often, when, and how Defender will scan

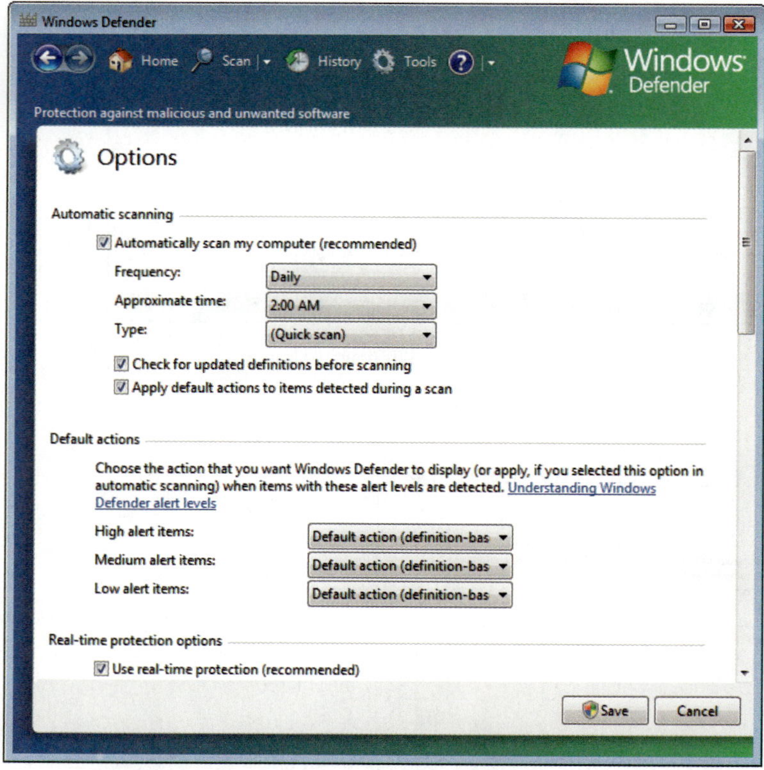

Figure 2-14 Configure Windows Defender options

the system and decide if all users can perform manual scans or only those with administrative rights. You can also turn Defender on and off using this window.

6. Software Explorer is new to Windows Vista; this tool works like a combination of Windows XP Task Manager and the System Configuration Utility (MSconfig). Return to the Tools and Settings window and click **Software Explorer** to see the Software Explorer window shown in Figure 2-15.

Figure 2-15 Use the Software Explorer window to view and manage installed software

7. Select a program listed in the left pane to see details about the program in the right pane and commands that can be applied to the program at the bottom of the window. In the figure, the category shown is Startup Programs; therefore, the programs listed are all launched at startup. Notice in the figure that other options for Category are Currently Running Programs, Network Connected Programs, and Winsock Service Providers. These last two items can be used to research the source of unwanted network activity. You can use Software Explorer to investigate programs installed or running on a system or to end, remove, or disable a program. You can also use this window to remove a program from the startup programs list so that it does not automatically launch at startup.

When Defender is running in real-time mode, monitoring the system for changes, and a monitored event occurs, Defender alerts the user of potentially unwanted changes and asks what to do. The user must allow or reject the change.

Some users prefer to use anti-adware and anti-spyware software rather than Windows Defender. Defender does not like being turned off and periodically displays a message asking to be turned back on. Users can find this message annoying, so to permanently disable

Defender, you will need to disable the Defender service. If you do not need Defender running on a system, disabling the service will save on memory, too. To do so, follow these steps:

1. In the Windows Defender window, click **Tools** and **Options**. On the Options window, under Automatic scanning, turn off **Automatically scan my computer (recommended)**. Under Real-time protection options, turn off **Use real-time protection**. Under Administrator options, turn off **Allow everyone to use Windows Defender**, and turn off **Use Windows Defender**.
2. Click **Save** and then respond to the UAC box. A dialog box appears informing you that Defender is turned off. Click **Close** to close the box.
3. To stop the Windows Defender service, click **Start** and enter **services.msc** in the Search box, press **Enter**, and respond to the UAC box. The Services console opens (see the left side of Figure 2-16).

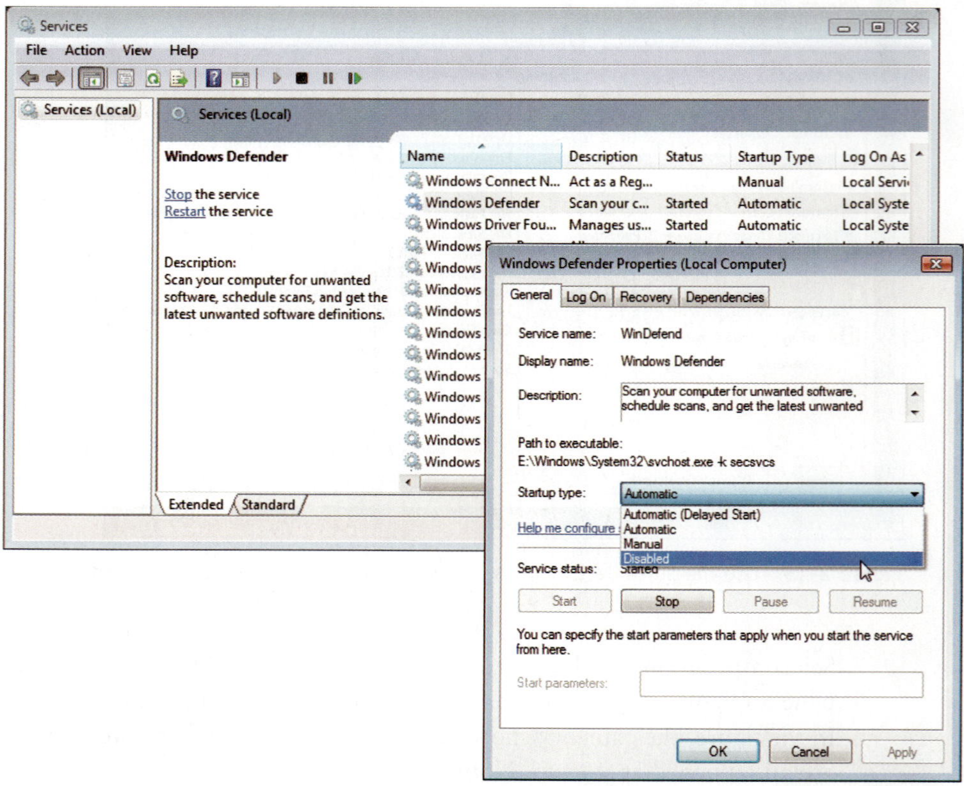

Figure 2-16 Use the Services console to disable Windows Defender

4. Scroll down to Windows Defender, right-click it, and select **Properties** from the shortcut menu. The Properties box opens (see the right side of Figure 2-16). In the Startup type list shown in the figure, select **Disabled** and click **Apply**. Click **OK** to close the Properties box and then close the Services console.

If you later want to use Defender, restore the Windows Defender service to Automatic and then go to Control Panel and open the Windows Defender window.

2

INTERNET EXPLORER SECURITY FEATURES

With malware on the rampage, Microsoft is always toughening up its defenses, especially with Internet Explorer, because malware often gets to computers through Web sites that trick users into accepting it or downloads and installs itself without user knowledge. New security features for Internet Explorer are discussed next.

PROTECTED MODE

Internet Explorer runs in Protected Mode to help prevent malware from secretly installing itself in the system. When Internet Explorer is in Protected Mode, Mandatory Integrity Control forces it into a low-integrity access level where it can write files only to the Temporary Internet Files folder and only change insignificant registry keys. However, sometimes a user might want Internet Explorer to install an add-on. To handle this situation, IE asks the user permission to move to a higher access level to perform the task. An information bar appears below the Internet Explorer menu bar as shown in Figure 2-17. When you click the bar, the drop-down menu appears as shown in the figure. Click Run ActiveX Control to allow the add-on to be installed.

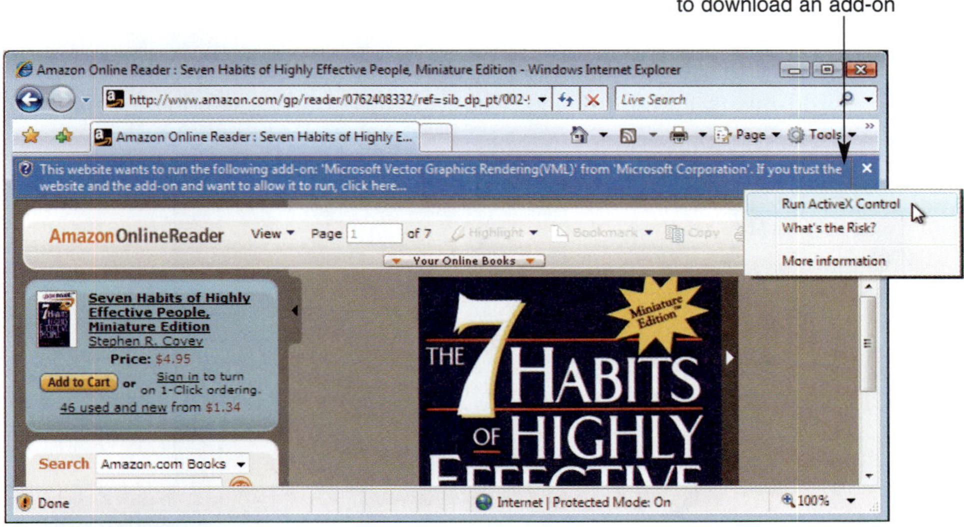

Figure 2-17 Internet Explorer is asking permission to install an add-on

MANAGING ADD-ONS

Sometimes problems arise with corrupt or malicious add-ons. Using Internet Explorer 7, you can temporarily disable all add-ons so that they can be eliminated as the source of a problem. To disable add-ons, do the following:

1. Click **Start, All Programs, Accessories, System Tools,** and **Internet Explorer (No Add-ons)**. Internet Explorer opens showing the information bar message in Figure 2-18.
2. You can now find out if the problem with Internet Explorer has disappeared. If it has disappeared, then you can assume the source of the problem is an add-on. You can next try disabling one add-on after another until you discover the one creating the problem.
3. To return Internet Explorer to run with add-ons, close the IE window and then open IE as usual.

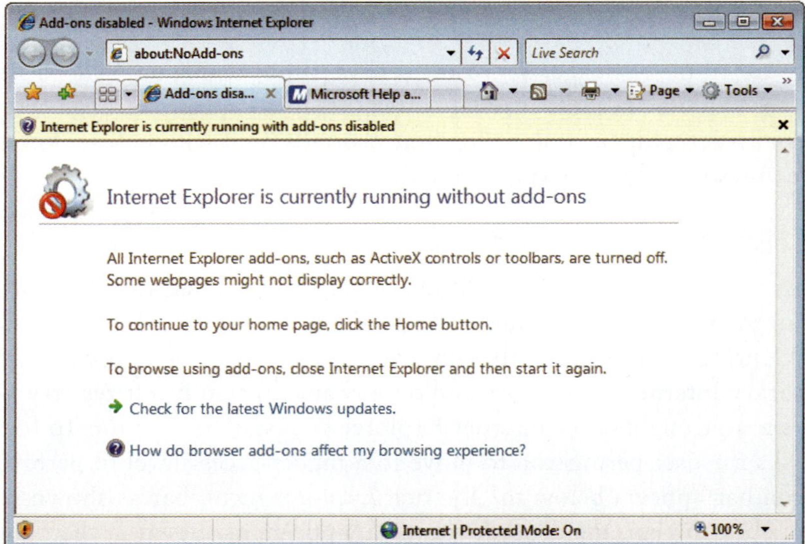

Figure 2-18 Internet Explorer is running without add-ons

To disable a specific add-on, do the following:

1. Open Internet Explorer. Click **Tools, Manage Add-ons,** and **Enable or Disable Add-ons** (see Figure 2-19). The Manage Add-ons window opens as shown in Figure 2-20.

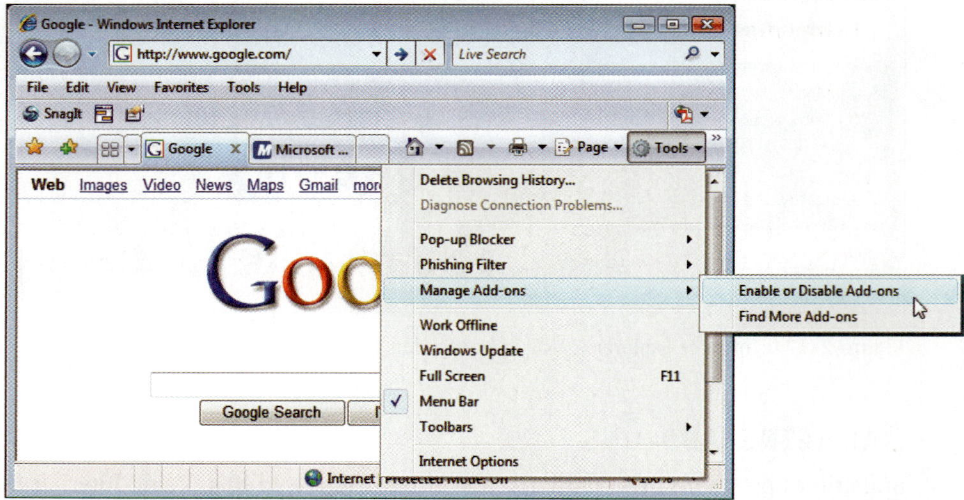

Figure 2-19 Manage add-ons using the Tools menu of Internet Explorer

2. The window displays currently loaded add-ons, but you can also display add-ons that have been used by IE. To disable any add-on, select it and click **Disable.** You can also delete ActiveX controls by selecting them and clicking **Delete.**

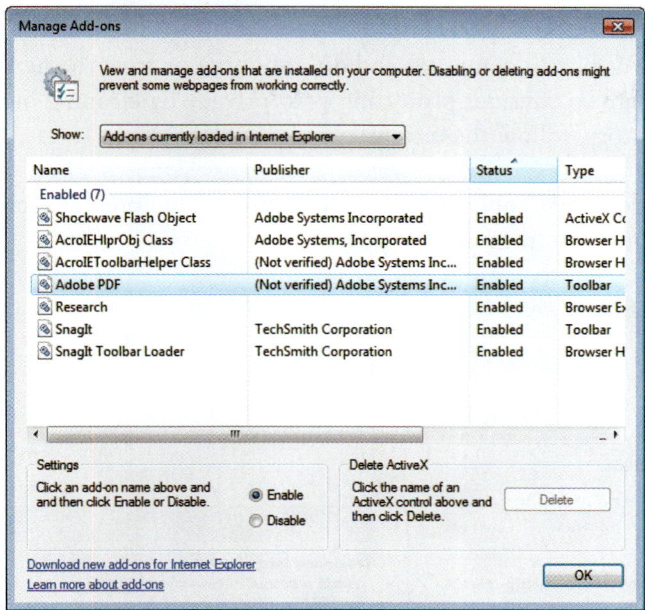

Figure 2-20 Use the Manage Add-ons window to disable or delete add-ons

PHISHING FILTER

Swindlers and cons have gone electronic, and lots of phishing Web sites are trying to lure in naïve users. Internet Explorer 7 offers a phishing filter to help you decide who you can trust. It works in three ways:

1. It compares the current Web site to a list of trusted sites stored on this computer.
2. It checks the current site for characteristics that indicate it is a phishing site.
3. It compares the site against an online database kept by Microsoft of known phishing sites.

You can use and manage the phishing filter using the Tools menu. Click Tools and Phishing Filter and the menu in Figure 2-21 appears. Using this menu, you can check the current Web site, turn the filter off and on, report a site to be a phishing site, and manage filter settings.

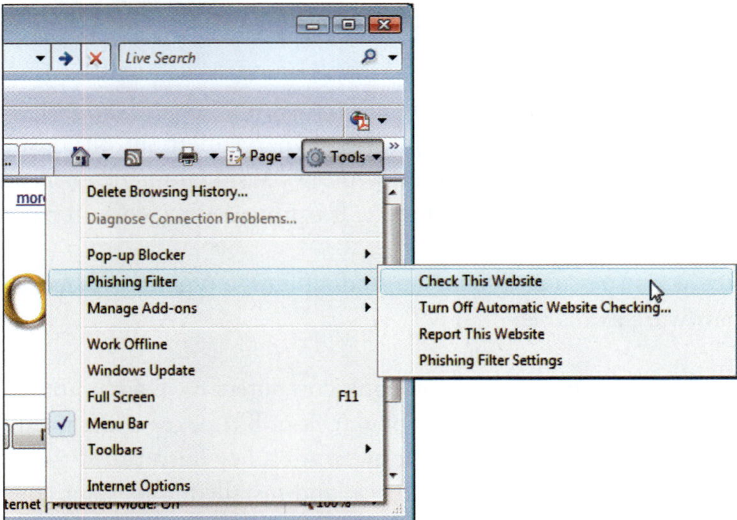

Figure 2-21 Use the Internet Explorer Phishing Filter to protect yourself against phishing

CLEANING THE BROWSER HISTORY

Next time you surf the Web on a computer and do not know or trust the next user(s) of this computer, you might want to consider protecting your privacy by cleaning out your browser history. To clean the history, follow these steps:

1. In Internet Explorer, click **Tools** and **Internet Options**. The Internet Options dialog box appears as shown on the left in Figure 2-22.

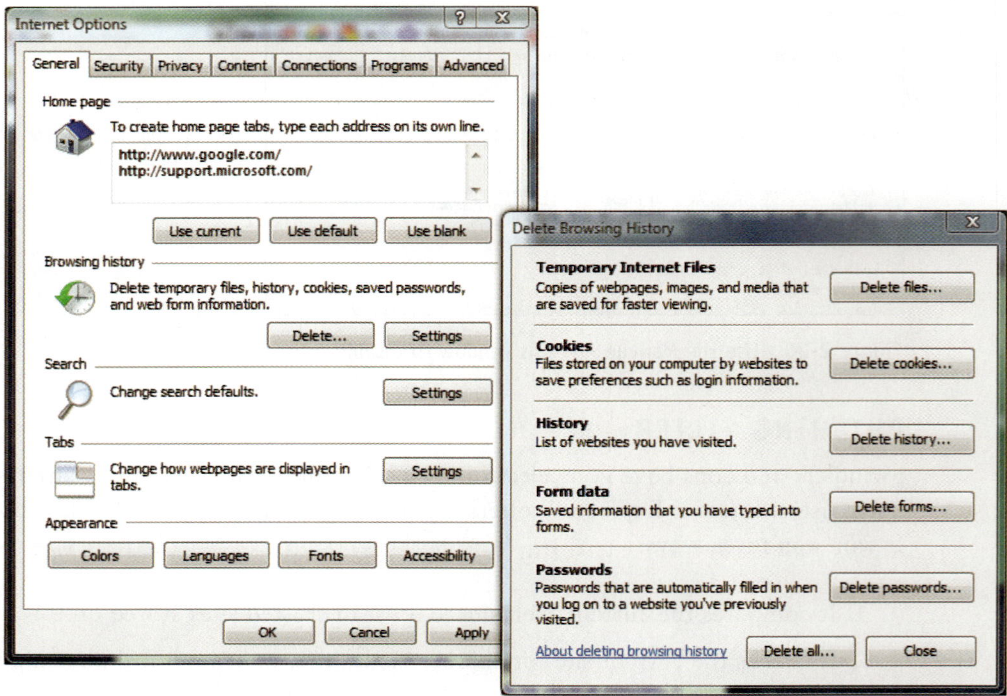

Figure 2-22 Internet Options dialog box

2. Under Browsing history, click **Delete**. The Delete Browsing History dialog box appears as shown in the right of Figure 2-22. You can select particular items to delete or click **Delete all** to clean out the entire browsing history.

BITLOCKER ENCRYPTION

Many folks carry around private data on their laptops. Just the thought of someone stealing the hard drive or even the entire laptop can cause hyperventilation! BitLocker Encryption, available with Windows Vista Enterprise or Windows Vista Ultimate, encrypts the entire Vista volume to prevent this kind of data theft. It is intended to work in partnership with EFS to protect data by encryption.

There are three ways to use BitLocker, depending on the type of protection you need and the computer hardware available:

- *Computer authentication.* Many notebook computers have a chip on the motherboard called the **TPM (Trusted Platform Module) chip**. BitLocker is designed to work with this chip; the chip holds the BitLocker encryption key (also called the startup key). If the hard drive is stolen from the notebook and installed in another computer, the data would be safe because BitLocker would not allow access without the startup key stored on the TPM chip. Therefore, this method authenticates the computer.

- *User authentication*. For computers that do not have TPM, the startup key can be stored on a USB flash drive (or other storage device which the computer reads before the OS is loaded), though the flash drive must be installed before the computer boots. This method authenticates the user. For this method to be the most secure, the user must never leave the flash drive stored with the computer. (The user might keep the USB startup key on his or her key ring.) This method does not assure you that the hard drive has not been moved to a different computer.
- *Computer and user authentication*. For best security, a PIN or password can be required at every startup in addition to TPM. Using this method, both the computer and the user are authenticated.

For BitLocker to work, the hard drive must have two partitions: the active partition used to boot the OS which will not be encrypted, and the system partition that will hold Vista and will be encrypted.

To make sure the hardware device that will hold the startup key is ready for BitLocker, do one of the following:

- If you are using TPM, make sure the TPM chip is enabled in CMOS setup. If TPM is present, the hard drive has already been prepared for BitLocker. In some cases, such as when you have upgraded a previous OS with Windows Vista, you might need to update BIOS so that your BIOS will be compatible with BitLocker.
- If you are using a USB flash drive to hold the startup key, make sure the system reads the flash drive before the OS is loaded.

After you have verified the startup key device is ready, then do the following to prepare the hard drive for BitLocker:

1. Click **Start, All Programs, Accessories, System Tools** and verify that **BitLocker** is listed as a system tool. If BitLocker is not in the list, the component might not be installed on your system. To install it, click **Start, All Programs**, and **Windows Update**. In the Windows Update window, click **View available updates**. In the list of updates under Windows Ultimate Extras, select and install **BitLocker and EFS enhancements** (see Figure 2-23).

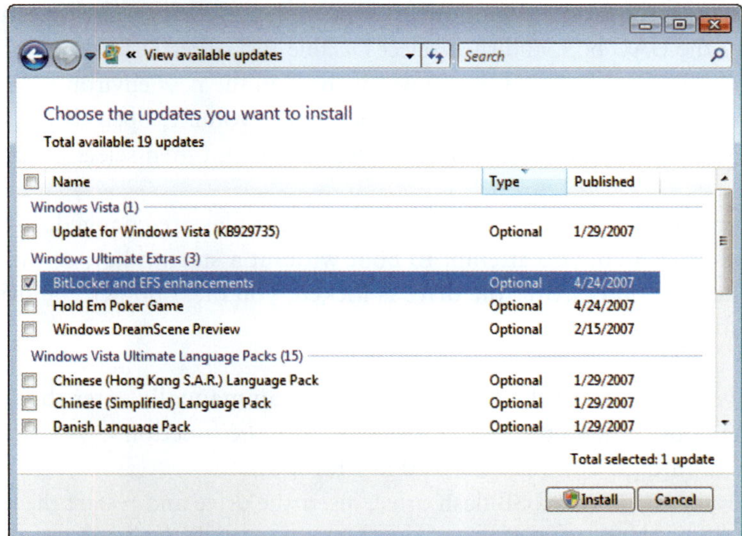

Figure 2-23 Select and install BitLocker and EFS enhancements

2. Now that you have verified BitLocker is installed, click **Start, All Programs, Accessories, System Tools, BitLocker**, and **BitLocker Drive Preparation Tool** and respond to the UAC box. Follow the onscreen directions, which create a new active partition used to boot the system which will not be encrypted. Restart your computer to complete the process.

Follow these steps to enable BitLocker Encryption:

1. Perform a full backup of the Vista volume and then use Chkdsk to check the volume for errors and repair them.
2. From Control Panel, click **Security**. On the Security window, under BitLocker Drive Encryption, click **Protect your computer by encrypting data on your disk**, and respond to the UAC box.
3. On the BitLocker Drive Encryption window, click **Turn on BitLocker** and follow directions on screen.
4. During the installation, if you chose to use a USB flash drive, you will be given the opportunity to insert the flash drive and Vista will write the startup key to the device.
5. You will also be given the opportunity to save a 48-digit recovery key to another USB flash drive or a folder, or you can print the recovery key. You can repeat this step more than once. It is a good idea to keep multiple copies of the recovery key in a secure location in case you lose your primary USB flash drive or you have problems with the TPM chip. If you are an administrator encrypting a volume for another user, be sure to keep a printout of the recovery key just in case the user calls you one day saying, "I've lost my startup key! Help!"
6. Finally, the encryption begins and BitLocker will be enabled.

Here are a few important tips about BitLocker:

- If you later want another copy of the recovery key or you want to change the PIN, use the Security window in Control Panel, and click Manage BitLocker keys.
- If you need to exchange the motherboard, flash BIOS, or upgrade the OS, you must first disable BitLocker so that BitLocker will not lock your hard drive. To temporarily disable BitLocker, open the Security window in Control Panel, click BitLocker Drive Encryption, respond to the UAC box, and then select Disable BitLocker Drive Encryption. When you later turn it on, the same startup key will be used in the new environment.
- To permanently turn off BitLocker and decrypt the volume, open the Security window in Control Panel, click BitLocker Drive Encryption, and then select Decrypt the volume.

A drive encrypted by BitLocker can lock down if boot files are changed, BIOS is modified, TPM is disabled or cleared, you attempt to boot without a startup key, or the drive is moved to another computer. After the drive is locked, you must unlock the drive using one of these methods:

- If you have a printout of the recovery key, you can manually enter the recovery key during the boot. When prompted for the key, use the function keys (F1 through F10) to enter the 48-digit key. (Use the F10 key for a 0.)
- If the recovery key is on a USB flash drive, insert the drive and restart the computer. If Windows Boot Manager attempts to launch recovery tools during the restart, do not follow these instructions because these recovery tools cannot read an encrypted volume.

BitLocker provides great security, but security comes with a price. For instance, you risk the chance your TPM will fail or losing all copies of the startup key. In these events, recovering the data can be messy. Therefore, use BitLocker only if the risks of BitLocker causing problems outweigh the risks of stolen data.

Notes

For more information about recovering encrypted data, see the Microsoft Knowledge Base article 928201 at *support.microsoft.com*.

SHARING AND SECURING FILES AND FOLDERS

In the following sections, you will learn how to secure and share folders for local users (users of the computer) and for network users (users on the network). Two tools used to share folders that you will learn about here are the new File Sharing Wizard and the Advanced Sharing window.

In this part of the chapter, let's begin by seeing how Vista manages local sharing and then we will look at how network sharing is accomplished.

LOCAL SHARING

When you want to share files and folders with other users of a single computer, you can use the Public folder, share files or folders within your user profile, or use folders that are not under the Users folder. Let's look at all three ways to share locally.

Use the Public Folder

When users on a single computer want to share files, the simplest way is to use the Public folder. Look at Figure 2-24 where two user accounts are set up on this PC. Jean Andrews is an administrator account and Joy Dark is a standard account. Because Jean is an administrator, she can access all folders on the drive including the folders in the C:\Users\Joy Dark profile, but Joy is a standard user; therefore, she cannot access folders in the C:\Users\Jean Andrews profile, the C:\Windows folder, or the C:\Program Files folders. If she were to try to access these folders, a UAC box appears asking for an administrator password. However, all users, administrators and standard users alike, can access folders in the C:\Users\Public profile without an administrator password.

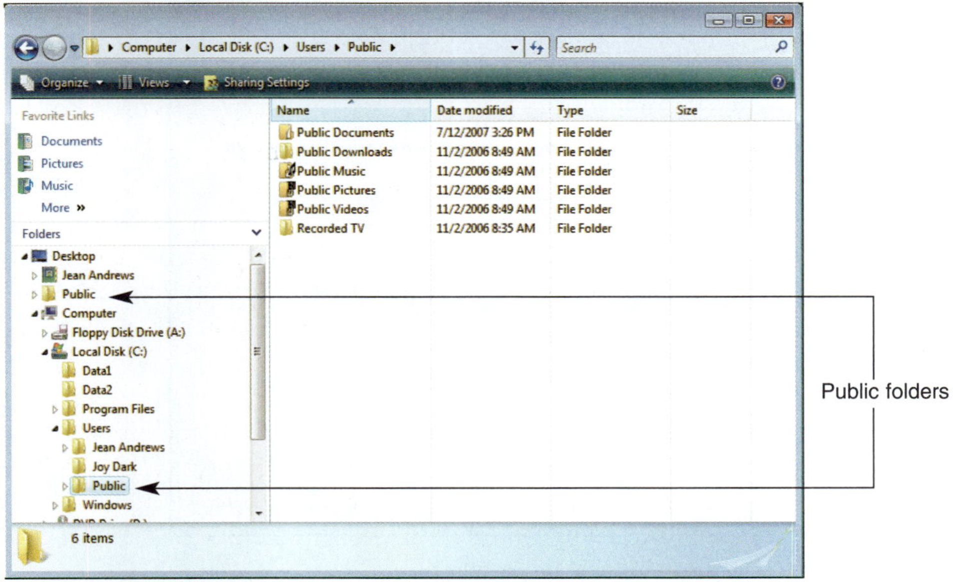

Figure 2-24 Users are encouraged to put shared files in the Public folder

Windows encourages users to share files using the Public folder by making it easy to find when using Windows Explorer. Click More in the Favorite Links section in the top left pane and select Public from the drop-down menu as shown in Figure 2-25. The Public folder is also conveniently listed near the top of the Folders list.

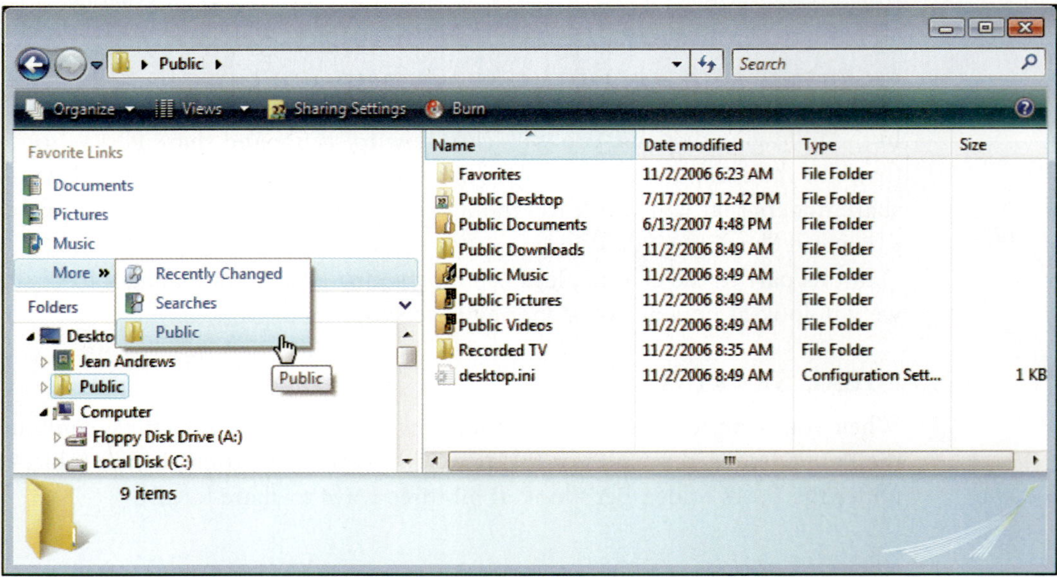

Figure 2-25 A user can easily find the Public folder using the Favorite Links section

Share Folders in Your User Profile

You can also share folders in your user profile; such sharing is called profile sharing. Follow these steps:

1. To share the Documents folder in your user profile, right-click the folder name and select **Share** on the shortcut menu. The File Sharing dialog box opens as shown in Figure 2-26.

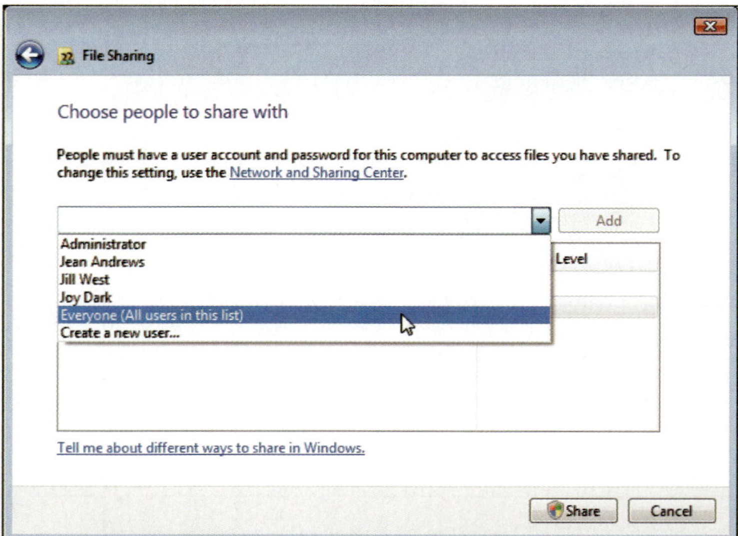

Figure 2-26 Choose people to share the folder

2. Click the down arrow to see a list of users of this computer. To allow everyone access, select **Everyone (All users in this list)** and click **Add**. (Alternately, you can select an individual user.) Whoever you add is assigned the permission level of Reader, as shown in Figure 2-27.

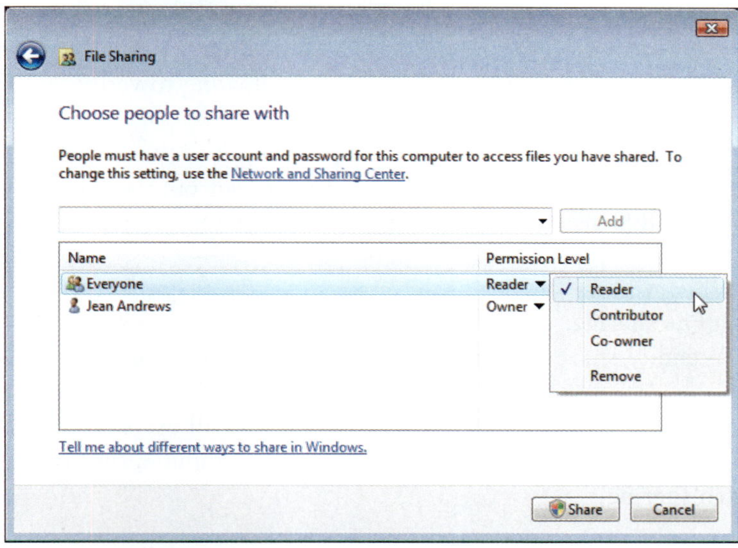

Figure 2-27 Change the permission level of a user

3. To allow the users the right to make changes to the folder, click the down arrow beside Reader. Notice the three choices of permission levels and the opportunity to remove the user from the list of users. Table 2-1 explains the meaning of the three permission levels. Select **Co-owner** from the shortcut menu as shown in Figure 2-27.
4. To close the box, click **Share** and respond to the UAC box. Then click **Done**.
5. Remember the serving hand icon under shared folders in Windows XP? Well, it is now replaced with the two-friends icon under shared folders in Windows Vista. Take a look at Figure 2-28.

Permission Level	Description
Reader	Can read but not write to the contents of the folder and its subfolders
Contributor	Can write new files and read existing files but cannot change existing files put there by others. Applies only to folder sharing.
Co-owner	Has full control over the folder in the same way the owner does, but is not identified as the folder owner.

Table 2-1 Permission levels for files and folders in Windows Vista

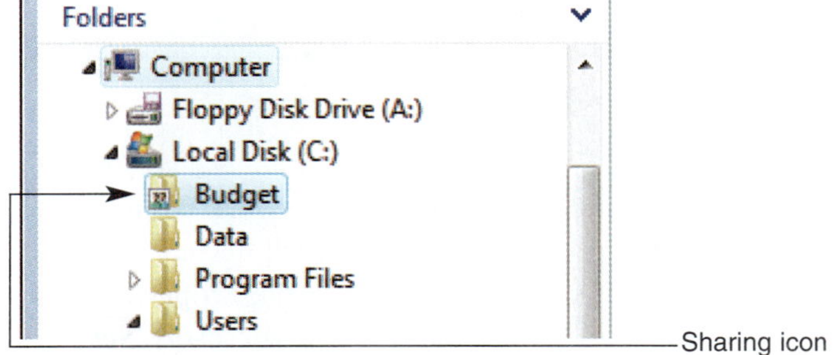

Figure 2-28 The two-friends icon indicates a shared folder

Use Other Folders

In addition to the Public folder and profile sharing, all users can access any folder created under the root directory of a drive, such as the C:\Data1 and C:\Data2 folders shown earlier in Figure 2-24.

NETWORK SHARING

To share folders on a network, you must first do the following to verify that network sharing options are enabled:

1. Click **Start**, right-click **Network** and select **Properties** from the shortcut menu to open the Network and Sharing Center. Under Sharing and Discovery, verify these items (see Figure 2-29):
   - Turn on **File sharing.**
   - If you intend to share the Public folder to the network, turn on **Public folder sharing.**
   - If you want the added protection of requiring that all users on the network must have a valid user account and password on this computer, turn on **Password protected sharing.**

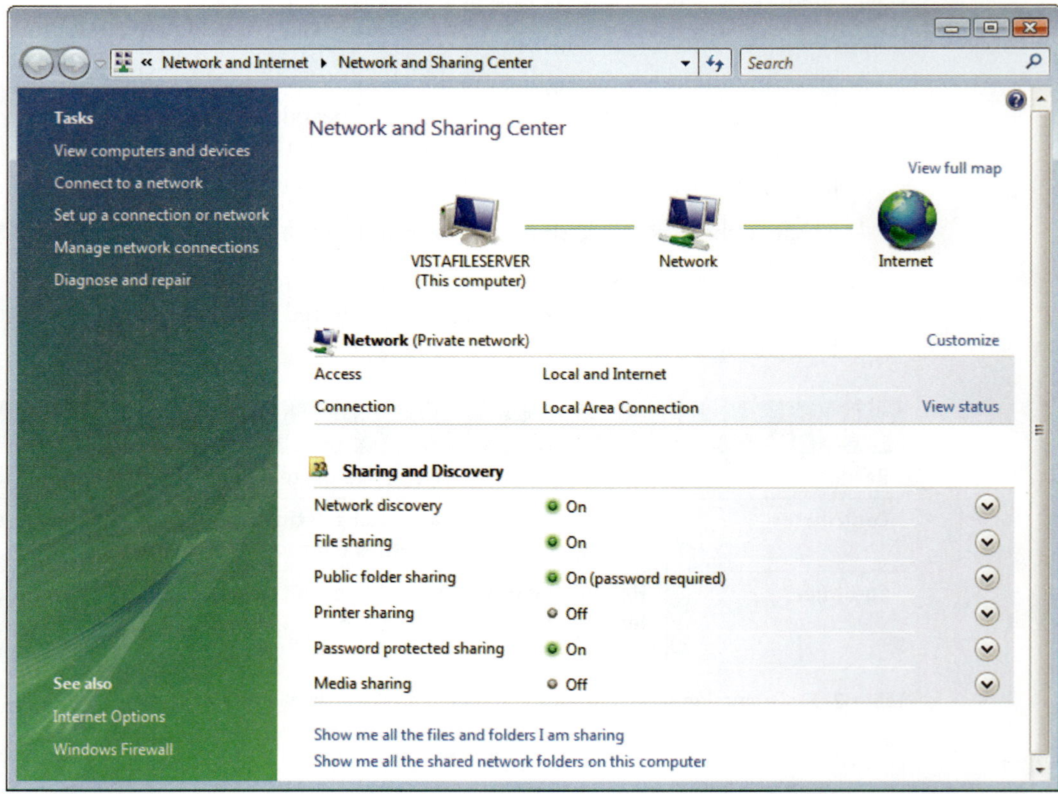

Figure 2-29 Verify file sharing options are enabled for network sharing

2. In the Network and Sharing Center, click **Manage network connections.** In the Network Connections window, right-click the network device, select **Properties** from the shortcut menu, and respond to the UAC box. In the Properties dialog box (see Figure 2-30), verify that **File and Printer Sharing for Microsoft Networks** is checked.

2

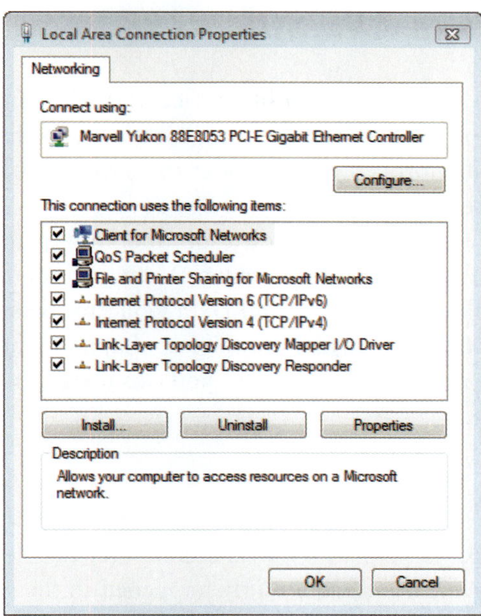

Figure 2-30 Verify the network adapter is configured for file and printer sharing

You are now ready to share specific folders. Using Windows Explorer, right-click the folder you want to share and select Share from the shortcut menu. Following instructions given earlier in the chapter, select the user or users with which to share and then select the level of sharing (Reader, Contributor, or Co-owner).

If you prefer, just as with Windows XP, you can also use the Advanced Sharing dialog box to manually configure shared permissions for each user or user group. To access the box, right-click a folder and select Properties. In the Properties dialog box on the Sharing tab, click Advanced Sharing and respond to the UAC box. In the Advanced Sharing dialog box (see Figure 2-31), click Share this folder. You can then click Permissions to add users and their permissions to the share. If later you have a problem with network sharing, always verify that the Network and Sharing Center shows that file sharing options are enabled. Sometimes Vista incorrectly sets a private network to public, which then disables file sharing options.

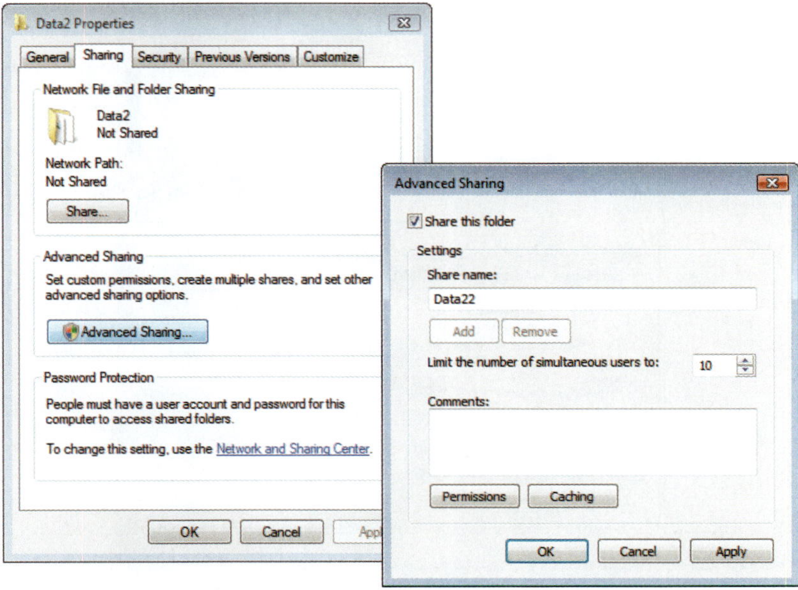

Figure 2-31 Use the Advanced Sharing dialog box to manually configure shared folders

TROUBLESHOOTING HARDWARE AND SOFTWARE

Every PC support technician will one day be faced with a device that refuses to work or a nasty application error the user cannot solve. When that day comes, know that Windows Vista offers some new tools and some improvements on older tools to help you troubleshoot problems with hardware and software.

In this part of the chapter, you will learn about the new tools and how to apply them to solve problems. Let's first look at troubleshooting tools new to Vista, including the Reliability Monitor, the Problem Reports and Solutions window, and Data Collector Sets. (One other new tool, Windows Memory Diagnostics, was covered in the last chapter.) After we have surveyed the new tools, we will turn our attention to strategies you can use to solve hardware and software problems.

RELIABILITY MONITOR

When a PC support person is called on to help a user with a computer problem, it is a great help to know the history of the problem, what has recently happened to the system, and how the system has performed in the past. Windows Vista offers a new tool to help you get these answers, the **Reliability Monitor**. Follow these steps to learn to use it:

1. Click **Start**, right-click **Computer**, select **Manage** from the shortcut menu, and respond to the UAC box. The Computer Management console opens. Under System Tools, expand **Reliability and Performance** and then expand **Monitoring Tools**. Click **Reliability Monitor**. The Reliability Monitor pane opens as shown in Figure 2-32.

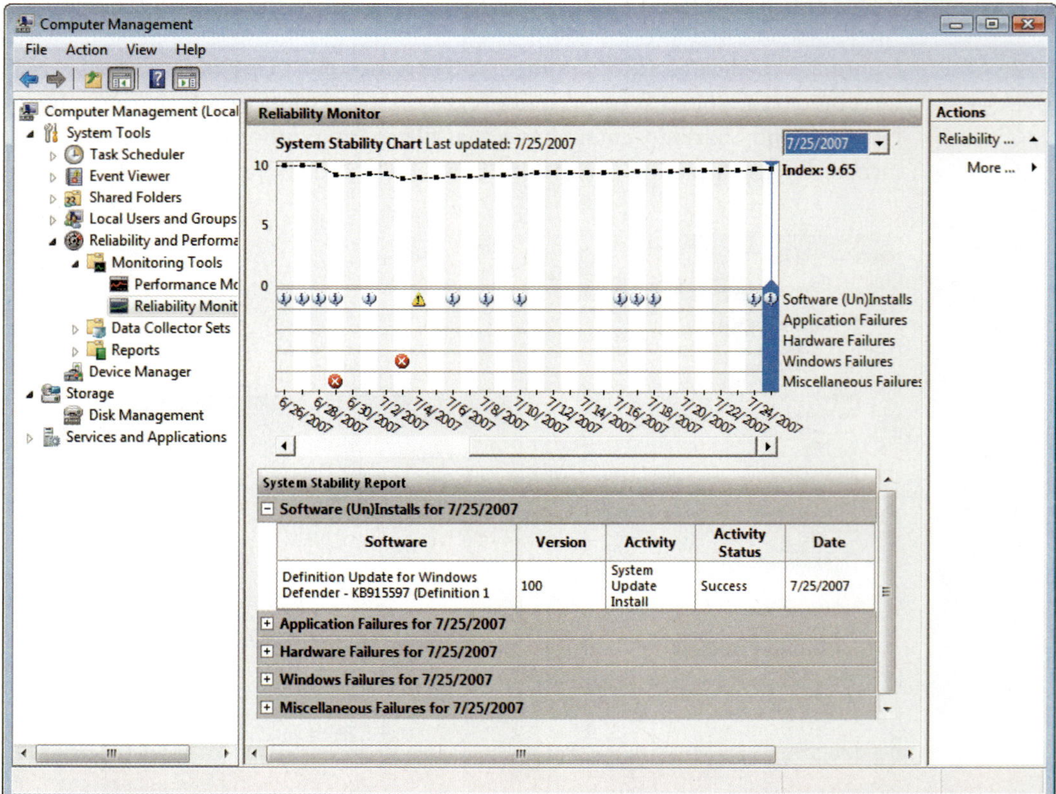

Figure 2-32 Use the Reliability Monitor tool to investigate a history of events on this computer

2. Click a day in the chart to see details about that day in the lower area of the pane. The monitor is tracking five types of events as shown in the pane (Software, Application, Hardware, Windows, and Miscellaneous Failures). To see details for each type event, click the + sign to the left of the event type. By selecting days in the chart where warnings and errors are marked by red circles and yellow triangles in the chart, you can quickly get a pretty good idea as to what has been happening with the system in the last few weeks. This information can be invaluable to help you understand the history and source of a computer hardware or software problem.

PROBLEM REPORTS AND SOLUTIONS

Another useful tool that can help with hardware problems, and occasionally with software problems, is the Problem Reports and Solutions tool. This tool, included with all versions of Vista, maintains a history of problems and solutions that you can view and use. To learn to use this tool, follow these steps:

1. Click **Start, All Programs, Maintenance,** and **Problem Reports and Solutions**. The Problem Reports and Solutions window shown in Figure 2-33 appears.

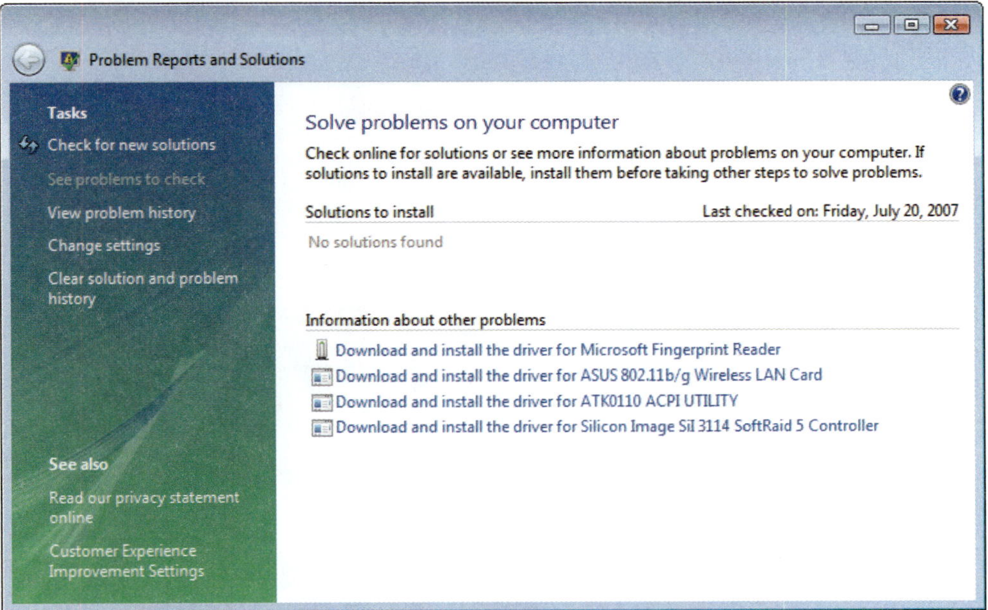

Figure 2-33 Use the Problem Reports and Solutions tool to help solve hardware problems

2. Notice the list of problems in the window not yet solved on this system. To see details about a problem, click it. For example, if you click the second item in the list, **Download and install the driver for ASUS 802.11b/g Wireless LAN Card,** the detail window shown in Figure 2-34 opens. From the information given, it appears that the wireless LAN card drivers need updating.

3. To follow through with this proposed solution, open **Device Manager,** right-click the card, and select **Properties** to open the Properties box as shown in Figure 2-35. Note that Device Manager reports the device is not working.

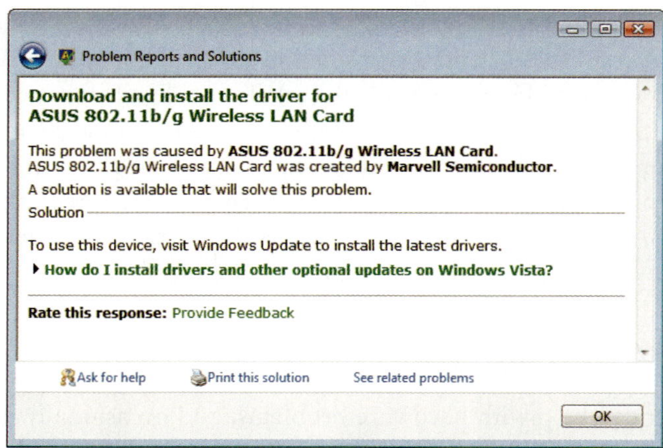

Figure 2-34 Details about a problem can lead to a solution

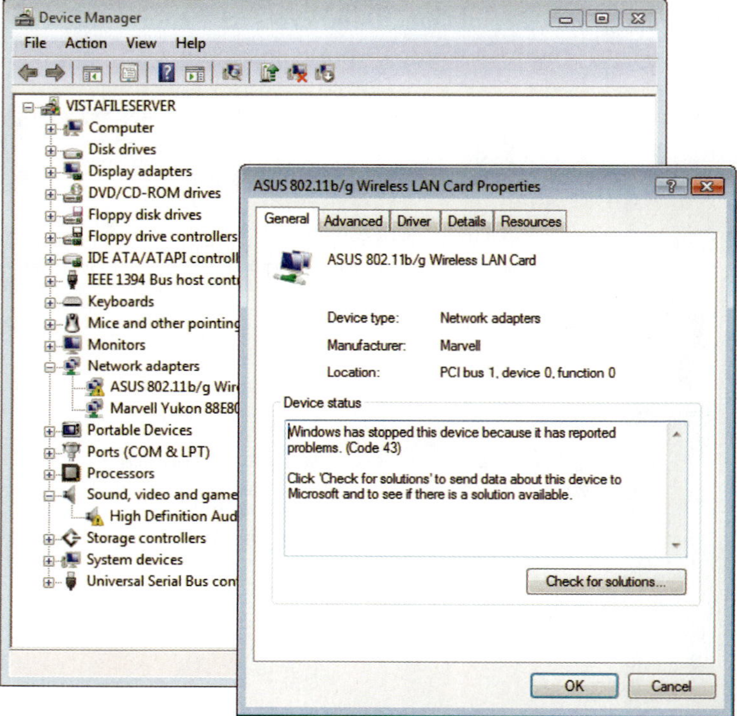

Figure 2-35 The device Properties box reports the device is not working

4. To update the drivers, click the **Driver** tab and then click **Update Driver**. On the next window (see Figure 2-36), you can decide to have Windows search online for the update or, if you have already downloaded the new driver update to your computer, click **Browse my computer for driver software** and follow the directions on screen to point to the update. After the drivers are updated, return to Device Manager to make sure the device is working without errors.
5. To see a history report of problems, in the Problem Reports and Solutions window (refer back to Figure 2-33), click **View problem history** in the left pane. A list of prior problems appears as shown in Figure 2-37. Double-click an item in the list to see details about the problem.

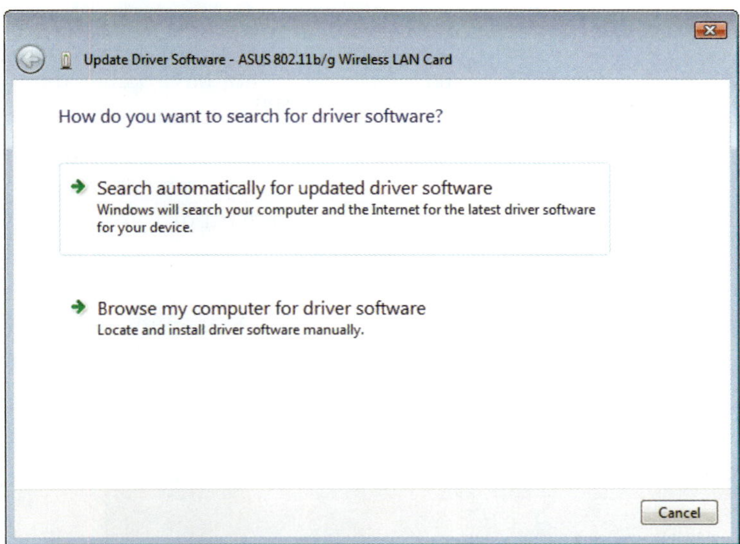

Figure 2-36 Decide where you want Windows to look for the driver update

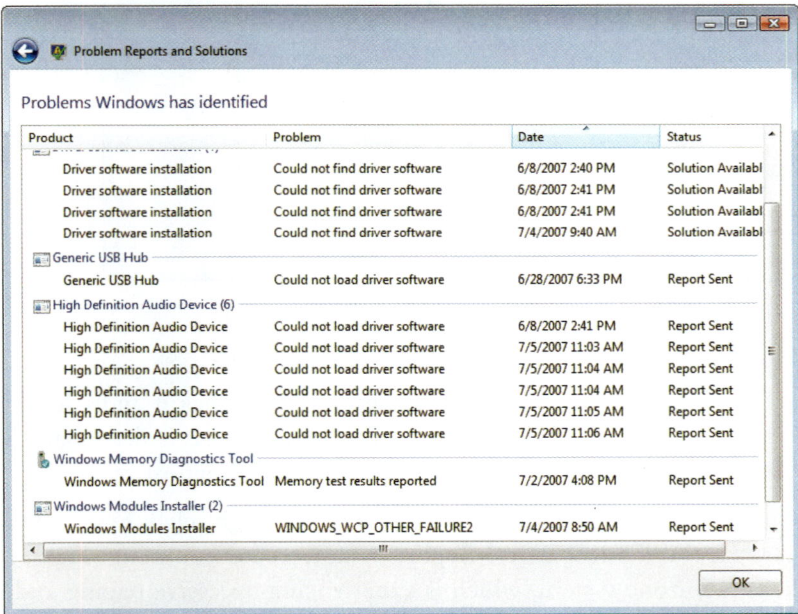

Figure 2-37 History of problems captured by Windows

6. Looking back at the Problem Reports and Solutions window, when you click **Check for new solutions**, Windows will search for new solutions not yet found for problems in the history list. To clean the history list, click **Clear solution and problem history**.

As you have seen, you can use the Problem Reports and Solutions window to give you an idea of previous problems found on the system and solutions presented that have not yet been applied.

DATA COLLECTOR SETS

When you have a problem with the system, but you do not have a clue about what is causing it, Vista has a tool that can help. You can use the **Data Collector Set utility**, available with all versions of Vista, to collect data about the system and report that data to you in ways that can help you zero in on a problem's source. These reports can also be useful when checking the performance of critical devices such as the hard drive or memory. To see how the tool works, follow these steps:

1. From the Computer Management console, expand **Reliability and Performance**, expand **Data Collector Sets**, and then click **System**. The four categories under System appear in the middle pane as shown in Figure 2-38.

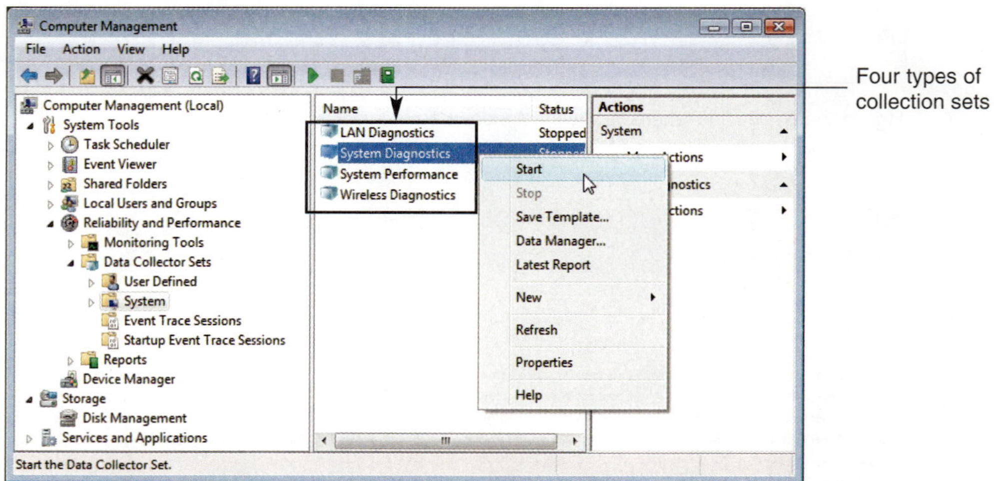

Figure 2-38 Four categories from which you can collect data to analyze

2. To collect data in one of these four categories, right-click it and select **Start** from the shortcut menu as shown in the figure. Wait while data is collected and then fills the middle pane. In our example, we are using System Diagnostics.
3. To view the system diagnostics data as a report, right-click **System Diagnostics** in the left pane and select **Latest Report** from the shortcut menu. Figure 2-39 shows the report for one system, which is experiencing excessive paging and needs more memory.

Let's now turn our attention to strategies you can use when troubleshooting hardware and software under Windows Vista.

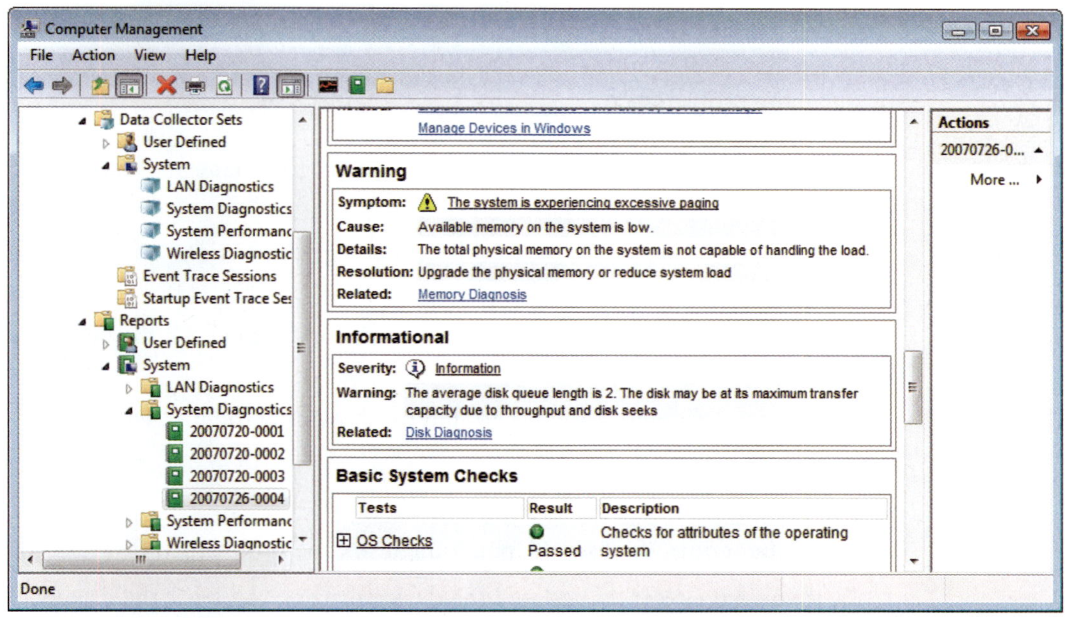

Figure 2-39 Reported results of collecting data about System Diagnostics

TROUBLESHOOTING STRATEGIES FOR NEWLY-INSTALLED HARDWARE

If you have just installed a device and the darn thing does not work, the general approaches to solving the problem under Windows XP still apply to Windows Vista. However, to make the chapter complete, we will briefly summarize the guidelines here:

1. If Vista will not start, see the sections later in the chapter on how to solve startup problems.
2. For an external device, check cable connections and power and make sure the device is turned on. For an expansion card, reseat the card in its slot.
3. Try updating Windows. The problem might be solved by applying a Windows patch.
4. Check Device Manager for errors. Try updating device drivers and updating the software which uses the device. Look for driver updates on the hardware manufacturer Web site.
5. Try uninstalling and reinstalling the device. Carefully check hardware manufacturer directions to install the device and follow the directions in detail. If you do not have the directions, try to find them on the manufacturer's Web site.
6. Check Event Viewer for errors. Device drivers often put events in the System log, but it is a good idea to check all logs.
7. Consider flashing BIOS or updating drivers for other hardware that you suspect might be contributing to the problem.
8. For USB devices, move the device to a different USB port and try installing a known good device on the original port. Is the port enabled and working?
9. Consider whether a cable might be bad. Replace the cable.
10. Try installing the device in another computer.

PROBLEMS WITH EXISTING HARDWARE

If a device has been working fine, but now is creating problems, these guidelines will help you solve the problem:

1. If Windows refuses to start, see instructions given later in the chapter on startup problems.
2. For external devices, check cable and power connections and make sure the device is turned on.
3. Use the Problem Reports and Solutions window to check the details given about the device and solutions offered.
4. Use the Reliability Monitor to find out how long the problem has existed and about related problems.
5. Check Event Viewer for any useful information.
6. Try updating Windows. A patch might fix the problem.
7. If you have recently updated the device drivers, roll back the drivers.
8. Check Device Manager for errors. Try updating device drivers and updating the software using the device. Look for driver updates on the hardware manufacturer Web site.
9. Check the hardware manufacturer Web site for problems and solutions. Search the Microsoft support site (*support.microsoft.com*) for known problems with the device. Use a search engine to look for known problems and solutions.
10. Try uninstalling any newly installed hardware that might be contributing to the problem.
11. Update device drivers for other devices in the system and flash BIOS. As strange as it might seem, updating drivers for one device can occasionally solve the problem of another.
12. Check your hard drive. Is there enough free space? Try running Chkdsk.
13. Move the device to another computer. If it works there, try reinstalling it on the original computer.
14. Replace cables. For internal expansion cards, reseat the card.
15. Try System Restore. Be aware of settings and user account information you might lose by applying an older restore point.

APPROACHES TO TROUBLESHOOTING SOFTWARE

Here is the general list of things to do when faced with a software program causing problems:

1. The first item of business is the user's data. Is it saved, backed up, corrupted? Try a different data file; the original file might be corrupted. Remember, the data is often the most valuable thing on a computer and saving it is much more important than fixing a software problem.
2. Try closing other applications, rebooting the PC, logging on as a different user (one with administrator privileges), or running the application as an administrator (right-click the program file and choose Run as administrator from the shortcut menu).

3. Use the help tools provided by the software manufacturer to search for answers. These tools might include documentation (printed, on CD, or online) or a help tool that is integrated into the software program.
4. When you update Vista, fixes are often applied to other Microsoft products, including Microsoft Office and Internet Explorer. Click Start, All Programs, and Windows Update. On the Windows Update window, click Check for updates. In the list of available updates, search for updates for the product giving trouble.
5. An especially powerful tool for solving software problems is the Internet. Check the software manufacturer Web site for solutions. Search the Microsoft support Web site for known problems with the software. Use a search engine to search on errors messages or problem description. You might even find a forum where others have had similar problems and can lend a hand.

The Vista tools you have available to help solve software problems are as follows:

- System Configuration Utility (MSconfig.exe), affectionately known "M-S-config", can be used to examine and temporarily disable processes configured to launch at startup. Use it to solve problems with a slow startup or a startup that gives errors. It is also helpful when Vista is running slowly to root out unneeded software taking up resources.
- Task Manager is used to view currently running processes and to stop them. Use it when an application hangs and you need to end it. It is also useful when researching processes that might be hogging resources including the network, CPU, and memory.
- Use Software Explorer to examine, remove, and disable startup programs and currently running programs. Recall from earlier in the chapter, you access it from the Windows Defender window, so Defender must be running to use Software Explorer.
- In Control Panel, select Programs and then select Programs and Features to uninstall, change, and repair programs installed on the system. If software is causing problems, click the software in this window. If Repair appears as an option, try this first. If Repair is not an option (the Repair link appears only if it is included in the original software installation), then try uninstalling and reinstalling the software. Be sure to uninstall the software before you attempt to install it a second time.

SUPPORTING VISTA STARTUP

Nothing is more frustrating to a user than a computer that refuses to start when he or she has work that cannot wait. As the support technician, your job in these situations is most likely to save the day by getting the computer up and going as quickly as possible. But, again, remember to always ask the user, "Is your data backed up?". If not, then focus on the data first and then the startup problem.

The good news is that Vista has some much improved tools to solve startup problems to make your work easier. In this section of the chapter, you will first learn about how Vista startup has changed from Windows XP, and then about new tools to solve startup problems. Finally, we will turn our attention to strategies to use when solving these problems.

UNDERSTANDING VISTA STARTUP

Table 2-2 lists the files necessary to start Vista. All the files except the first three in the list are also required for Windows 2000/XP to load. Recall that under Windows 2000/XP, the boot loader program, Ntldr, managed Windows startup and the Boot.ini text file kept startup parameters. In Windows Vista, Ntldr has been replaced by two Vista components: The

File	Path	Description
BootMgr	Root directory of boot partition (C:\)	Windows Boot Manager manages the initial startup of the OS
BCD	\Boot folder of the boot partition (C:\Boot)	Boot Configuration Data file contains boot parameters
WinLoad	*%systemroot%*\System32 (C:\Windows\System32)	Windows Boot Loader loads and starts essential Windows processes
Ntoskrnl.exe	*%systemroot%*\System32 (C:\Windows\System32)	Vista kernel
Hal.dll	*%systemroot%*\System32 (C:\Windows\System32)	Dynamic-link library handles low-level hardware details
Smss.exe	*%systemroot%*\System32 (C:\Windows\System32)	Sessions Manager file responsible for loading user mode graphics components
Csrss.exe	*%systemroot%*\System32 (C:\Windows\System32)	Win32 subsystem
Winlogon.exe	*%systemroot%*\System32 (C:\Windows\System32)	Logon process
Services.exe	*%systemroot%*\System32 (C:\Windows\System32)	Service Control Manager starts and stops services
Lsass.exe	*%systemroot%*\System32 (C:\Windows\System32)	Authenticates users
System registry hive	*%systemroot%*\System32\Config\System (C:\Windows\System32\Config\System)	Holds data for the HKEY_LOCAL_MACHINE key of the registry
Device drivers	*%systemroot%*\System32\Drivers (C:\Windows\System32\Drivers)	Drivers for required hardware

Table 2-2 Files needed to start Windows Vista

Notes

One more major change in Vista startup is that the hardware profiles used in Windows 2000/XP are no longer needed under Vista, because Vista automatically detects different hardware configurations at startup.

Windows Boot Manager (BootMgr) and the Windows Boot Loader (WinLoad). In addition, Boot.ini has been replaced by the Vista Boot Configuration Data (BCD) file. Also notice in Table 2-2 that the BootMgr file and the BCD file are stored in the boot partition (the active partition) and the other files are stored in the system partition. For most Vista installations, the boot partition and the system partition are the same partition (drive C).

The **Vista Boot Configuration Data (BCD)** file is structured the same as a registry file and contains configuration information about how Vista is started. Here is the type of information contained in the BCD file:

Notes

In a normal Vista installation, the boot and system partitions are the same partition (drive C). However, when Vista is installed in a dual boot configuration, the boot partition and the system partition are different partitions. Another situation where the boot and system partitions are different partitions is when Vista BitLocker Encryption is used.

- Settings that control BootMgr and WinLoad
- Settings that control WinResume.exe, the program that resumes Vista from hibernation

- Settings that start and control the Windows Memory Diagnostic program (\Boot\MemTest.exe)
- Settings that launch Ntldr to load a previous OS in a dual boot configuration
- Settings to load a non-Microsoft operating system (such as the Mac OS or Linux)

STEPS IN VISTA STARTUP

Now let's look at the steps to start a Vista computer. Study these steps carefully because the better you understand startup, the more likely you will be able to solve startup problems.

1. Just as with all computers, startup BIOS performs POST (power-on self test) to verify that essential hardware devices are working and looks to CMOS (firmware) to find out the boot sequence. The BIOS then turns to the first device in the boot sequence to find and load an OS. Most likely, this device is the hard drive.
2. The BIOS finds and launches the small program in the master boot record (MBR) of the hard drive. This program points to the BootMgr program stored in the root of the boot partition. BootMgr is launched.
3. BootMgr starts in 16-bit mode and switches the processor to 32-bit or 64-bit mode. (Starting in 16-bit mode is necessary because all processors start in 16-bit mode, also called real mode.)
4. BootMgr reads the BCD file. The next step depends on these factors:

   - If the user presses the spacebar, the Windows Boot Manager window appears, as shown in Figure 2-40.
   - If the computer is set up for a dual-boot environment, BootMgr displays the Windows Boot Manager window, as shown in Figure 2-40, with the two operating systems listed for your selection.

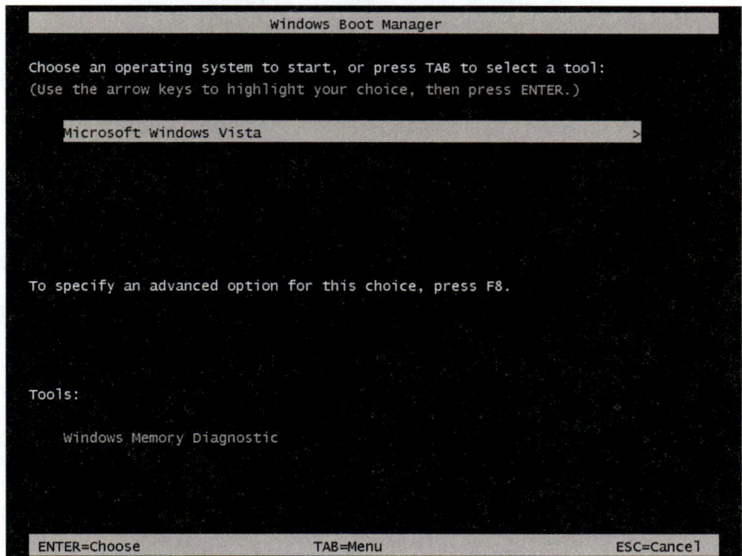

Figure 2-40 Press the spacebar to force the Windows Boot Manager window to appear

   - If the user presses F8, BootMgr displays the Advanced Boot Options windows, as shown in Figure 2-41.
   - If Windows was previously stopped abruptly, the Windows Error Recovery window (see Figure 2-42) appears.
   - For normal startups that are not dual booting, no menu appears and BootMgr finds and launches Windows Boot Loader (WinLoad).

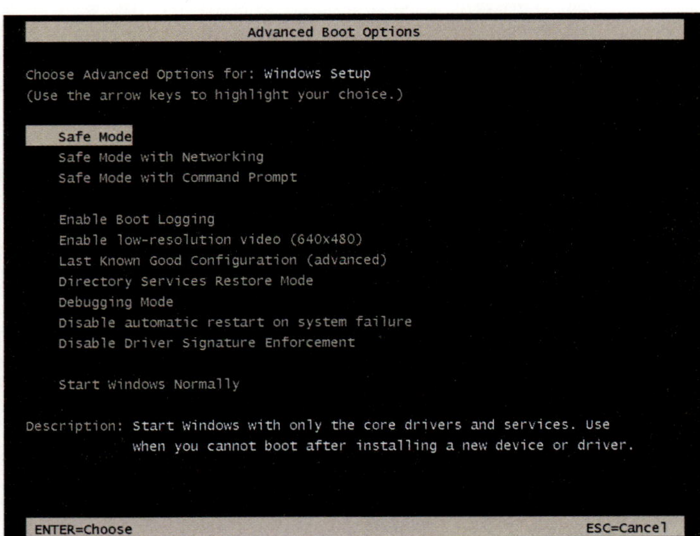

Figure 2-41 Press F8 to see the Advanced Boot Options window

Windows Error Recovery
Windows failed to start. A recent hardware or software change might be the cause. To fix the problem:

1. Insert your Windows installation disc and restart your computer.
2. Choose your language settings, and then click "Next."
3. Click "Repair your computer."

Other options:
If power was interrupted during startup, choose Start Windows Normally.
(Use the arrow keys to highlight your choice.)

Safe Mode
Safe Mode with Networking
Safe Mode with Command Prompt
Last Known Good Configuration (advanced)
Start Windows Normally

Description: Start Windows with its regular settings.

ENTER=Choose

Figure 2-42 This window appears if Windows has been abruptly stopped

5. WinLoad loads the OS kernel (Ntoskrnl.exe) into memory but does not yet start it. WinLoad also loads the hardware abstraction layer (Hal.dll) into memory, which will later be used by the kernel.
6. WinLoad loads the system registry hive (C:\Windows\System32\Config\System) into memory.
7. WinLoad then reads the registry key just created, HKEY_LOCAL_MACHINE \SYSTEM\Services, looking for and loading device drivers that must be launched at startup into memory. The drivers are not yet started. It also reads data from the HKEY_LOCAL_MACHINE\SYSTEM key that tells the OS if the user wants to start the OS using the Last Known Good Configuration.
8. WinLoad starts up the memory paging process and then turns over startup to the OS kernel.
9. The kernel (Ntoskrnl.exe) activates the HAL, reads more information from the registry, and builds the registry key HKEY_LOCAL_MACHINE\HARDWARE into memory, using information that has been collected about hardware.

10. The kernel then starts critical services and drivers that are configured to be started by the kernel during the boot. Recall that drivers interact directly with hardware and run in kernel mode, and services interact with drivers. Most services and drivers are stored in C:\Windows\System32 or C:\Windows\System32\Drivers and have a .exe, .dll, or .sys file extension.
11. After all services and drivers configured to load during the boot are started, the kernel starts the Session Manager (Smss.exe), which runs in user mode.
12. Smss.exe starts the part of the Win32 subsystem that displays graphics and the Windows **progress bar** displays on the screen (see Figure 2-43). When you see the progress bar, you know the Windows kernel has loaded successfully. Smss.exe then starts Csrss.exe, which also runs in user mode. Csrss.exe is the Win32 subsystem component that interacts with applications.

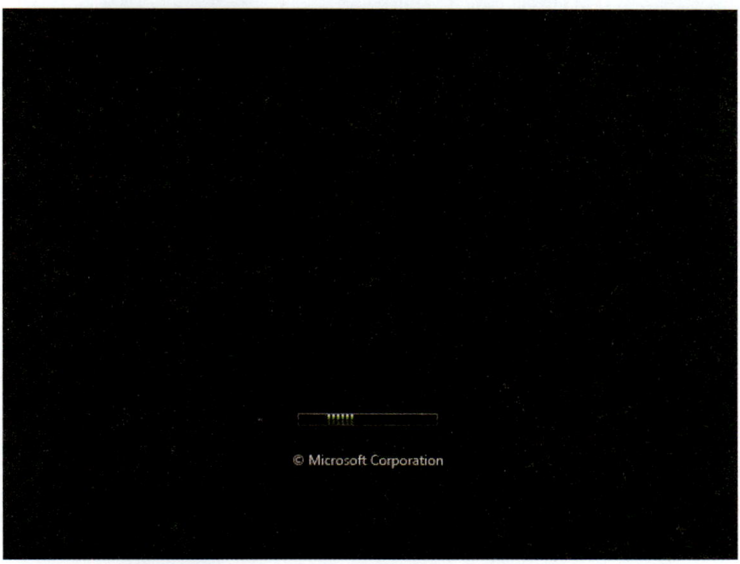

Figure 2-43 The progress bar indicates that the Windows graphics subsystem is running and the kernel has successfully loaded

13. Smss.exe starts the Logon Manager (Winlogon.exe) and reads and executes other commands stored in the registry, such as a command to replace system files placed there by Windows update.
14. Winlogon.exe starts the Service Control Manager (Services.exe). Services.exe starts all services listed with the startup type of Automatic in the Services console.
15. Winlogon.exe starts the Local Security Authority process (Lsass.exe). The logon screen appears (see Figure 2-44), and the user account and password are passed to the Lsass.exe process for authentication. The Last Known Good Configuration information in the registry is updated.
16. Winlogon.exe launches Userinit.exe and the Windows desktop (Explorer.exe).
17. Userinit.exe applies Group Policy settings and any programs not trumped by Group Policy that are stored in these registry keys and folders:
    - HKLM\SOFTWARE\Microsoft\Windows\CurrentVersion\Runonce
    - HKLM\SOFTWARE\Microsoft\Windows\CurrentVersion\Policies \Explorer\Run

Figure 2-44 Windows Vista logon screen

- HKLM\SOFTWARE\Microsoft\Windows\CurrentVersion\Run
- HKCU\Software\Microsoft\Windows NT\CurrentVersion\Windows\Run
- HKCU\Software\Microsoft\Windows\CurrentVersion\Run
- HKCU\Software\Microsoft\Windows\CurrentVersion\RunOnce
- *Systemdrive*\ProgramData\Microsoft\Windows\Start Menu\Programs\Startup
- *Systemdrive*\Users*username*\AppData\Roaming\Microsoft\Windows\Start Menu\Programs\Startup

The Windows startup is officially completely when the Windows desktop appears and the wait circle disappears. (The familiar hourglass is gone forever!)

APPLYING CONCEPTS — DIGGING DEEPER INTO THE REGISTRY AND VISTA STARTUP

It is interesting to dig a little deeper into how Windows Vista manages services using the registry and the Services console. Remember that knowledge is power, and what you will learn in this section is sure to help when a critical service fails. Let's first look at how the registry is organized and generally used and then we will turn our attention to how it is specifically used to help with the startup process.

Understanding the Registry

The registry is a hierarchical database that contains configuration information for Windows, users, software applications, and installed hardware devices. Windows builds the registry from the five registry hives, the current hardware configuration, and the Ntuser.dat database file. The registry is stored in memory and remains there until Windows shuts down. During startup, Windows builds the registry and then reads from it to obtain information about the startup process. After Windows is loaded, it continually reads from many of the subkeys in the registry.

The five hives that hold information used to build the registry are stored in the C:\Windows\System32\config folder and are named System, SAM, Security, Software, and Default. If you check the folder, you will find a .LOG file and a .SAV file for each hive. The .LOG files hold logged information about the hive activity, and the .SAV files are backup copies of each hive created during Windows Vista setup.

The registry is divided into six keys and each serves a specific purpose for the normal functioning of the operating system. Figure 2-45 shows the high-level keys displayed by the Registry Editor and is followed by a description of each key:

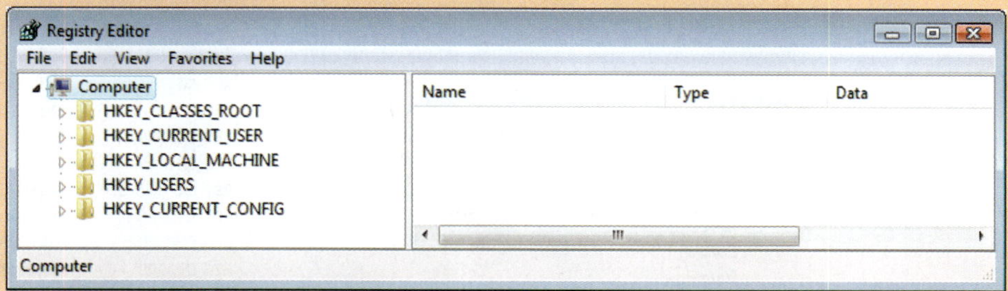

Figure 2-45 The Registry Editor shows the high-level keys of the registry

Notes

Device Manager reads data from the HKLM\HARDWARE key to build the information it displays about hardware configurations. You can consider Device Manager to be an easy-to-view presentation of this HARDWARE key data.

- ***HKEY_LOCAL_MACHINE (abbreviated HKLM)*** is the most important key and contains hardware, software, and security data. The data is taken from four hives: the SAM hive, the Security hive, the Software hive, and the System hive. In addition, the HARDWARE key of HKLM is built when the registry is first loaded based on data collected about the current hardware configuration.
- ***HKEY_CURRENT_CONFIG (abbreviated HKCC)*** contains hardware configuration data including Plug and Play information. Some of the data is gathered from the current hardware configuration when the registry is first loaded into memory. Other data is taken from the HKLM key, which got its data from the System hive.
- ***HKEY_CLASSES_ROOT (abbreviated HKCR)*** contains data about applications and associated file extensions. Data is gathered from HKLM key and the HKCU key.
- ***HKEY_USERS (abbreviated HKU)*** contains data about all users and is taken from the Default hive.
- ***HKEY_CURRENT_USER (abbreviated HKCU)*** contains data about the current user. The key is built when a user logs on using data kept in the HKEY_USERS key and data kept in the Ntuser.dat file of the current user. The Ntuser.dat file is stored in the C:\Users*username* folder.
- ***HKEY_PERFORMANCE_DATA*** is a pass-through placeholder for performance data. This key is used only as a reference point for Windows processes, does not contain data, and, therefore, is not displayed by the registry editor.

Understanding How Drivers and Services are Loaded at Startup

During Vista startup, the kernel reads the registry looking for drivers and services that need to be started at this stage of the boot and then starts them. Later, the Services process starts other services. Follow these steps to examine how all this works.

1. Be careful! You are about to open the registry editor to view important keys. Please do not change these registry keys as you work! Click **Start**, enter **regedit** in the Search box, press **Enter**, and respond to the UAC box. The registry editor window opens.

2. Drill down to this key: HKEY_LOCAL_MACHINE\SYSTEM\CurrentControlSet\Services.
3. The key contains many subkeys that hold information about services. For example, click the subkey ACPI and the left pane in Figure 2-46 shows information about that subkey.

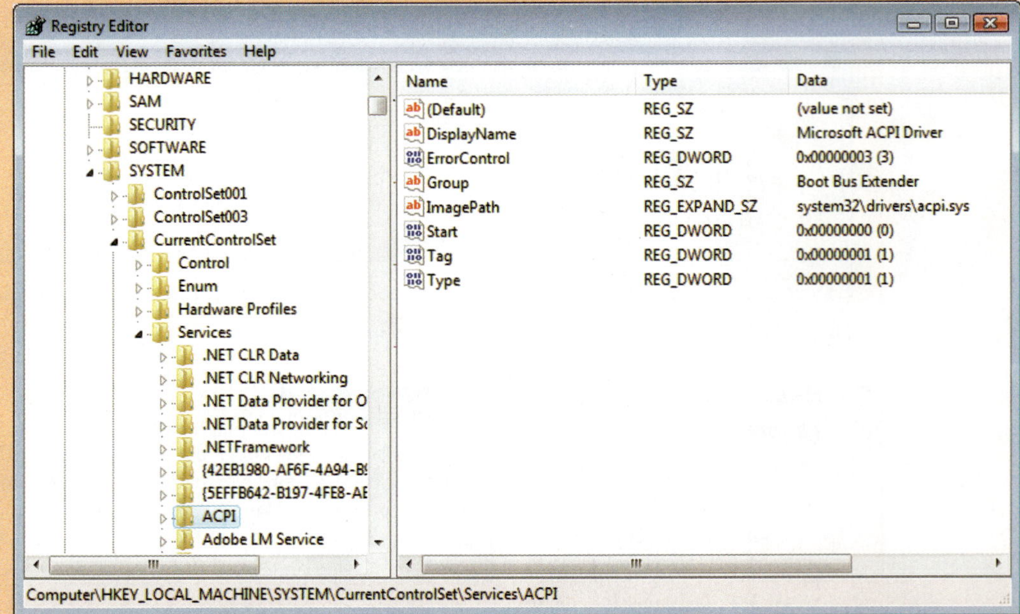

Figure 2-46 The Services key lists keys for each installed service

4. To understand how Vista manages a service, it is important to understand the purpose of each name and data value in the right pane of Figure 2-46. These items are explained in Table 2-3. A service or driver might not use every name in the table.

Name	Value
DependOnGroup	The service is dependent on the listed item, which must be started first
DependOnService	The service is dependent on the listed service, which must be started first
DisplayName	Describes the service
ErrorControl	Identifies what must happen if the driver will not start. Possible values are: 0x0 = Continue with startup 0x1 = Record in the System event log and continue with startup 0x2 = Record in the System event log and use the Last Known Good Configuration (LKGC) 0x3 = Record in the System event log and use the LKGC. If the LKGC is already being used, display a Stop error and halt.
Group	All services or drivers in this group will start together as a group

Table 2-3 Names and descriptions for values used to manage a service or driver

Name	Value
ImagePath	Path and filename to the service or driver
ObjectName	Account that a service logs on with
Start	When the service or driver starts. Values are: 0x0 = Loaded by BootMgr and started by WinLoad 0x1 = Loaded and started by WinLoad 0x2 = Started by Services.exe or Smss.exe. (Listed as Automatic in the Services console) 0x3 = Started manually as needed (Listed as Manual in the Services console) 0x4 = Disabled (Listed as Disabled in the Services console) 0x5 = Started shortly after startup. These services are not critical to startup and have a delayed start so that the system can more quickly provide a logon screen to user (Listed as Automatic, Delayed Start, in the Services console).
Tag	The order a driver starts within its driver group
Type	Service or driver

Table 2-3 Names and descriptions for values used to manage a service or driver (continued)

5. When you compare the list of services and drivers listed under this registry key to the list in the Services console, you will see that the Services console does not list every item in the key. That is because the Services console manages only some services, not all. To open the Services console, click **Start**, enter **Services.msc** in the Search box, press **Enter**, and respond to the UAC box. The Services console opens (see Figure 2-47). Notice in the figure that the first service listed is the Adobe LM Service, which is also listed near the bottom of Figure 2-46. This service has a start value of 0x3, meaning it will be loaded on demand. Also notice in Figure 2-47 that the ACPI driver is not listed and, therefore, not managed by the Services console. Knowing how to investigate a service or driver in this way can be invaluable when smoking out problems with when or how a process is loaded.

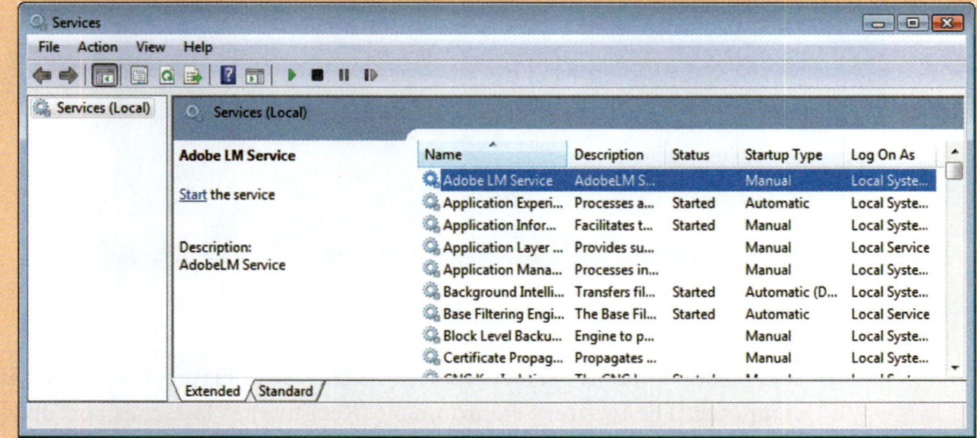

Figure 2-47 The Services console lists the services that it manages

Now that you have a pretty good idea about what happens when Windows Vista starts, you are ready to learn about the tools available in Vista to solve startup problems.

EXPLORING VISTA STARTUP AND RECOVERY TOOLS

The Windows Vista Recovery Environment (Windows RE) and the BCD registry file are new to Vista. In this part of the chapter, you will see how Windows RE works and how you can make changes to the BCD file.

EXPLORE WINDOWS RE

The major change in the recovery tools used to solve startup problems is that the Windows XP Recovery Console has been replaced by the Windows Vista Recovery Environment. The **Recovery Environment** (RecEnv.exe), also known as **Windows RE**, is an operating system launched from the Vista DVD, which provides both a graphical and command line interface. Recall that the Windows XP Recovery Console is a command-line OS launched from the Windows XP CD. Windows RE provides more tools and is easier to use than the Recovery Console. The goal in this section is to help you become familiar with Windows RE, and in later sections of the chapter, you will learn to use it to solve startup problems.

Follow these steps to explore Windows RE:

1. Using a computer that has Windows Vista installed, boot from the Vista setup DVD. (To boot from a DVD, you might have to change the boot sequence in CMOS setup to put the optical drive above the hard drive.) The screen in Figure 2-48 appears. Select your language preference and click **Next**.

Figure 2-48 Select your language preference

2. The Install Windows screen appears as shown in Figure 2-49. Click **Repair your computer**. The recovery environment (RecEnv.exe) launches and displays the System Recovery Options dialog box (see Figure 2-50).
3. Select the Vista installation to repair and click **Next**.
4. The System Recovery Options window in Figure 2-51 appears, listing recovery options.

Figure 2-49 Launch Windows RE after booting from the Vista DVD

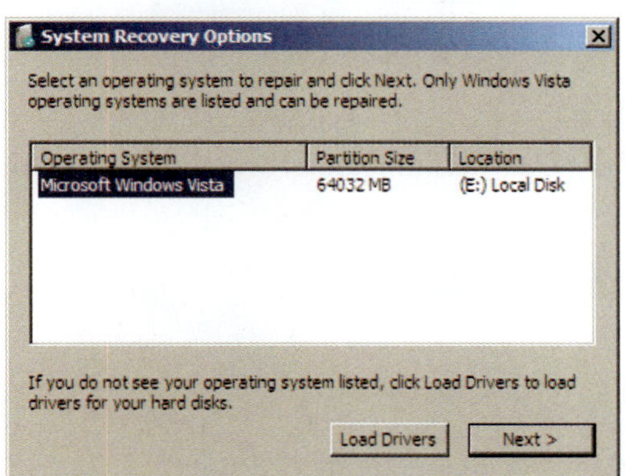

Figure 2-50 Select an installation of Vista to repair

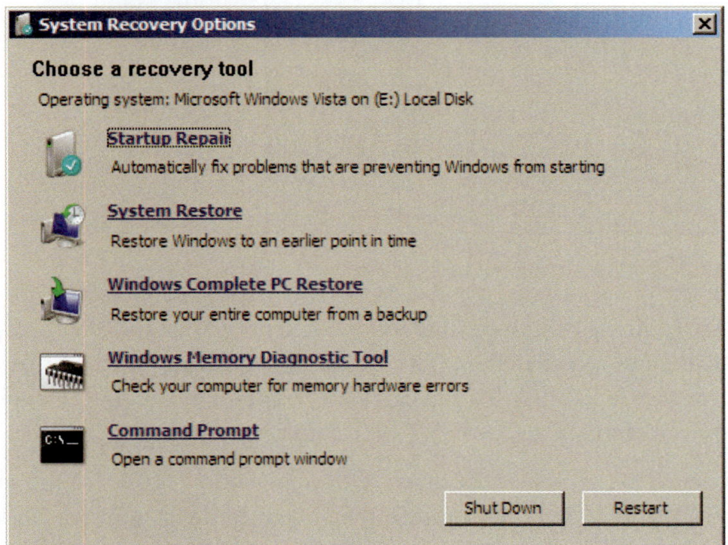

Figure 2-51 Recovery tools in Windows RE

5. The first tool, Startup Repair, can automatically fix many Windows problems, including those caused by a corrupted BCD file and missing system files. You will not cause any additional problems by using it and it is easy to use; therefore, it should be your first recovery option. Click **Startup Repair** and the tool will examine the system for errors (see Figure 2-52).

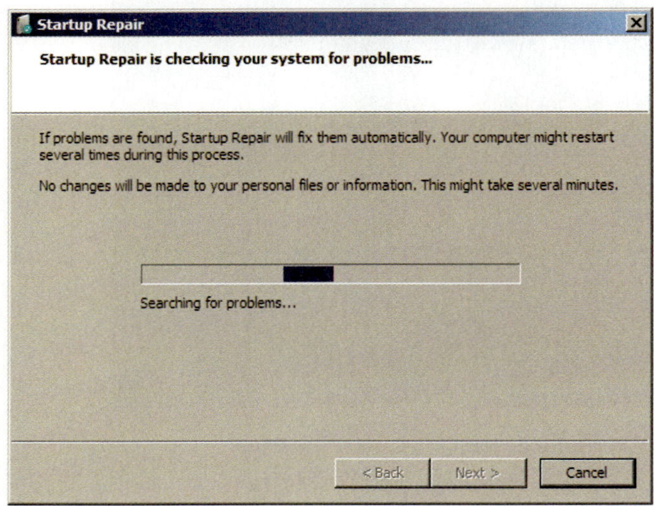

Figure 2-52 Startup Repair searches the system for problems it can fix

6. Based on what it finds, it will suggest various solutions. For example, it might suggest you use System Restore or that you immediately reboot the system to see if the problem has been fixed (see Figure 2-53).

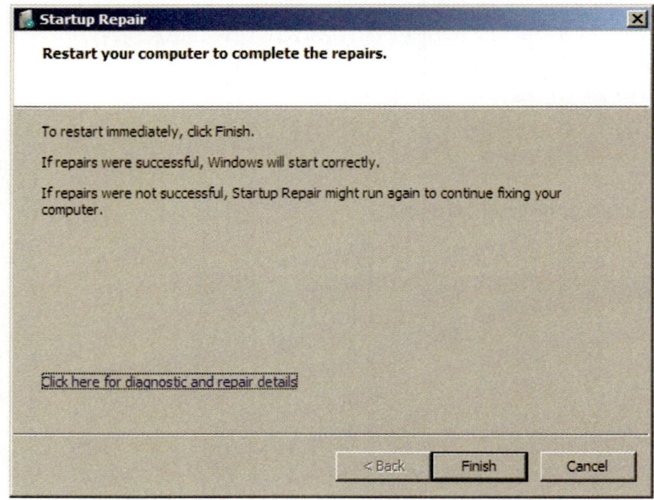

Figure 2-53 Startup Repair has attempted to fix the problem

7. To see a list of items examined and actions taken by Startup Repair, click **Click here for diagnostic and repair details**. The dialog box showing the list of repairs appears as shown in Figure 2-54. A log file can also be found at the following location: C:\Windows\System32\LogFiles\SRT\SRTTrail.txt.

8. System Restore in the System Recovery Options window works in the same manner as Windows XP System Restore to return the system to the state it was in when a restore point was made. Click **System Restore** and a list of restore points appears (see Figure 2-55). Select the most recent restore point to make the least intrusive changes to the system.

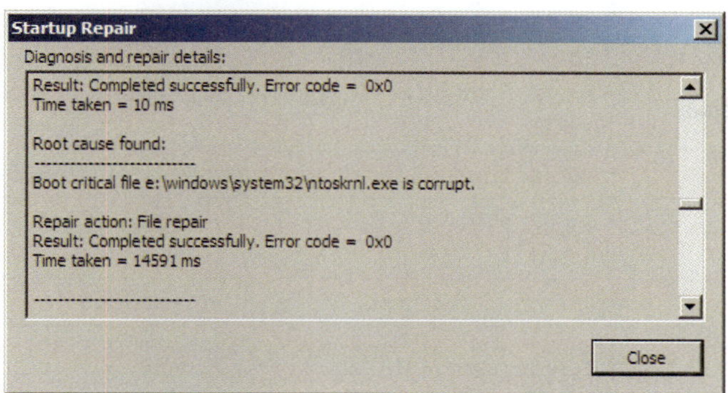

Figure 2-54 Details of actions taken by Startup Repair

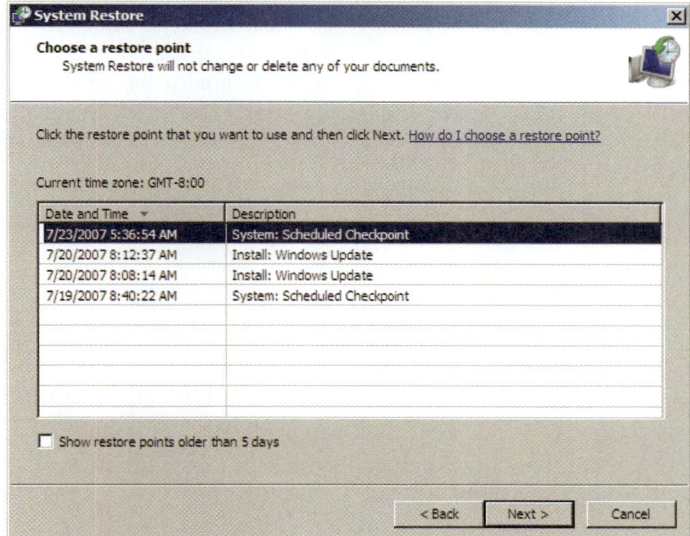

Figure 2-55 Select the most recent restore point to make fewer changes to the system

9. Two other tools in the System Recovery Options window are Windows Complete PC Restore and the Windows Memory Diagnostic Tool, which you learned to use in the last chapter. Use the first tool to restore the system to a previous backup and use the second tool to test memory.

10. Click **Command Prompt** to open a command prompt window (see Figure 2-56). Table 2-4 lists some of the commands new to Vista that can help you repair a

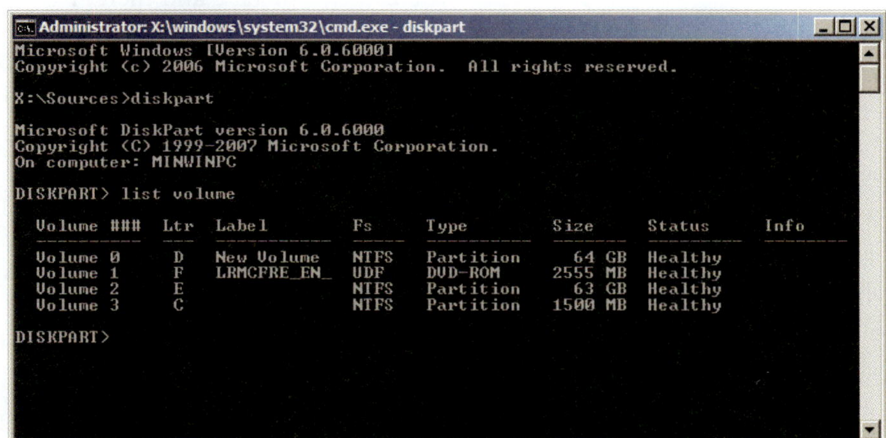

Figure 2-56 The command prompt window resembles the Windows XP Recovery Console

Command Line	Description
`Bootrec /scanOS`	**Scans the hard drive for Windows installations not stored in the BCD**
`Bootrec /rebuildBCD`	**Scans for Windows installations and rebuilds the BCD**
`Bcdedit`	**Manually edits BCD. Be sure to make a copy of the file before you edit it.**
`Bootrec /fixboot`	**Repairs the boot sector of the system partition**
`Bootrec /fixmbr`	**Repairs the master boot record (MBR)**
`Diskpart`	**Manages partitions and volumes. Use these commands within Diskpart:** ◢ ***List disk*—Lists installed hard drives** ◢ ***List partition*—Lists partitions on selected drive** ◢ ***Select disk*—Selects a hard drive** ◢ ***Select partition*—Selects a partition on the selected drive** ◢ ***Active*—Makes the selected partition the active partition** ◢ ***Inactive*—Makes the selected partition inactive**
`Bootsect`	**Repairs problems with dual booting PCs**

Table 2-4 Commands used in the command prompt window of Windows RE

system. To get helpful information about a command, enter the command followed by `/?`, such as `bcdedit /?`. Most Recovery Console commands, including commands to recover valuable data, such as `Copy`, `Ren`, `Dir`, and `CD`, work in this Vista command prompt window.

11. As you use a tool in the System Recovery Options window, be sure to reboot after each attempt to fix the problem to make sure the problem has not been resolved before you try another tool. To exit the Recovery Environment, click **Shut Down** or **Restart**.

> **Notes**
>
> For a complete list of Diskpart commands, go to the Microsoft support site (*support.microsoft.com*) and search on "DiskPart Command-Line Options".

MAKING CHANGES TO THE BCD FILE

Previous versions of Windows stored startup parameters in the Boot.ini text file, but Vista stores similar information in the BCD registry file. The following are the ways in which you can edit this file and thereby change startup options:

- ***System Properties box.*** In the System Properties box, under Startup and Recovery, click Settings. The Startup and Recovery dialog box opens (see Figure 2-57). This method is the preferred method of editing the BCD file.
- ***System Configuration utility (MSconfig.exe).*** Use the Boot tab on the MSconfig box to change boot settings (see Figure 2-58).

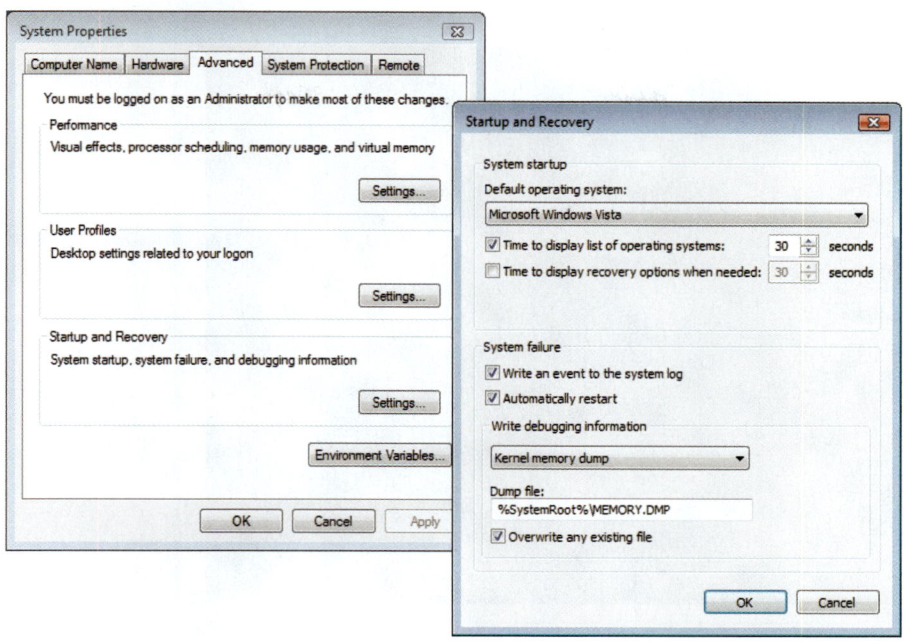

Figure 2-57 Use the Startup and Recovery dialog box to change startup options

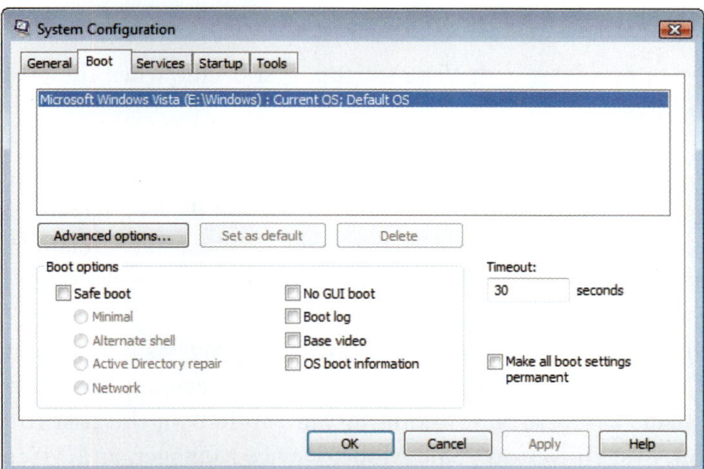

Figure 2-58 Use MSconfig to change boot parameters

- *BCDedit.exe*. Use the command `bcdedit` followed by parameters to view, copy, and edit the BCD file. Use `bcdedit /?` to browse the command options. The command can be used from a command prompt window in Windows (use the *Run as administrator* option) or in the Recovery Environment. Figure 2-59 shows the results of the command with no parameters, which displays the contents of the BCD file.

You are now armed with a lot of information about Vista startup and recovery tools. With this information in hand, you are ready to learn about troubleshooting strategies for startup problems.

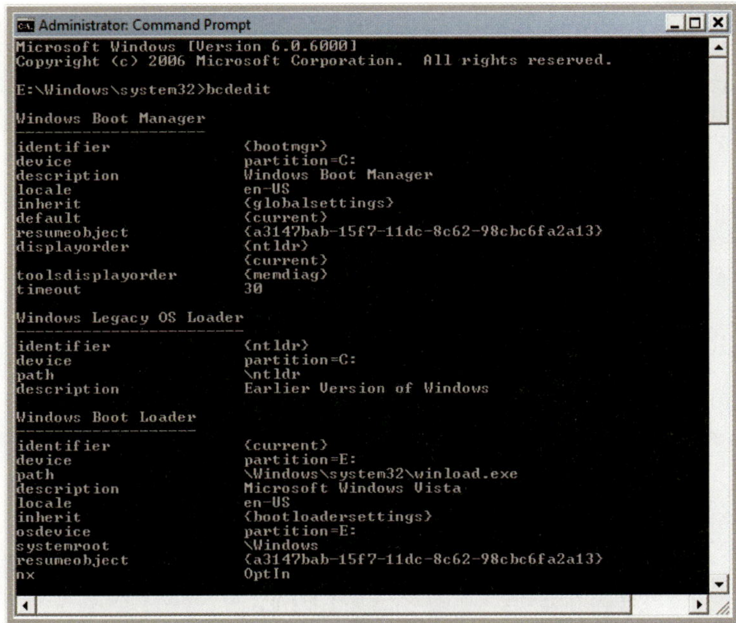

Figure 2-59 Contents of the BCD file displayed by the `bcdedit` command

TROUBLESHOOTING STARTUP PROBLEMS

When troubleshooting problems with Vista startup, first decide when the problem occurs in one of three startup stages of the boot:

- ***Before the progress bar.*** When you see the Microsoft progress bar appear, you know the Windows kernel, including all critical services and drivers, has loaded. Any problems that occur before the progress bar appears are most likely related to corrupt or missing system files or hardware. Your best Vista tools to use for these problems are Startup Repair and System Restore.
- ***After the progress bar and before logon.*** After the progress bar appears, user mode services and drivers are loaded and then the logon screen appears. Problems with these components can best be solved using Startup Repair, the Last Known Good Configuration, System Restore, Safe Mode, Device Manager, and MSconfig.
- ***After logon.*** After the logon screen appears, problems can be caused by startup scripts, applications set to launch at startup, and desktop settings. When you hold down the Shift key during logon, certain startup programs are not launched. Other useful tools to solve the problem are MSconfig, Software Explorer, and Safe Mode.

Now let's take a closer look at how to address problems at each of these three stages.

PROBLEMS BEFORE THE PROGRESS BAR APPEARS

As you perform each troubleshooting step described below, be sure to restart the system to see if the problem is solved before you apply the next step. Remember, if the progress bar has not yet appeared, some portions of the Vista kernel and critical drivers and services to be started by the kernel have not yet started. Therefore, the problem is with hardware or these startup files. Here are the steps to fix the problem:

1. As always, check with the user to find out if important data is on the hard drive and not backed up. Make every effort to copy the data to a safe location before you start troubleshooting the original problem.

2. If startup BIOS displays a message about not being able to find a boot device, the problem is probably caused by hardware. Check CMOS setup to make sure the hard drive is listed as the first boot device and reboot. You can also listen to the drive for a spinning sound or look for lights on the front panel that indicate the drive is physically working. Check internal cable connections.
3. Following directions earlier in the chapter, boot from the Vista DVD, launch Windows RE, and run Startup Repair. If the problem is not solved, you can check the log file, C:\Windows\System32\LogFiles\SRT\SRTTrail.txt, for clues.
4. Restart the system and run System Restore from Windows RE.
5. Restart the system and press F8 during the boot to launch the Advanced Boot Options menu (shown earlier in the chapter in Figure 2-41). If the boot menu does not appear, chances are the problem is a corrupted boot sector. If the boot menu appears, chances are the BCD file or other startup files are the problem. If you do see the menu, enable boot logging and reboot. Then check the boot log (\Windows\ntbtlog.txt) for the last entry, which might indicate which system file is missing or corrupt.
6. If the boot menu does not appear, return to the Recovery Environment, launch the command prompt window and attempt to repair the boot sector. Try these commands: `bootrec /fixmbr` and `bootrec /fixboot`. Also try the `Diskpart` command followed by the command `list volume`. Does the OS find the system volume? If not, the entire partition might be lost.
7. If the boot menu does appear, return to the Recovery Environment, launch the command prompt window and attempt to repair the BCD file. Try this command: `bootrec /rebuildbcd`.
8. When startup files are missing or corrupt, sometimes Vista displays an error message similar to the one shown in Figure 2-60, which names the file causing the problem. You can replace the file by going to a healthy Vista computer and copying the file to a removable media. Then on the problem computer, boot to the Recovery Environment, open the command prompt window, and copy the replacement file to the hard drive. Be sure to back up the original file first, so you can backtrack if necessary.

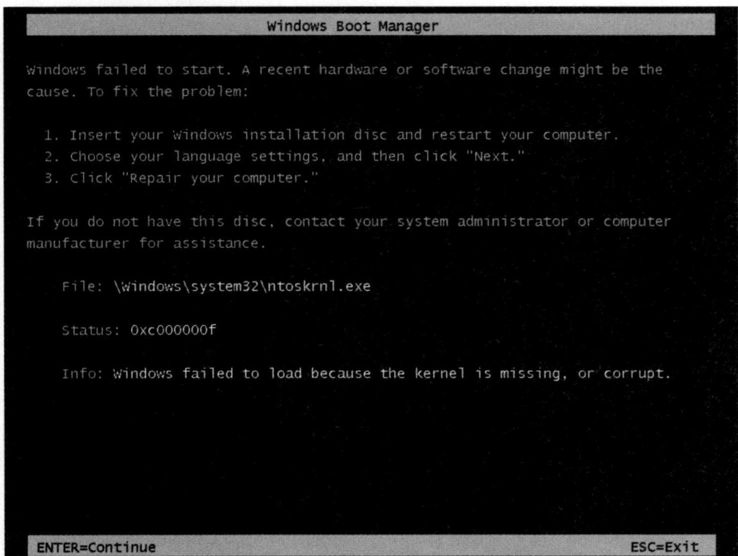

Figure 2-60 Windows Vista might display a screen similar to this one when a critical startup file is missing or corrupt

9. If the problem is still not solved, the problem is related to hardware or the Vista installation is corrupted. You might be forced to reinstall Windows.

Options to Recover from a Corrupted Vista Installation

Depending on available backups, you have these choices to restore a corrupted installation:

- If you have a Complete PC backup, use it to restore the system to the last backup. If data is on the hard drive that has not been backed up, make every effort to copy this data to a safe place before you restore the system.
- If you do not have a Complete PC backup but you do have backups of the data on the hard drive, install Vista on the partition, formatting the hard drive during the installation. You will need to install all applications again and then restore the data.
- If you do not have either a Complete PC backup or backups of the data on the drive (worst case scenario), try to copy the data and then perform a reinstallation of Windows Vista. Even if you cannot copy the data, you might be able to recover it after the reinstallation. The following are steps to reinstall Vista.

Steps to Reinstall Windows Vista

Follow these steps to reinstall Vista when the OS refuses to boot and there is important data on the drive:

1. Boot from the Vista DVD, select your language, click **Next**, and then select **Install now** from the opening menu. Follow directions on screen to install the OS.
2. When given the opportunities, enter the product key and accept the license agreement. For the type of installation, select **Custom (advanced)**.
3. When asked where you want to install the OS, select the partition on which Vista is installed.

Vista setup will move all folders of the old installation into the \Windows.Old folder, including the \Windows, \Users, and \Program Files folders. A fresh, clean installation of Vista will then be installed in the \Windows folder. If you suspect the hard drive might be failing or need reformatting, immediately save all important data to a removable media and reinstall Windows Vista a second time, this time reformatting the hard drive. If you believe the hard drive is healthy, then follow these steps to get things back to their original order:

1. Install all applications and device drivers.
2. Create all user accounts and customize Vista settings. Then copy all user data and other data folders from the \Windows.Old folder to the new installation.
3. Delete the \Windows.Old folder.

PROBLEMS AFTER THE PROGRESS BAR APPEARS AND BEFORE LOGON

When you see the Microsoft progress bar appear during the boot, you know the Windows kernel has loaded successfully, critical drivers and services configured to be started by the kernel are running, and the Session Manager (Smss.exe) running in user mode has started the Win32 subsystem necessary to provide the graphics of the progress bar. If the logon screen has not yet displayed, most likely the problem is caused by a corrupted driver or service that is started after the kernel has finished its part of the boot. Your general plan of attack to fix the problem is to isolate and disable the Windows component, service, or application causing trouble.

Follow these steps:

1. Run **Startup Repair** from the Recovery Environment. It cannot do any harm, it is easy to use, and it might fix the problem.
2. Reboot and press **F8** to launch the Advanced Boot Options menu. Then select the **Last Known Good Configuration.** It is important to try this option early in the troubleshooting process, because you might accidentally overwrite a good Last Known Good Configuration with a bad one as you attempt to log on with the problem still there.

> **Notes**
>
> The Last Known Good Configuration is updated after you log on normally to Vista. However, logging onto a computer when booting into Safe Mode does not update the Last Known Good Configuration.

3. Boot to the Recovery Environment and use **System Restore.** Select the latest restore point. If that does not fix the problem, try an earlier one.

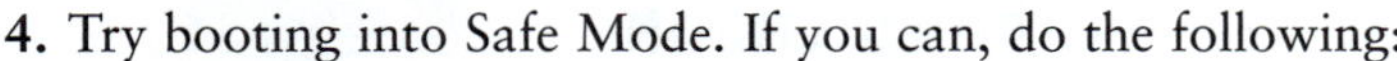

4. Try booting into Safe Mode. If you can, do the following:
   - Immediately run antivirus software to eliminate a virus as the problem.
   - Run Chkdsk to check and repair the hard drive.
   - Examine all the logs in Event Viewer for errors that might point to the problem.
   - Use Software Explorer and MSconfig to stop any applications just installed. Then uninstall and reinstall the application.
   - Use Device Manager to check for hardware errors and disable any devices just installed. If you have just updated a driver, roll back the driver.
5. Boot to the Advanced Boot Options menu and select **Enable Boot Logging.** Windows starts, logging information to the log file, \Windows\Ntbtlog.txt. Every file that is successfully loaded is written to the file. The last entry is most likely the one giving problems.
6. The easiest way to view the log is to boot into **Safe Mode** and view the file with Notepad. If you cannot boot into Safe Mode, you can still view the file using the command prompt window in the Recovery Environment. Try replacing the program file listed last in the log or disabling the device or service. If that does not work, then you will need to dig a little deeper to identify the culprit. Here are some tips for identifying a device or service causing the problem:
   - Try to boot into **Safe Mode.** Then use MSconfig to disable all nonessential services and devices. Reboot normally. If the problem goes away, you can enable one after another until you find the one causing the problem.
   - In Safe Mode, examine Event Viewer **Application** logs, **Security** logs, and **System** logs for errors.
   - In Safe Mode, use System Information (**msinfo32.exe**) to find the program filenames of drivers and services. Useful information can be found at these locations: Services in the Software Environment group and Problem Devices in the Components group.
   - Compare the entries in the Ntbtlog.txt file when booting in Safe Mode to the entries when booting normally. Consider that the culprit might be any item that is loaded for a normal boot but not loaded for Safe Mode.
   - If the computer will not boot into Safe Mode, compare the Ntbtlog.txt file to one created on a similar computer booted into Safe Mode. Look for a service or driver listed as loaded on the good computer that is not loaded or is missing on the bad computer.

7. After you believe you have identified the problem service or device, if you can boot into Safe Mode, first use Device Manager to disable the device or use the Services console to disable the service. Then reboot, and, if the problem goes away, restore the program file and enable the driver or service.
8. If you cannot boot into Safe Mode, open the command prompt window of the Recovery Environment. Then open the Registry Editor using the regedit command, and drill down to the service or device key. Recall from earlier in the chapter, the key can be found in this location:

   HKEY_LOCAL_MACHINE\SYSTEM\CurrentControlSet\Services
9. Disable the service or driver by changing the Start value to 0x4. Close the Registry Editor and reboot. If the problem goes away, use the Copy command to replace the program file, and restart the service or driver.

PROBLEMS AFTER WINDOWS LOGON

Problems that occur after the user logs onto Windows are caused by applications or services configured to launch at startup. Programs can be set to launch at startup by placing their shortcuts in startup folders, by Group Policy, or by software installation processes.

Do the following to disable programs put in startup folders:

1. Reboot the system and hold down the **Shift** key as you log on and the desktop loads. This prevents startup programs in these folders from loading:
   - C:\Users*username*\AppData\Roaming\Microsoft\Windows\StartMenu\Programs\Startup
   - C:\ProgramData\Microsoft\Windows\Start Menu\Programs\Startup
2. If the problem goes away, one of these startup programs is the problem. Move one after the other to a different folder until the problem is fixed. Alternately, you can use MSconfig to temporarily disable the program.

You can use Group Policy (gpedit.msc) to manage startup programs. Follow these steps:

1. Click **Start**, in the **Search** box, enter **gpedit.msc**, press **Enter**, and respond to the UAC box. The Group Policy Object Editor console opens.
2. Drill down to **Computer Configuration, Administrative Templates, System**, and **Logon**. A list of Logon policies appears in the right pane (see Figure 2-61). To change an entry, double click it; its Properties box appears as shown in Figure 2-62. If the policy is enabled, you can disable it by clicking **Disabled**, clicking **Apply**, and then clicking **OK**.
3. Now drill down and check the entries in the **User Configuration, Administrative Templates, System**, and **Logon** policies. During startup, policies in the Computer Configuration are applied first, followed by policies in the User Configuration, so you must check both areas.

To permanently remove a startup program, do one of the following:

- In Control Panel, use the Programs link to uninstall an application.
- Remove the entry from a startup folder or from Group Policy.

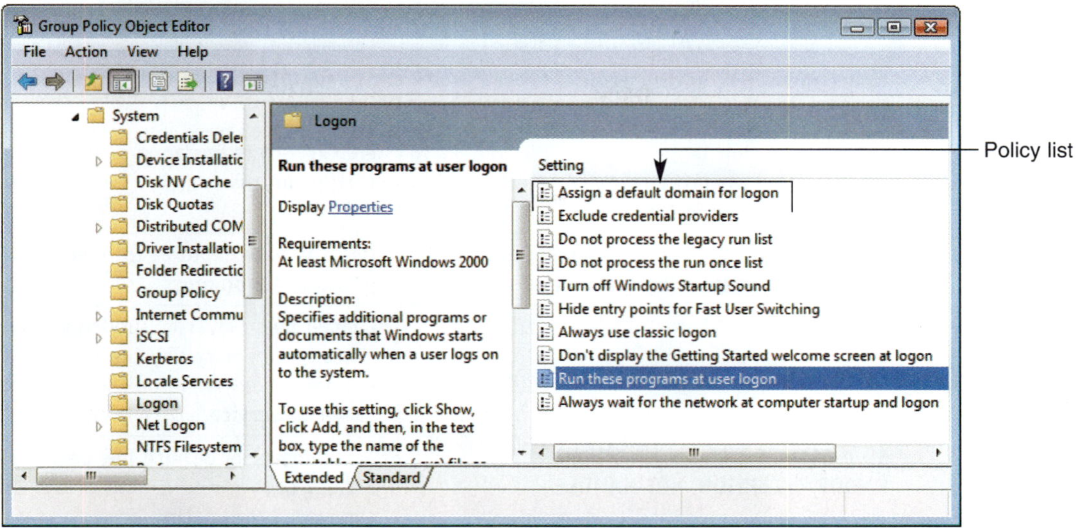

Figure 2-61 The list of policies that affect the logon event

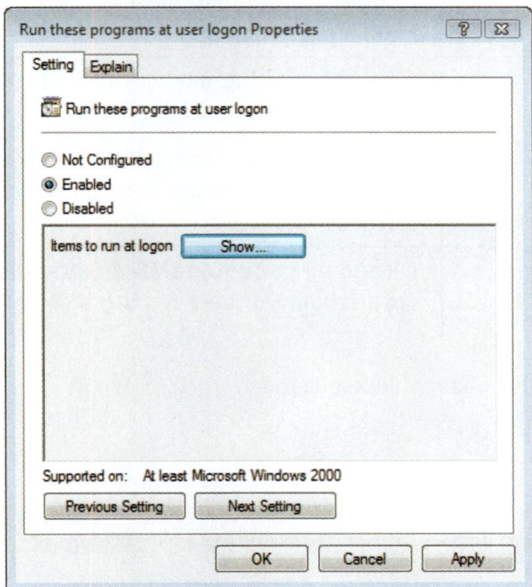

Figure 2-62 Manage a policy using its Properties box

- Use the Services console to disable a service.
- Use Software Explorer to remove or disable an entry in the startup programs list.

Table 2-5 summarizes some error messages, including stop errors, you might encounter during the boot and what to do about them. Stop errors occur when the Windows kernel encounters an error in a kernel mode process, which most likely points to a hardware or driver problem.

Error or Error Message	Description and What To Do
Non-system disk or disk error Replace and press any key when ready	Startup BIOS could not find a boot device.
Invalid partition table Error loading operating system Missing operating system	MBR record is damaged or the active partition is corrupt or missing.
An application is launched at startup that gives errors or takes up resources.	Use Software Explorer to remove it from the list of startup programs.
Stop 0x0A or IRQL_NOT_LESS_OR_EQUAL	Caused by a driver or service making an illegal access to memory. Try the Last Known Good Configuration. Then look for an incompatible driver or service.
Stop 0x1E or KMODE_EXCEPTION_NOT-HANDLED	A bad driver or service has performed an illegal action. Look for corrupted or bad drivers or services. Try updating firmware.
Stop 0x24 or NTFS_FILE_SYSTEM	Suspect a failing hard drive or bad third-party disk utility tools.
Stop 0x2E or DATA_BUS_ERROR	A hardware problem most likely caused by failing memory or a corrupted hard drive.
Stop 0x50 or PAGE_FAULT_IN_NONPAGED_AREA	Caused by failing memory or bad software.
Stop 0x7B or INACCESSIBLE_BOOT_DEVICE	Windows cannot access the hard drive; probably caused by installing bad or incorrect hard drive drivers.
Stop 0xFE or BUGCODE_USB_DRIVER	Caused by corrupted USB drivers. Update the motherboard drivers for the USB ports.

Table 2-5 Error messages during startup and what to do about them

>> CHAPTER SUMMARY

- Under Windows Vista, administrators have more control over a system so that they can control what a user can or cannot do with security settings, such as connecting to a public wireless network, changing Firewall settings, using removable media, and use EFS encryption.
- Internet Explorer is better secured by using Protected Mode.
- The User Account Control (UAC) dialog box is intended to protect against careless administrators and malware.
- BitLocker Drive Encryption encrypts the Windows system volume and requires a startup key each time the system is booted.
- An elevated command prompt window has more privileges than a normal command prompt window.
- Mandatory Integrity Control (MIC) assigns four levels of privileges to a process to prevent less trustworthy processes from infecting or corrupting a system.

- Windows Firewall applies one of three security profiles (domain, private, and public) to the system depending on the type of network being used.
- Windows Defender is an integrated part of Windows Vista and is designed to protect the system from software installing itself without the user's permission.
- Software Explorer is part of Defender and is used to manage installed programs.
- The Internet Explorer phishing filter can help the user determine if a Web site is legitimate.
- Using Internet Explorer, a user can clean out the entire IE browser history by clicking one button to protect his or her privacy.
- BitLocker Encryption can use a PIN, a TPM chip on the motherboard, or a flash drive to provide a startup key at startup. The PIN together with a TPM or a flash drive authenticate both the user and the computer.
- Two tools used to manage file and folder sharing are the File Sharing Wizard and the Advanced Sharing window.
- For local file sharing, users are encouraged by Windows to use the Public folder. In addition, users can share folders in their user profile; this process is called profile sharing.
- For network sharing, the Public folder or any folder on the hard drive can be shared with other users on the network.
- Tools new to Vista that are helpful to solve hardware problems include the Reliability Monitor, Problem Reports and Solutions window, Data Collector Sets, and Windows Memory Diagnostics.
- The Reliability Monitor is helpful to find out the history of problems on a computer.
- The Problem Reports and Solutions window can also provide a history of problems that Windows has encountered as well as solutions offered.
- A Data Collector Set can help identify weaknesses and problems in a system.
- Vista tools useful to solve problems with applications are the System Configuration Utility, Task Manager, Software Explorer, and Programs and Features window.
- Startup files new to Windows Vista include the BootMgr, BCD, and WinLoad files. The BCD file replaces the Windows XP Boot.ini file. BootMgr manages the initial boot process and WinLoad is responsible for loading the kernel.
- A tool new to Vista to solve startup problems is the Recovery Environment, which includes Startup Repair, System Restore, Windows Complete PC Restore, the Windows Memory Diagnostic Tool, and a command prompt window. The command prompt window replaces the Windows XP Recovery Console.
- When troubleshooting a Windows Vista startup problem, first decide whether the problem occurs before the Microsoft progress bar appears, after it appears but before the logon event, or after the logon event. When the progress bar appears, you know the Windows kernel has successfully loaded.
- When you need to reinstall Vista, know that the old Vista installation files will be moved to the \Windows.Old folder.

>> KEY TERMS

Boot Configuration Data (BCD) file – The Windows Vista registry file named BCD that is stored in the \Boot folder of the active or boot partition and holds configuration data used during Vista startup.

Data Collector Set utility – A tool in the Computer Management console used to collect data about different aspects of the system and present that data in a report which can help you identify the source of a computer problem.

domain profile – The profile settings that Windows Firewall uses when the firewall recognizes the computer is connected to a domain. This profile provides the least degree of protection because it is assumed the domain has security features in place to protect the computer. Also see *private profile* and *public profile.*

elevated command prompt – A command prompt window that allows commands to run at the privileged administrative level. To access the window, right-click Command Prompt in the Start menu and select Run as administrator.

high-integrity access level – Mandatory Integrity Control assigns this level to trusted processes, such as those started by administrators. The process can install files in the Program Files folder and write to areas of the registry that affect the entire system, such as the HKEY_LOCAL_MACHINE key. Also called administrative level.

low-integrity access level – Mandatory Integrity Control assigns this level to a process that is untrusted, such as a program downloaded from the Internet. Also called untrusted level.

Mandatory Integrity Control (MIC) – A Vista feature that assigns one of four integrity levels to a process which determines the privileges the process has. The four levels are low, medium, high, and system access level. Also see *low-integrity access level, medium-integrity access level, high-integrity access level,* and *system access level.*

medium-integrity access level – Mandatory Integrity Control assigns this level to most processes. The process can access areas of the registry that are user specific, such as the HKEY_CURRENT_USER key, and has access to the user's Documents folder. Also called user level.

private profile – The profile settings that Windows Firewall uses when the computer is not logged onto a domain and all active networks (wired and wireless, including Bluetooth) are configured as private networks. The profile uses a medium level of protection. Also see *domain profile* and *public profile.*

progress bar – A graphical bar that appears on the screen during Windows Vista startup. When you see the bar, you know that the Windows kernel (ntoskrnl.exe) and all its kernel mode components are running and the Win subsystem running in user mode has started, displaying the progress bar. Up to this point in the boot, all displays have been in text mode.

public profile – The profile settings that Windows Firewall uses when the firewall recognizes the computer is connected to a public network. This profile offers the highest level of protection. Also see *domain profile* and *private profile.*

Recovery Environment – A recovery OS loaded from the Vista setup DVD that includes both graphical and command-line interfaces. Tools available in the environment are Startup Repair, System Restore, Windows Complete PC Restore, Windows Memory Diagnostic Tool, and the Command Prompt. Also see *Windows RE.*

Reliability Monitor – A tool in the Computer Management console that can report the past history of problems on the computer, including the history of Software, Application, Hardware, Windows, and Miscellaneous Failures.

system-integrity access level – Mandatory Integrity Control assigns this level to system processes.

TPM (Trusted Platform Module) chip – A chip on a motherboard designed to hold an encryption key used at startup to allow access to an encrypted partition on a hard drive. If the chip is present, BitLocker Drive Encryption stores its encryption key on the chip.

Vista Boot Configuration Data (BCD) file – A file that is structured the same as a registry file and contains configuration information about how Vista is started.

Windows Boot Loader (WinLoad) – The Windows Vista startup program named WinLoad that is stored in the \Windows\System32 folder of the system partition (most likely drive C). This program is responsible for loading into memory essential Windows components including the Vista kernel program, Ntoskrnl.exe.

Windows Boot Manager (BootMgr) – The Windows Vista startup program named BootMgr that is stored in the root directory of the active or boot partition (most likely C:\BootMgr) that is responsible for beginning Vista startup. It reads the BCD file and then searches for and loads the Windows Boot Loader (WinLoad).

Windows RE – Another name for the Recovery Environment, which is an operating system launched from the Vista DVD. Also see *Recovery Environment*.

>> REVIEWING THE BASICS

1. What is the operating mode used by Internet Explorer 7 which allows it to only write files to the Temporary Internet Files folder?
2. List the four integrity levels that can be assigned to a process by Mandatory Integrity Control.
3. List the steps to open an elevated command prompt window.
4. What are the three types of security profiles used by Windows Firewall?
5. What is the primary purpose of Windows Defender?
6. What does a Windows Defender quick scan check? What does a full scan check?
7. How can you authenticate both the user and the computer using BitLocker Encryption?
8. In what situation does the User Access Control dialog box require the user to enter a password?
9. Which folder is intended to be used to share files among local users of a computer?
10. What are the three permission levels that can be assigned to a user given rights to a shared folder? Which level has the greatest power?
11. Which Windows tool can temporarily disable startup programs and services to help troubleshoot a startup problem?
12. What component must a computer have before BitLocker Encryption can authenticate the computer?
13. Explain the difference between local sharing and network sharing.
14. Which Windows tool can tell you what happened to the system on a particular date, including software installations as well as software, hardware, and Windows failures?
15. The Data Collector Set tool is a part of which console?
16. List four Windows tools that can give you a history of problems that have occurred on a computer.
17. Which Windows tool can be used to permanently disable or remove a startup program?
18. In Windows Vista, what file replaces the Boot.ini file of Windows XP?
19. Which registry key contains a key for every service or driver installed in the system?
20. Which program is responsible for providing the Recovery Environment when you boot from the Vista DVD to recover a failed system?
21. What two Windows Vista startup programs replace the Ntldr startup program of Windows XP?

22. Is the Bootmgr file stored in the active partition or the system partition?
23. In which folder is the Winload file stored?
24. Which Windows component is responsible for starting the loading of user mode graphics components during the Windows Vista startup process?
25. What program file is responsible for resuming Windows Vista from hibernation?
26. During the Vista boot, the small program stored in the master boot record looks for which program file in the boot partition?
27. Which key do you press to launch the Advanced Boot Options window during Windows startup?
28. Which registry hive is loaded first during the Vista boot?
29. What displays on the screen during the boot that indicates the kernel has successfully loaded?
30. Which program is responsible for the Windows desktop?

>> THINKING CRITICALLY

1. In a dual boot configuration using Windows XP and Windows Vista, which files are stored on the boot partition?
   a. Boot.ini, Ntldr, BCD, and Bootmgr
   b. Boot.ini, Btldr, BCD
   c. BCD, Bootmgr, and Winload
   d. Ntldr, Bootmgr, and Winload
2. A Vista administrator needs to configure a system so that Microsoft Word starts each time a user named Nancy logs on. Where does he or she store the shortcut to the Winword.exe program?
   a. In the registry key HKLM\SOFTWARE\Microsoft\Windows\CurrentVersion\Run
   b. In the Services console
   c. In the folder *Systemdrive*\Users\Nancy\AppData\Roaming\Microsoft\Windows\Start Menu\Programs\Startup
   d. In the folder *Systemdrive*\ProgramData\Microsoft\Windows\StartMenu\Programs\Startup
3. Windows Vista refuses to start and the error message says something about the WinBoot program file missing. Which action is the best way to fix the problem?
   a. Boot from the Vista DVD and use the command prompt window to copy the WinBoot file from a working PC to this PC.
   b. Boot from the Vista DVD and use the Startup Repair tool.
   c. Use the latest Complete PC backup to restore the system.
   d. Boot into Safe Mode and restore the program from backup.

4. An error message displays during Vista startup before the progress bar appeared about a missing services program file. You try to boot into Safe Mode, but get the same error message. Next, you use the Vista DVD to boot into the Recovery Environment. Select the best two tasks to fix the problem and order them correctly.
   a. Use System Restore to restore the system to previous restore point
   b. Use the command prompt to disable and then replace the service
   c. Startup Repair
   d. Complete PC Restore

>> HANDS-ON PROJECTS

PROJECT 2-1: Investigate Microsoft Resources

Research the Microsoft Web site and other sites concerning resources available to help with Windows Vista and answer the following questions or print web pages showing your answers:

1. Briefly describe the content of the book, *Windows Vista Resource Kit*. What other resource(s) are included with the book? How much does it cost?
2. What is one other book that you think would be your next choice of books to help with supporting Vista? Why did you choose this book?
3. Using the Microsoft site as your source, list and describe the eight parameters of the Chkdsk command.
4. Using the Microsoft site as your source, what is the purpose the /S and /D parameters used with the Attrib command?
5. Using the Microsoft Web site as your source, list five stop errors not listed in Table 2-5 and the meaning of the stop error.

PROJECT 2-2: Troubleshooting Vista Startup

Sabotage your Vista system so that it refuses to boot and displays a screen similar to the one in Figure 2-60. Then repair the problem and answer the following questions:

1. What steps did you use to sabotage the system and make the error message display?
2. What was the exact error message?
3. What steps did you use to fix the problem?

PROJECT 2-3: Sharing Folders

Working with another student on a network, do the following to practice sharing folders:

1. Share the Public folder so that the other student can access it from the network. List the steps you took.
2. Share a folder in your user profile so that the other student can access it from the network. List the steps you took.

PROJECT 2-4: Practice Using the Recovery Environment

Boot from the Vista DVD and launch the Recovery Environment. Then do the following:

1. Execute the Startup Repair process. What were the results?
2. Execute System Restore. What is the most recent restore point? (Do not apply the restore point.)
3. Execute the command prompt window. Open the Registry Editor. What command did you use? Close the editor.
4. Using the command prompt window, copy a file from your Documents folder to a flash drive. Where you able to copy the file successfully? If not, what error message(s) did you receive?

PROJECT 2-5: Practice Using the Elevated Command Prompt

One command that requires an elevated command prompt is the Ipconfig command. Do the following to practice using the command prompt windows:

1. Open a standard command prompt window and execute this command: `ipconfig /all`.
2. Execute the command `ipconfig /release`. What error message do you get?
3. Open an elevated command prompt window and execute the command again. What is the result?
4. Execute the command `ipconfig /renew`. What is the result?
5. Close both command prompt windows.

>> REAL PROBLEMS, REAL SOLUTIONS

REAL PROBLEM 2-1: Helping End Users Learn Windows Vista

Users often call on PC support technicians to help them learn about a new operating system. Savvy technicians can help empower their users by teaching them to turn to the Microsoft Web site for information and instructions about Windows. One very useful entry point into the Microsoft site is *windowshelp.microsoft.com*, which provides links to both technical and non-technical information (see Figure 2-63).

Go to the site and browse through its links. Then answer the following questions:

1. Jose, an end user, asks the question, "Why won't my computer turn on or off quickly?" What are the six suggestions the site offers to solve this problem?
2. Linda, an end user, asks you to teach her how to use the Windows Sidebar and gadgets. How can you direct her to an easy-to-read overview of these Vista features?
3. Janice, an end user, does not like the picture that appears when she logs onto her user account. What is the link that can explain to Janice how to change that picture?

2

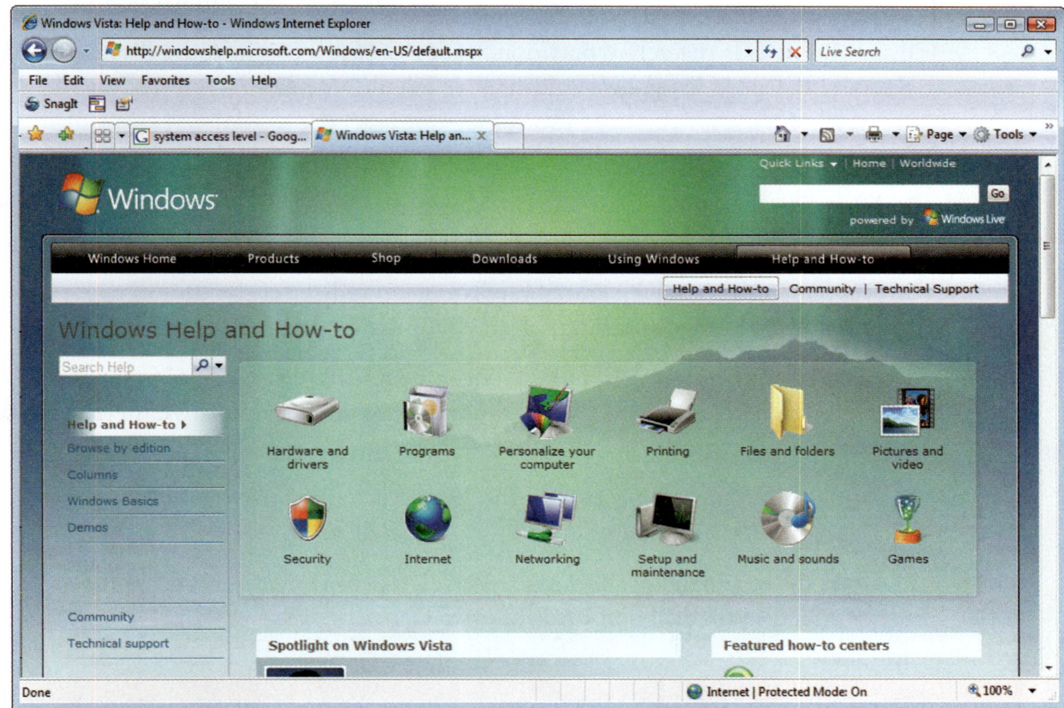

Figure 2-63 End users find the Windows Help and How-to site full of useful information

4. Blogs are an excellent way to join the community of Vista users and support technicians. List five Microsoft blogs that include information about Windows Vista. Which blog do you think would be most useful to you or your users? Why?
5. Why is it better to direct end users to the Microsoft site rather than answering each question yourself?

REAL PROBLEM 2-2: Removing Windows Vista from a Dual Boot Configuration

Joan purchased an upgrade version of Windows Vista Home Edition and installed it in a dual boot configuration with Windows XP on her laptop computer. She discovered after the installation that her laptop manufacturer does not provide Vista drivers for all her laptop components. She has come to you asking for help. You first congratulate her on not upgrading Windows XP to Vista, which would have made it necessary to reinstall XP. In discussing her options, you discover that her desktop computer does qualify for Vista. She is most happy to move the Vista installation to her desktop.

One step in that process is to delete the Vista installation from her laptop. Recall that when Vista installs, it changes the MBR program on the hard drive so that the program searches for Bootmgr rather than Ntldr. The command to reinstate the Windows XP Ntldr program as the boot loader is: `C:\Boot\Bootsect.exe -NT52 All`. The command is executed from an elevated command prompt. Using this command, list the steps to uninstall Vista from Joan's laptop, freeing the hard drive space.

REAL PROBLEM 2-3: Removing Windows XP from a Dual Boot Configuration

Larry wanted to try out Windows Vista without overwriting his Windows XP installation, so he decided to install Vista in a dual-boot configuration with Windows XP. He partitioned his hard drive so that drive D contains Vista and drive C contains Windows XP. Now that

Vista is up and working well, he wants to remove Windows XP to increase free space on his drive. Drive C is the active partition, and, therefore, contains the Bootmgr and BCD files. Reorder the steps listed below to remove Windows XP:

1. Delete the C:\Windows folder and other Windows XP folders on drive C.
2. Using the command prompt in the Vista Recovery Environment, use the `Bootrec /fixmbr` command to fix the MBR.
3. Reboot to the Vista Recovery Environment and select the option to repair startup, which reinstalls Bootmgr and builds a new D:\Boot folder.
4. Booting to the Vista Recovery Environment, use the Diskpart command to make drive D the active partition. The Diskpart commands used are *list disk, select disk 0, list partition, select partition 1*, and *active*.
5. Using the command prompt in the Vista Recovery Environment, use the `Bootrec /rebuildBCD` to build a new BCD file on drive D.
6. Using the command prompt in the Vista Recovery Environment, use the `Bootrec /fixboot` command to fix the boot sector of drive D.

INDEX

X

NOTES

NOTES

NOTES